D0840999

MCAT® Verbal Reasoning Mastery

The Complete Reading Comprehension Program

MCAT® Verbal Reasoning Mastery

The Complete Reading Comprehension Program

CHARLES A. CHANEY

CHARLES L. CHANEY, EDITOR

IvyHall Review™

MCAT is a registered trademark of the Association of American Medical Colleges

Published by IvyHall Review
P.O. Box 4151
Mission Viejo, California 92690

Copyright ©2008 Copyright ©2009 second printing by Charles A. Chaney. All rights reserved. IvyHall Review and the colophon are trademarks of IvyHall Review.

No part of this publication may be reproduced, stored in a retrieval system, or transmitted in any form or by any means, electronic, mechanical, photocopying, recording, or otherwise, without permission in writing from its publisher, IvyHall Review.

Requests to the Publisher for permission should be addressed to the Legal Department, IvyHall Review, P.O. Box 4151, Mission Viejo, California 92690. e-mail: ivyhallreview@gmail.com.

Trademarks: All brand names and product names used in this book are trademarks, registered trademarks, or trade names of their respective holders. IvyHall Review is not associated with any product or vendor in this book.

Library of Congress Cataloging-In-Publication Data
Library of Congress Control Number: 2008927125

ISBN 13: 978-0-9816721-0-6
ISBN 10: 0-9816721-0-8

Printed in the United States of America

10 9 8 7 6 5 4 3 2

About the Author

Charles A. Chaney has taught countless clients how to read critically and boost comprehension, especially on standardized tests. After earning a master's degree from Johns Hopkins University, he created Neuro-Visual Programming, the system of learning that integrates reading comprehension with visual memory. His methods have allowed students to achieve excellent scores on the MCAT, GMAT, GRE, and DAT, and gain admission to top graduate schools.

During his time teaching MCAT preparatory courses, he worked with numerous students who had been forced to set aside medical dreams due to low Verbal Reasoning scores. He made it his mission to uncover the secrets of excellent reading comprehension, and to share them with others. Charles is proof of his own methods, having turned a low VR score of 6 into 11s and 12s consistently (along with a perfect writing score of T).

His belief is that people of all backgrounds can become superb readers and writers. The goal is to realize the power of the mind to its full extent.

The mind is not a vessel that needs filling, but wood that needs igniting. - Plutarch

Table of Contents

Part I: On the Mountaintop: Exploring MCAT Verbal Reasoning

Part II: Angels are in the Details: Scrutinizing Passages and Questions

Part IV: The Journey of a Thousand Miles Begins with a Single Word: Reading

11 What Should You Read for Practice? 193

12 Student Perspectives: Q&A with Top Performers 205

Part V: Elevens for the Wise: Invaluable Information to Help You Succeed on the MCAT

13 Eleven False Assumptions about Verbal Reasoning 223

14 Eleven Things You Must Do on Test Day 235

15   Eleven Ways to Reduce Anxiety Before and During the MCAT **249**

Part VI. Reading Comprehension and Memory Exercises

Preface

The goal of this book is to maximize your performance on the Verbal Reasoning (VR) section of the Medical College Admission Test (MCAT). Each year, thousands of examinees face the possibility of disastrous results on this section of the test. This book guides you to transform those struggles into successes. First, it analyzes VR passages and question types with an emphasis on strategies for handling them effectively. Second, it discusses poor reading habits and presents methods for overcoming them. Third, the book offers extensive methods for improving reading comprehension by introducing new reading exercises and techniques. Fourth, it lays out a training timeline with suggested MCAT-quality books and journals as practice material.

MCAT Verbal Reasoning Mastery seeks to give you every help possible to discover a level of reading proficiency that you may have never reached before. It will show you how to realize various levels of meaning that the written word contains. You will practice techniques that improve reading memory by employing a new system of learning called Neuro-Visual Programming, which can serve you well for the rest of your life.

Also addressed in this book are the false assumptions that unfortunately deter examinees from reaching their full potential. Furthermore, you will find a series of interviews with top performing students who have achieved scores of 11 or better on Verbal Reasoning. Their advice will prove extremely useful to anyone seeking success on this very difficult section of the MCAT. Finally, you will find at the end of the book, 150 pages of exercises aimed at improving visual memory, reading memory, reading speed, and comprehension.

As you complete the journey of Verbal Reasoning mastery, you will hopefully develop excellent memory, critical thinking, reading mechanics, and focus. By mastering these abilities you will realize a higher aptitude for reading and writing, a thorough command of which are indispensable to medical professionals.

WHY THIS BOOK IS SO SPECIAL

This is the first published book to teach extensive reading techniques, provide advice from top performers, and map out training programs specifically aimed at maximizing performance on the Verbal Reasoning section of the MCAT. The techniques and exercises in this book are designed to boost reading memory, focus, speed, and comprehension.

This book can be part of an overall curriculum, or a helpful manual with useful guidelines for self-directed study. Put simply, this book promises to elevate Verbal Reasoning scores if one follows its training and direction diligently.

ORGANIZATION

This book is organized into five major sections:

PART I: ON THE MOUNTAINTOP: EXPLORING MCAT VERBAL REASONING

This part gives an overview of both the MCAT and the Verbal Reasoning section.

PART II: ANGELS ARE IN THE DETAILS: SCRUTINIZING PASSAGES AND QUESTIONS

This section delves into the passage and question types of Verbal Reasoning. These two chapters provide a thorough analysis of the Natural Science, Social Science, and Humanities passages, as well as key strategies for how to tackle them.

PART III: BUILDING THE FOUNDATION: DEVELOPING YOUR COMPREHENSION, MEMORY, AND ACTIVE READING SKILLS

The third part is a journey into enhancing critical reading and thinking skills. These four chapters teach how to master reading comprehension, diagnose and improve poor reading habits, and develop visual memory. Readers should be careful to follow the techniques and strategies diligently.

PART IV: THE JOURNEY OF A THOUSAND MILES BEGINS WITH A SINGLE WORD: READING

In the fourth part, three chapters provide sample training schedules, books and journals to read for practice, and essential interviews with top performers.

PART V: ELEVENS FOR THE WISE: INVALUABLE INFORMATION TO HELP YOU SUCCEED ON THE MCAT

The final part comprises three chapters that are devoted to the proper mental and physical aspects of top performance. These chapters address false assumptions about Verbal Reasoning, discuss proactive habits for test-taking success, and recommend techniques for reducing anxiety.

FEEDBACK

To share comments and suggestions about the book, you are invited to contact the author by e-mail:

verbalbook@gmail.com

All thoughts are welcome. Your feedback is invaluable for continuing to make this book a vital source for future pre-medical students. Success stories are also greatly appreciated.

FURTHER INSTRUCTION

If you are interested in receiving further Verbal Reasoning instruction, either on an individualized consulting basis, or at a possible Verbal Reasoning Mastery seminar in your area, then contact the author at the same e-mail address above.

The author also provides personalized consultation services to students applying to medical schools. Be sure to include your email and a brief message indicating your interest.

ACKNOWLEDGEMENTS

This book would not exist without the outstanding help of my parents, Julia and Charles, whose sacrifice and enduring love have sustained me throughout life. Their belief in the importance of this project has been a true blessing. Their encouragement and guidance have been invaluable, especially the critical editorial skills so ably wielded by my father, an author in his own right. His contribution is deeply appreciated.

I want to thank Dr. David Verrier for his generous review and recommendation, and Dennis Taylor for his expert post-production work.

I also thank the extraordinary pre-medical students who contributed to this book. Their enthusiasm and insight have been invaluable for helping others realize the dream of a medical career. Thanks, as always, to my personal students who have had faith in me and the kindness to let me share in their success.

Gratias maximas vobis ago.

PART I

On The Mountaintop:
Exploring MCAT
Verbal Reasoning

CHAPTER

1

The MCAT Explained

IN THIS CHAPTER

The days of enduring a room full of test-takers cramped in small chairs at a strange location, such as the ballroom of a hotel or the lecture hall of a law school, are long gone for the MCAT examinee. In an air-conditioned and tightly controlled environment, the administration of the computer-based MCAT takes place at testing centers throughout the United States, Canada and 15 other countries.

The relatively new testing centers provide advanced identity verification, video monitoring, staff monitoring, and noise control. Thanks to electronic finger-scanning technology, discreet cameras, vigilant employees, and shooting-range noise-reduction headphones, examination integrity is excellent. Gone are the mandatory 8:00 am MCAT tests that proved near-fatal for the nervous test-taker who could not fall asleep until 5:00 am the night before, and who subsequently went home defeated. Now examinees have a choice: to take the exam at 8:00 am, or at noon. This may not be as flexible or as generous as the administration of some other exams like the GRE, but it is a step in the right direction.

Now that the MCAT is totally computer-based, some people wonder whether the test is adaptive. On some other exams, like the GMAT, the

---

level of difficulty of questions change according to how you answer. If you answer a question correctly, then the next question is more difficult, and vice-versa. On the MCAT, however, the questions do not become harder or easier based on your answers. Each passage that appears on the computer screen has been constructed in advance, which means that the questions are not going to change. Does this compromise your ability to skip ahead or look back at questions? The answer is no. Examinees may review and change answers to questions within a current test section.

I. MCAT EXAM CONTENT

The Medical College Admission Test (MCAT) is a standardized exam that consists of four sections offered in the following order: Physical Sciences, Verbal Reasoning, the Writing Sample, and Biological Sciences. According to the AAMC, the purpose of the test is to measure the knowledge and skills that medical educators and physicians have identified as key prerequisites for medical school success and beyond.

The MCAT evaluates your knowledge and understanding of physics, general chemistry, organic chemistry, and biology. The exam also tests your ability to write essays, in which your logic, development of thought, strength of argument, grammar, syntax, and everything else that contributes to a strong essay will be evaluated. The Physical Sciences section covers physics and general chemistry, while Biological Sciences covers biology, organic chemistry, genetics, and some fundamental physiology and biochemistry. Both sections consist of multiple-choice questions (A through D), and the Writing Sample consists of two essays.

> The computerized MCAT is nearly one-third shorter in length than the former paper MCAT.
>
> Total time on the computer is a little over five hours.

PHYSICAL SCIENCES

The Physical Sciences section covers the subjects of physics and general chemistry (inorganic). Many of the questions on Physical Sciences will test for a firm conceptual understanding of **general physics**. There are very few number-crunching questions, and calculus-based problems do not appear at all. Hence, reading a good high school physics book can be very helpful. When you study, focus on concepts, not equations. You will need to know your physics equations, but these should come **after** you understand all of the concepts.

PHYSICS TOPICS

✓ translational motion
✓ force and motion, gravitation
✓ equilibrium and momentum
✓ work and energy
✓ waves and periodic motion
✓ sound
✓ fluids and solids
✓ electrostatics and electromagnetism
✓ electronic circuit elements
✓ light and geometrical optics
✓ atomic and nuclear structure
✓ unit and dimensional conversions
✓ graphing techniques

Learn the concepts first.
Let the equations confirm your understanding of the concepts.

The approach for **general chemistry** is similar. You should begin your chemistry studies by reading a high school chemistry book. After finishing this, pick up a college (freshman level) inorganic chemistry textbook and work through the majority of the exercises. This is excellent preparation for the MCAT. Many college chemistry books have an accompanying study guide. **Purchase the study guide and use it thoroughly.** Like physics questions, the majority of chemistry questions will test your understanding of **concepts**. Be prepared to crunch through a few chemistry calculations on the MCAT, but be sure to have mastered general chemistry concepts before taking the test.

GENERAL CHEMISTRY TOPICS

- ✓ electronic structure and periodic table
- ✓ bonding phase and phase equilibria
- ✓ stoichiometry
- ✓ thermodynamics and thermochemistry
- ✓ rate processes in chemical reactions
- ✓ gasses
- ✓ solution chemistry
- ✓ acids and bases
- ✓ electrochemistry

For learning concepts: get your hands on physics and chemistry books typically found at the **high school** level. Titles of these books will be some variation of Conceptual Physics or Conceptual Chemistry.

For developing problem-solving skills: acquire **college** level text books and work through the exercises. Using four books or more to prepare for Physical Sciences should not scare you.

VERBAL REASONING

Verbal Reasoning, arguably the most difficult section and the one feared most, evaluates the ability to comprehend and apply information presented in passages that are typically 600 words in length. The passages are taken from scholarly articles found in the **humanities**, **social sciences**, and various areas of the **natural sciences**.

Following each passage are five to seven questions of varying difficulty. Some questions assess your fundamental comprehension of the text, while others require you to analyze information, evaluate the validity of an argument, determine the opinion of an author, identify implied ideas, or apply knowledge to other contexts.

WRITING SAMPLE

The Writing Sample consists of two essays that are administered consecutively. You have 30 minutes to write a response to each prompt. **You are not graded on your outside knowledge of the particular topic to which the prompt pertains.** Instead, the graders look for the following elements:

- ✓ solid arguments
- ✓ strong examples and support
- ✓ logical development of ideas
- ✓ cohesive and effective style
- ✓ spelling
- ✓ syntax
- ✓ grammar

Luckily, you will not see topics dealing with biology, physics, or chemistry, or any dealing with emotionally-significant issues such as religion.

BIOLOGICAL SCIENCES

The Biological Sciences section covers topics in biology and organic chemistry. The best way to begin preparing for Biological Sciences is to study a college (freshman level) biology text, skipping plant biology. Start with this. Once you have covered all of the basics of biology, you will know over half of the required material for this section. You should also make time to study genetics, as well as an abridged version of human physiology and biochemistry.

The next step in your preparation should include practicing as many Biological Science passages as possible. Enrolling in a MCAT class provided by test preparatory companies would be most wise. Practicing sample passages is crucial because many questions deal with experiments that you have never seen, and you need to develop a system for applying known concepts to new circumstances.

Questions pertaining to biology evaluate your ability to analyze new facts and unusual experimental design. Always remember that the MCAT tests your critical thinking.

BIOLOGY TOPICS

> ✓ enzymes and metabolism
> ✓ DNA and protein synthesis
> ✓ eukaryotes
> ✓ prokaryotes
> ✓ genetics
> ✓ microbiology
> ✓ physiologic systems

A smaller portion of Biological Sciences assesses your understanding and knowledge of organic chemistry. Organic chemistry constitutes approximately 25% or less of all Biological Science questions. You will be responsible for the following organic chemistry topics:

ORGANIC CHEMISTRY TOPICS

- ✓ covalent bonds
- ✓ molecular structure and spectra
- ✓ separations and purifications
- ✓ hydrocarbons
- ✓ oxygen-containing compounds
- ✓ amines
- ✓ biological molecules
- ✓ classifications of compounds
- ✓ reactions and reaction mechanisms
- ✓ stereochemistry
- ✓ nomenclature

The following table summarizes the various parts of the MCAT with information about timing and the number of questions per section.

Table 1.1 Timing Breakdown of the MCAT.

Test Section	Time	Details
Non-Disclosure Agreement		required
Tutorial	10 min	optional
Physical Sciences	70 min	52 questions
Break	10 min	optional
Verbal Reasoning	60 min	40 questions
Break	10 min	optional
Writing Sample	60 min	2 essays
Break	10 min	optional
Biological Sciences	70 min	52 questions
Survey	10 min	optional

Total time = 5 hours, 10 min

II. WHY IS THE COMPUTER FORMAT SO GREAT?

While most students are running scared from long passages on computer screens, a select few are rejoicing. Why? What makes the computer format preferred to the traditional paper exam? The computer format offers advantages in the following areas:

- ✓ timing
- ✓ essay-writing
- ✓ scoring accuracy
- ✓ proctoring behavior
- ✓ testing environment

Students would be wise to turn their fears (if they happen to exist) of the computer format into hopes.

TIMING ADVANTAGE

Before the dawn of the computer-based MCAT, students took the exam in large rooms where proctors used desk clocks to keep track of time. Nobody could predict when, exactly, the proctor would announce the end of a section, despite the five-minute warnings. Supposedly, sometimes a proctor would end a section a minute too early, sometimes a minute too late. The five-minute warning might have been followed by a loud "Pencils down!" four minutes later. Some students reported that the proctor forgot to give the five-minute warning.

You can imagine the annoyances. For many examinees, such unpredictability meant that students had to rush through a section and finish a good minute or two before they anticipated its actual end. Other students simply pulled out their hair.

Now, the inevitable element of human error regarding proctoring is no more. The computer provides a clock at the bottom of the screen that counts down quietly each second, so that every examinee may see, at any moment, how much time remains on a given section. This is a real blessing, and one that may improve your score (especially on Verbal Reasoning).

> The clock on the screen provides the key to mastering your ability to pace yourself, a critical strategy that you will read more about in Chapter 8.

NO MORE WRITING BY HAND

If you have great handwriting, raise your hand. If your hand is still on the table, do not feel embarrassed. After all, when was the last time you met a doctor with legible handwriting?

The paper-based MCAT forced students to write neatly under extreme pressure. The circumstances forced them to synthesize a cohesive and legible essay with few, if any, grammatical and spelling mistakes. Under this sort of stress, writing neatly became a difficult task. And, if doctors are not required to write neatly, then why are you?

The computer format is blessing to the essayist. Now examinees are reunited with their favorite friend, the word processor (although what the computer MCAT offers is hardly considered a fully functional word processor). In addition to typing their essays, examinees can copy and paste text, use the space bar, move the cursor to any location using the mouse, delete text using the backspace key, and introduce a new line with the return key.

However, that is about all. Apart from the letter and numeric keys, most of the other keys are non-functional. You cannot tab the cursor forward. The delete key will do nothing. Forget about using key combinations with the Ctrl or Alt keys.

There are, however, buttons on the screen above the main text box (where you type your essay) that allow you to copy and paste material. This is the extent of any use of shortcuts.

All in all, the transition to a limited version of a word processor is a welcome and advantageous change for the student. You can move sentences around, spot misplaced commas and other incorrect punctuation, fix spelling errors with ease, and proofread much more quickly and efficiently than your paper-based ancestors ever could. Hurrah!

SCORING ACCURACY ADVANTAGE

Infamous for causing the scoring machine to detect heavy eraser marks that should have been ignored, the forms on which you had to fill in the bubbles (known as Scantron forms in some circles) caused many an upset stomach. Similarly, a well-prepared student may have intended to answer the first question, but filled in the bubble for the second one by mistake. These kinds of errors occurred easily on the paper-based MCAT.

With the arrival of the computer exam, pencil and eraser mistakes were history. The computer eliminated any human error that may result from filling in the wrong bubble, or erasing too lightly, or any other mishaps related to selecting answers with paper and pencil.

Now, examinees simply move the mouse pointer and click on the bubble next to the correct answer on the screen. This saves time, prevents scoring inaccuracies, and minimizes careless mistakes. Also, no more time is lost jumping back and forth between the answer sheet and the booklet.

PROCTORING ADVANTAGE

Having a proctor pacing around a room watching you take an exam for several hours can be bothersome to say the least. Typically in the past, two or more proctors monitored each paper-based MCAT examination.

While proctors may have had quiet footsteps, their sheer movement and close proximity probably contributed to the stress of the situation. Things are much different now that the MCAT is administered at testing centers, care of the Thomson Prometric Global Testing Center Network. Thomson Prometric is a global leader in technology-enabled testing and assessment services, and has an exclusive agreement with the AAMC to provide MCAT testing.

Each testing center is built similarly to ensure a consistent and equivalent testing experience for all. A testing center is comprised of a front room, furnished with lockers and chairs for those waiting to check in, and typically two large rooms in the back, each seating approximately twenty examinees in walled cubicles. Each cubicle has a dedicated computer, and only test-takers are allowed in these isolated rooms during the exam. Proctors, called Testing Center Administrators (TCA), do not walk around the computer room during the exam. However, they do watch from a glass window and via overhead cameras. One wall of the isolated testing room is actually a large window, the other side of which sits the administrators. In this manner, the examinees can remain totally focused and immersed without the visual or verbal distractions of someone pacing around the room.

CONTROLLED ENVIRONMENT ADVANTAGE

Knowing your surroundings before test day is certainly nice. In the past, the disconcerting small size of your desk, the discomfort of a room without air-conditioning, plus the noise of the public beyond the walls of the room all proved very bothersome during the MCAT.

Now that the test is administered at dedicated centers, you need not worry about such annoyances. Each center places the examinee in a room that is comfortable and free of noise. Noise reduction headsets are available as well (you **cannot** bring your own earplugs). The chairs are on par with those used in professional offices, and the ambient temperature is always at a comfortable setting (no simulations of being inside a refrigerator).

✓ A strong suggestion is to visit the center where you plan to take the MCAT a week or two before the exam; this will familiarize you with the testing environment and relieve you of any anxieties about the uncertainties of the setting.

WHAT HAPPENS SHOULD SOMETHING GO WRONG?

Technology does not function flawlessly all of the time. Incidences of technical problems during test administrations are extremely rare, but can happen. So what should you do if something goes wrong?

Luckily, **the computerized MCAT has been designed with a recovery feature.** The creators of the MCAT recognize that, inevitably, technical issues can occur even on the best systems. If you experience technical difficulties, immediately notify your Test Center Administrator who will watch from outside the room. The TCA will be able to resolve the problem, usually with no loss of time or information from your testing session.

In the vast majority of cases, either your system will be restarted, or you will be moved to a different system and resume your test exactly where you left off. **No time will be lost or deducted.** In extremely rare cases where resumption is not possible, the exam will be rescheduled **at no cost to you.**

III. APPROXIMATE CORRELATION BETWEEN CORRECT ANSWERS AND SPECIFIC SCORES

For each of the three multiple choice sections of the MCAT – Physical Sciences, Verbal Reasoning, and Biological Sciences – scores range from 1 to 15 (highest). Thus, a score of 45 is the highest combined score possible on the MCAT.

Written below are rough estimates of how many questions you must answer correctly to achieve a certain score on each of the three MCAT sections. These estimates were derived from scoring metrics used on the available MCAT exams released by the AAMC.

Remember that these are not exact correlations to true grading metrics, but only estimates.

PHYSICAL SCIENCES - 52 QUESTIONS TOTAL

Questions Correct (out of 52)	Estimated Score	Percent correct
41	10	79
44	11	85
46	12	87
49	13	94
50	14	96
51	15	98

VERBAL REASONING - 40 QUESTIONS TOTAL

Questions Correct (out of 40)	Estimated Score	Percent correct
31	10	78
34	11	85
37	12	93
38	13	95
39	14	98
40	15	100

BIOLOGICAL SCIENCES - 52 QUESTIONS TOTAL

Questions Correct (out of 52)	Estimated Score	Percent correct
39	10	75
43	11	83
46	12	88
47	13	90
50	14	96
51	15	98

WRITING SAMPLE - 2 ESSAYS

Scaled Score (J - T)	Percentile Rank
M	25th
O	50th
Q	75th

The writing sample is assigned a letter score ranging from J to T, T being the highest. How does this score come about? One grader is a human, and the other is a computer (say hello to Hal), and each assigns a numbered score to an essay. The scores range from 1 to 6 (highest) for a total of four scores (24 is perfect) for the two essays combined.

These four scores translate to a final letter grade between J through T as witnessed on the MCAT score report. On the report you will see only the letter grade. Keep in mind that admissions officers at medical schools can request to see your essays, so be sure to give your best effort on this section. **Some medical schools add a point to your total MCAT score if you receive an R, S, or T (for example, a 34T carries the weight of a 35 at some institutions).**

In case you were wondering, the computer grader is actually called IntelliMetric. According to Vantage Learning, the makers of IntelliMetric, the system is an artificial intelligence program capable of scoring open-ended and constructed-response questions with documented levels of accuracy and reliability exceeding that of human expert scorers. It consistently applies the pooled knowledge (scoring rubric) of expert scorers to the essays from MCAT examinations.

WHAT CONSTITUTES A DECENT SCORE?

Sure, we would all love to score a perfect 45T, but wants and wills are the difference between dreams and reality. In some years nobody scores a 45, or even a 44. The MCAT is no walk in any park. So what should you aim for, and what is considered a competitive score?

✓ Your target score depends on your goals and background. Generally speaking, you should shoot for a **minimum of 10 on each section with a writing score of at least a Q to have a decent chance at a medical school.**

However, a score of 30 may not be high enough. Examinee data from

2007 revealed that the average MCAT score for students who actually matriculated was a 31. Your goal should be to achieve two 10s and an 11 as your **minimum**.

If you wish to enter the front gates of a top-twenty medical institution, you should aim for at least an 11 or 12 on each section, with a writing score of R or better. Of course there are exceptions, but the competition for medical school admission is remarkably fierce. **Every year, tens of thousands of fine and talented candidates never receive an acceptance letter from any medical school.**

For a few imprudent students, studying for the MCAT comes down to cramming at the last minute for several weeks. For the rest of the world, however, achieving three 10s requires hard work and lots of preparation, patience, and perseverance.

> 42,315 students applied to US medical schools in 2007.
> Only 17,759 were accepted.

AFTER THE FINAL QUESTION, WHAT HAPPENS?

When you finish the last question on Biological Sciences, you will remain in your chair. Going to your car and falling asleep is not an immediate option (as much as you may want to).

You will see on the screen a brief survey asking about your testing experience and environment. Feel free to give several brief answers if your brain is still functioning. Next, you will be given the option to cancel or accept your exam. You will not, however, be able to see your scores, and must decide based on intuition. The computer will ask you to think carefully about your choice, but be careful not to overanalyze yourself. Feelings often fool us.

✓ Be careful about negating your test. Unless you faced unusual hardship during the exam that may have drastically affected your performance, or you know for sure that you failed an entire section, you should resist the temptation to cancel your score.

IV. REGISTERING FOR THE MCAT

As of 2008, the MCAT exam is administered multiple times from late January through early September, and offered at hundreds of test sites in the United States, Canada, and throughout the world.

You will want to take the exam either the year before applying to medical school, or the year during. For example, if you are applying in 2008 for entrance to medical school in 2009, you should take the exam in in either 2007 or 2008. Medical schools will, however, accept scores dating back two or three years. If you plan to take the MCAT more than once, then be sure to check the application policies of each school to which you are applying.

Once you have selected a test date, register as soon as possible. You should choose the testing date that affords you enough time to prepare your personal statement and AMCAS application early in the application cycle. This means that **you should take the MCAT in January, April, or May in any given year.**

If you anticipate having to take the MCAT twice or three times in the same year, then plan your first attempt for January, April, or May. Since you can only reserve one seat at a time, making your first attempt in June or July may preclude you from finding a local testing center by the time you can register for August and September.

Taking the MCAT close to where you live is optimal. **The AAMC processes MCAT exam registrations in the order in which they are received.** Early registration gives you a much better chance at taking the test at a center near you.

All registrations for the MCAT take place online at www.aamc.org. There is no walk-in registration. You will be able to register approximately 12 weeks prior to each test date, and there are both regular and late registrations. The regular registration **deadline** is 14 calendar days prior to the test. Those who miss the regular deadline can register during the late registration period and pay a late fee.

For the best chance at obtaining a preferred test date and location, you should register 60 days or more in advance of the exam day.

Regular Registration Fee	$210
Late Registration*	$50
International Test Site*	$60
Date Reschedule*	$50
Change of Test Center Location*	$50

* These fees are added to the regular registration fee

For a complete list of dates and times that the MCAT is offered, please refer to the official MCAT Web site hosted by the AAMC at:

www.aamc.org/mcat

If you have additional questions regarding the MCAT exam, please refer to the **MCAT Essentials** PDF that is available on the official AAMC Web site: www.aamc.org/mcat

CHAPTER 2	# Why Focus on Verbal Reasoning?

IN THIS CHAPTER
   I.   MCAT Results May Predict Medical School Performance
   II. Possible Link Between Verbal Reasoning and Board Scores

---

Why do we care so much about Verbal Reasoning? First, an admissions officer could possibly use your Verbal score as a predictor of your medical school success. Second, how well you read will certainly have an impact on how well you perform in medical school, and on the board exams. Third, since board exam scores heavily influence a student's residency options, poor reading skills could very well limit your choice of a medical practice. Therefore, take your preparation for Verbal Reasoning very seriously.

Overall, the need to focus on Verbal Reasoning is three-fold:

1. Preparation material for VR is more limited than that for other MCAT sections;

2. Many students require the most help on this section;

3. The VR score can play an important and decisive role in medical school admissions decisions.

If you are not an excellent reader at this point, then you should strive to become one. In a shocking study of reading performance in the USA, the National Endowment for the Arts found three unsettling trends:

---

(1) Americans are spending less time reading; (2) reading comprehension skills are eroding; and (3) these declines are having serious social, cultural, and economic repercussions.[1]

The study also revealed a male-female gap in reading proclivity and achievement levels, favoring the female student.

I. MCAT RESULTS MAY PREDICT MEDICAL SCHOOL PERFORMANCE

Over the years, studies have shown that a relation exists between preadmission academic variables (ie. MCAT scores, undergraduate GPA, etc.) and medical school performance in both osteopathic and allopathic contexts.[2-5] Medical schools have traditionally used MCAT scores and undergraduate grade point averages in the selection of candidates for admission. Most studies have focused on how well these variables relate to medical-licensing examination scores as performance measures.

Experts have reported that preadmission academic variables correlate with performance on the United States Medical Licensing Examination (USMLE) Step 1.[2-4]   Elam and Johnson found that the Biological Sciences MCAT subscore was the significant preadmission predictor of USMLE Step 1 performance.[2] Another study using data from 14 allopathic medical schools reported that MCAT performance and undergraduate GPAs were good predictors of USMLE Step 1 scores.[3]

II. POSSIBLE LINK BETWEEN VERBAL REASONING AND BOARD SCORES

Several studies have taken the next step to demonstrate a link between Verbal Reasoning scores and medical board exam performance. Dr. Donna Dixon analyzed test results of 174 students at the New York College of Osteopathic Medicine of New York Institute of Technology, and identified the Verbal Reasoning MCAT subscore as a predictor for COMLEX–USA Level 2 performance.[5] The COMLEX-USA series is the osteopathic equivalent to the USMLE series, and is designed to assess osteopathic medical knowledge and clinical skills. In another study, Dr. Claudio Violato and his colleagues published an article in the Journal of Academic Medicine reviewing performance on the MCAT exam and the Medical Council of Canada (MCC) qualifying examination.[6] They found that of the four subsections of the MCAT (Verbal Reasoning, Physical Sciences, Biological Sciences, and Writing Sample), **only Verbal Reasoning correlated significantly** with performance on the second part of the MCC qualifying examination. Since part two of the MCC examination is structured similarly to both parts of the USMLE Step 2 exam, the correlation between Verbal Reasoning scores and USMLE performance seems very reasonable.

You can safely conclude that medical school admissions committees give significant weight to the Verbal Reasoning score.

High science scores do not rescue a low verbal score.

1. National Endowment for the Arts. "To Read or Not to Read: A Question of National Consequence." Research Report #47.

2. Elam CL, Johnson MM. "NBME Part 1 versus USMLE Step1: predicting scores based on preadmission and medical school performances." Acad Med. 1994; 69:155.

3. Wiley A, Koenig JA. "The validity of the Medical College Admission Test for predicting performance in the first two years of medical school." Acad Med. 1996; 71(10 Suppl): S83 -S85.

4. Silver B, Hodgson CS. "Evaluating GPAs and MCAT scores as predictors of NBME I and clerkship performances based on students' data from one undergraduate institution." Acad Med. 1997; 72:394 -396.

5. Dixon D, "Relation Between Variables of Preadmission, Medical School Performance, and COMLEX–USA Levels 1 and 2 Performance." JAOA, 2004; Vol 104, No 8: 332-336

6. Violato C, Donnon T. "Does the Medical College Admission Test Predict Clinical Reasoning Skills? A Longitudinal Study Employing the Medical Council of Canada Clinical Reasoning Examination." AcadMed. 2005; 80(10): S14-16S.

CHAPTER 3

Brief Overview of Verbal Reasoning

IN THIS CHAPTER

QUESTION:
What is feared more by pre-medical students than cafeteria food?

ANSWER:
A difficult Verbal Reasoning passage on the MCAT.

In 2007, I polled a few hundred MCAT test-takers and found that 89% of students voted Verbal Reasoning to be the most difficult section to improve.

Some say that Verbal Reasoning is not only the most difficult section of the MCAT, but also the most important. As we saw in Chapter 2, of the three multiple-choice MCAT sections – Physical Sciences, Verbal Reasoning, and Biological Sciences – Verbal Reasoning might best predict how students will perform during their medical education. Achieving a VR score of 10 or better is not only impressive to admissions officers, but also imperative.

I. ANALYSIS OF VERBAL REASONING

Greatly diminishing the application success of thousands of students each year, the Verbal Reasoning section involves reading seven passages and answering 40 questions in 60 minutes.

Each of the seven passages is about 600 words long. A passage is followed by 5 to 7 questions which test the comprehension of material that comes only from the passage. **You do not need to (and should not) apply any outside knowledge to the questions because all of the information is contained therein.**

---

7 PASSAGES

40 QUESTIONS
5 TO **7** QUESTIONS PER PASSAGE

1 HOUR

The questions will assess your ability to:

✓ comprehend information

✓ apply concepts to situations

✓ interpret facts

✓ make inferences

✓ draw conclusions

✓ analyze the author's intent and tone

✓ recognize key assumptions

✓ understand the purpose and construction of arguments

DEALING WITH THE COMPUTER SCREEN

For those accustomed to taking paper and pencil tests, reading the complex passages on a computer is the last thing one wishes to do for one hour.

THE REALITY

Being able to flip pages of a book is esthetically pleasing and convenient, and paper tests offer the advantage of underlining, circling, and writing in the margins.

For many students, words on a screen do not register in the mind as efficiently as do words on a page. Woe to the traditional reader. The Information Age of instant access has arrived, and the computer is its favorite tool.

If you are one of the many students who struggle with reading on a computer, feel free to stomp your feet. When you are finished, follow this advice: starting tomorrow (after you have read this chapter), **begin reading articles on the Internet at the same hour of the day as the hour your MCAT begins.**

Work into your daily studies at least one hour of reading scholarly articles on a computer.

Subscribe to an online journal (see Chapter 11 for a suggested list), and access its archives on a daily basis.

If you plan to take the 8:00 am test, then start reading articles at 8:00 am every day. This way you will become accustomed to reading at the hour when you will actually begin your MCAT.

THE LAYOUT

You will see that your screen is divided into two vertical halves. On the left half will appear the passage. You will be able to scroll up and down to read it in its entirety. On the right half will appear the questions. You will also be able to scroll up and down to see every question, and the two halves can scroll independently of each other.

The computer does allow examinees to advance forward or backward through neighboring passages without having to answer questions. A test-taker can also open a master page that lists all questions, and by selecting the corresponding question, he or she can open the passage containing that specific question. (Note that the layout of this master list on the MCAT is somewhat difficult to read, so bring your glasses if you need them).

II. WHAT DOES VERBAL REASONING MEASURE?

Verbal Reasoning measures your ability to understand, evaluate, and apply information based on facts and arguments. Every future physician should have no trouble doing this. And whether you agree or not, Verbal Reasoning also measures to some extent your future success in understanding the material that will be covered in medical school.

As mentioned previously, the questions on Verbal Reasoning assess your ability to comprehend key information, apply concepts to new situations, apply new information to passage ideas, interpret facts, make inferences, draw conclusions, identify key assumptions, understand the author's intent and tone, and discern the purpose and construction of arguments. This section also tests your ability to read passages and answer questions in a rapid manner under pressure.

III. THE SCORING

The spread of Verbal Reasoning scores is unusual in that **the typical bell curve seen on other sections does not exist for VR results.** Typical examinee data of those who score in the 6 to 11 range on Verbal Reasoning reveals, surprisingly, a plateau. For example, examinee data from 2006 shows that 11.6% of all test-takers scored a 7 on VR, while another 11.6% scored an 11. In addition, the distribution of Verbal scores is spread more broadly than those for other sections.

Since there are only 40 questions on Verbal Reasoning, the grading scale is quite steep.

On AAMC practice tests, an examinee can miss no more than nine questions to score a 10. To achieve a score of 11, a student can miss only four to six questions. For a 12, an examinee must get 37 questions correct. The examinee who misses two questions receives a 13. For those who miss just one question, the VR score is a 14. The elusive score of 15 is given only to a perfect performance on AAMC tests.

IV. COMMON TOPICS FOUND IN VERBAL REASONING

Here is a quick overview of **various topics** that are popular on the Verbal Reasoning section. We will cover the various kinds of passages in more detail later in this book.

On any given MCAT exam, the collection of topics on Verbal Reasoning passages is diverse. You will see passages based on the

Natural Sciences, Social Sciences, and Humanities. These will be of varying difficulty, from straightforward, to long and complex. In a single Verbal Reasoning section, there are usually two or more easier passages, about three moderately-challenging passages, and two or so difficult passages.

✓ You will probably find that one of the seven passages seems to be much harder that the rest. Be on the lookout for that one extremely challenging passage. Since passages are presented in no particular order, it may appear first, last, or anywhere in the middle.

The list below provides a quick overview of the kinds of passages frequently encountered, each falling into one of the three main categories of Natural Sciences, Social Sciences, and Humanities. Many libraries organize their book collections around these categories, or ones very similar to them.

- Anthropology
- Economic Theory
- Humanities
- Literary Theory
- Natural Science
- Philosophy of Science
- Political Science
- Psychology
- Art Criticism
- Sociology

V. PACING OVERVIEW OF VERBAL REASONING

OVERALL:

    60 MINUTES TOTAL

    7 PASSAGES

    40 QUESTIONS

PER PASSAGE:

    8.5 MINUTES

    5 TO 7 QUESTIONS

        =   3.5 MINUTES TO READ, 5 MINUTES TO ANSWER QUESTIONS

TIMING (SEE CHAPTER 8 FOR INSTRUCTIONS):

    MINUTE 60:00 BEGIN PASSAGE I

    MINUTE 51:00 BEGIN PASSAGE II

    MINUTE 43:00 BEGIN PASSAGE III

    MINUTE 34:00 BEGIN PASSAGE IV

    MINUTE 26:00 BEGIN PASSAGE V

    MINUTE 17:00 BEGIN PASSAGE VI

    MINUTE 9:00 BEGIN PASSAGE VII

PART II

Angels Are in the Details:
Scrutinizing Passages
and Questions

CHAPTER

4

Verbal Reasoning Passage Types and Strategies

Many students wonder what, exactly, will appear on the Verbal Reasoning section of the MCAT.

While there is no way of predicting what will appear, trends do exist regarding the subject matter that students may anticipate seeing. As we mentioned in Chapter 3, Verbal Reasoning passages follow three overarching classifications:

- Natural Sciences

- Humanities

- Social Sciences

One thing is certain - Verbal Reasoning will not test your knowledge of material beyond that of the passage. In fact, **bringing outside knowledge to the passage will most likely mislead you.** This chapter will introduce the three kinds of passages. The goal is to help you pinpoint your strengths and weaknesses regarding passage topics.

I. HOW TO DEFINE NATURAL SCIENCES, SOCIAL SCIENCES, AND HUMANITIES

NATURAL SCIENCES
Traditionally understood, Natural Science is the study of nature which involves the physical aspects of animals, the earth, and the universe beyond. Subjects that comprise the Natural Sciences include mainly astronomy, biology, chemistry, and physics.

SOCIAL SCIENCES
Social Science is the study of human society, civics, and populations. In general, the broad academic area of the Social Sciences includes sociology, anthropology, economics, psychology, political science, education, and history.

HUMANITIES
The third major subdivision is the Humanities, which is the study of the cultural aspects of humanity. Generally, the fields of art, language, literature, communication, religion, and philosophy, are grouped into the broader academic area referred to as the Humanities.

II. THE NATURAL SCIENCE PASSAGE

Most MCAT students feel comfortable reading science passages in general. After all, you probably declared a major in a scientific discipline since you plan to spend the rest of your professional career in medicine (presuming that your Verbal score is high enough).

Thinking that you will perform best on Natural Science passages can hurt you. When you encounter your first practice MCAT exam, you will discover a very different story that points to the difficulty of these types of passages.

The Natural Science passage is, in fact, challenging for a number of reasons. First, science passages tend to be lengthy and full of details that test your comprehension, not memorization. Second, on science passages full of facts, examinees tend to focus on details and gloss over underlying ideas. Third, examinees expect questions that test their recollection of facts.

> Students assume that science passages are rather straightforward with predictable questions about facts. Thus, many students are caught off guard on the MCAT when they encounter in-depth conceptual questions on Natural Sciences passages.

Keeping track of details is not the sole purpose of the Natural Science passage, or any other passage for that matter. While the passage contains many facts and details that you should keep in mind, your mission is to **understand the ideas and arguments** lurking in the shadows.

Facts in a passage are to be treated as pieces of evidence supporting a conclusion, with certain assumptions. Your job is to identify the **conclusions** and **assumptions** of each paragraph (which this book will cover in more detail in Chapter 5). In addition, since the MCAT loves to throw curve balls, expect to see many questions asking about concepts (not simply facts).

> Your job is to identify the conclusions and assumptions of each paragraph, and remember them when you answer the questions.
>
> In addition, apply the new learning technique called Neuro-Visual Programming to remember key facts (see Chapter 9).

READING STRATEGIES FOR THE NATURAL SCIENCE PASSAGE

When carefully reading Natural Science passages, look for two or more theories. Understand who supports which theory, especially that of the author. Each theory (or argument) is supported by evidence, and one or more key assumptions. Locating assumptions is covered in Chapter 5.

When you encounter a Natural Science passage full of details, do not panic. If you have mastered Neuro-Visual Programming (see Chapter 9), then keeping track of many details should happen readily. Whether or not you use NVP, you should follow two strategies when dealing with many details: **remember where exactly each detail appears in the passage, and be sure to form conclusions in your mind based on the facts.**

The following strategies will help guide you on Natural Science passages:

1. Read for concepts AND details.
Students often overlook the **point** of each paragraph. Remember, MCAT passages provide questions that are designed to test your comprehension, not your memory, as such. (Unfortunately, some study guides recommend skimming over details and referring back to them later, but this tends to hurt students because it takes too much time.)

2. Read the passage for ideas and arguments, and remember the order in which they are presented.
Take a quick second to **summarize the main message of each paragraph as you read**, and the order in which they occur. Make a mental list of these so you do not forget them. This requires a decent amount of practice.

3. Look for two or more competing arguments or hypotheses.
Nearly every verbal passage mentions two or more arguments. You must keep track of which details support or weaken which arguments. (The reading technique called Neuro-Visual Programming can be of great value here.)

Remember, MCAT passages love to discuss theories, hypotheses, and arguments. You need to identify them, as well as the people who support and refute them.

QUESTION STRATEGIES FOR THE NATURAL SCIENCE PASSAGE

Students expect to find a laundry list of details in Natural Science passages, but the MCAT is known for asking for what you least expect. **Some Natural Science passages may have, unexpectedly, very few details.** Their focus may be on issues instead of facts. Indeed, the Social Science and Humanities passages may be the ones laden with details.

Whether or not your Natural Sciences passage contains many details, you should be prepared to answer questions that test your understanding of supporting or weakening evidence, main ideas, suggestions, and viewpoints of the author.

Follow these strategies to ace Natural Science questions:

1. Natural Science questions often ask about hypothetical opponents or supporters of various theories found in the passage.
Identify the main arguments of the passage, and ask yourself which group would support one hypothesis over another.

2. Read answer choices A through D extremely carefully for each question, and eliminate wrong answers as you proceed.
Take special note of extreme words like *always*, *never*, *not*, and *must*.

3. Natural Science questions often ask about the assumptions made by a group of scientists or experts.
Identify the assumptions of each hypothesis as you read. Ask yourself, "This hypothesis is true because it assumes what?"

4. Read the passage first, and then attack the questions.
Many students think that reading the questions first is a good approach. In fact, skimming the questions before reading the passage is **counterproductive** for a number of reasons:

> 1. A single question may require the deep understanding of several portions of the passage. By keeping a question in mind as you read, you tend to search for only the most relevant part of the passage dealing with that question. By having the question already in your mind, your attention becomes too focused.

> 2. By the time you finish reading the passage the first time through, you will have forgotten a few of the questions. You will have to read the questions a second time, and probably the passage again to find their answers. This wastes too much time. You should only have to read the passage in its entirety, and each question, **once**.

> 3. For many students, trying to remember something while reading becomes a big distraction from fully comprehending the material.

5. Be vigilant of all dates and time periods mentioned in the passage.
Natural Science questions will most likely test your understanding of when events occurred.

6. Pay attention to which arguments the author supports or rejects.
The authors of Natural Science passages usually have an opinion about the ideas presented in a passage.

7. Do not overanalyze Natural Science questions.
Read them at face value.

8. Eliminate wrong answers.
Look for obvious wrong answers and use the strikethrough feature to eliminate them. One or two should jump out at you as being false. The obvious wrong answers are those that are clearly opposite to what is stated in the passage.

III. THE SOCIAL SCIENCE PASSAGE

Some students make the mistake of assuming that Social Science passages contain a bunch of fluffy ideas with few details. While many articles found in coffee-table magazines seem easy to read and comprehend, the difficulty of MCAT Social Science passages should not be underestimated. These passages come from academic journals and books, and are unusually challenging. Many examinees, upon encountering Social Science passages filled with facts and dates, are grimly reminded of a daunting Natural Science passage.

The Social Science passage can cover a very broad range of topics, ranging from sociology, anthropology, economics, and psychology, to political science, education, and history. Like its Natural Science counterpart, there is a common element found in nearly all Social Science passages - **the discussion of two or more opinions, arguments, or hypotheses. Always look for these in the text.**

READING STRATEGIES FOR THE SOCIAL SCIENCE PASSAGE

You might assume that Social Science passages are nearly the opposite of Natural Science passages, that Social Science questions deal more with inferences and less with explicitly stated facts. This is not necessarily the case.

When you read the Social Science passage, be prepared to read about cultural or political movements, along with important dates, time periods, and key arguments. The following strategies will help you achieve a higher score on Social Science passages:

1. Look for comparisons made by the author.
MCAT passages rarely stick to just one idea. The author will present two or more arguments, including those of critics.

2. Pay attention to the argument supported by the author compared to others that he or she writes about.
Where does the author stand in relation to other ideas?

3. On Social Science passages, you need to identify the assumptions of the author.
What biases does the author have, if any?

4. Identify other assumptions in the passage that are relevant to the arguments made by competing experts.

5. What groups of people would support or reject various theories or ideas presented in the passage?

6. Read every sentence.
Do not read faster than you can comprehend, and try to remember as much material as possible.

7. Social Science passages usually have implied ideas woven into them.
Try to identify implied ideas as you read.

QUESTION STRATEGIES FOR THE SOCIAL SCIENCE PASSAGE

The questions on Social Science passages are no different in their complexity than those for Natural Science or Humanities passages. Expect to encounter questions that cover not only global topics, but also extreme details. Do not presume that only Natural Science passages test for detail.

Follow the strategies below when answering Social Science questions:

1. Social Science questions often ask about influences of certain political or social movements.
Be prepared to answer questions about such influences.

2. Social Science questions often test your understanding of how certain views relate to statements from the passage.
Ask yourself what groups of people would support or refute opinions expressed in the passage.

3. Pay attention to the *tone* of the author.
An author may be **subtle** about his or her tone, so try to discern it. Rarely will an author express an **extreme** view or tone.

4. Many Social Science questions ask about the intentions of the author.
Why did the author use a special word to describe an event, or use a particular phrase to describe a person? Be prepared for these kinds of "intent" questions.

5. Read the passage first, and then answer questions.
Again, skimming the questions before reading the passage will waste valuable time ultimately.

6. Read each answer choice A through D <u>twice</u> to make sure you understand each completely.
Again, take special note of extreme words like *always*, *never*, *not*, and *must*.

A common mistake is to misunderstand exactly what a question is asking. This is especially true on Verbal Reasoning, since questions often contain subtleties. Pick up and internalize every word of a question.

IV. THE HUMANITIES PASSAGE

One of the best ways to prepare for Verbal Reasoning is to read books dealing with topics within the Humanities. Pre-med students generally have poor exposure to subjects in this broad field, and should make it a daily habit to read books from this genre. Contained within the typical Humanities passage are competing ideas that test your ability to compare and contrast concepts. Whether the passage deals with art, language, literature, communication, religion, or philosophy, you can expect to see two or three differing views on a given subject.

When you read the Humanities passage, be prepared for many details and facts that may include important dates, time periods, artistic or literary movements, cultural groups, etc. **Artistic, literary, and cultural movements are hot topics on Verbal Reasoning.**

On a slightly brighter note, Humanities passages are sometimes more interesting to read than Natural Science or Social Science passages. The Humanities subject matter can be much more fascinating than a typical dry science passage, and the style is usually more engaging.

READING STRATEGIES FOR THE HUMANITIES PASSAGE

As you read the Humanities passage, look for arguments the author is conveying. Do not get caught up in fancy descriptions about beautiful art.

Many times, the author will leave out one or two key conclusions because the author expects you to figure them out. It will be helpful to use Neuro-Visual Programming (see Chapter 9) on Humanities passages due to the very visual subject matter of these passages. However, for dry philosophy passages that tend to use many abstract and unusual terms, Neuro-Visual Programming will require much greater skill on the part of the reader.

The following points serve as strategies for reading Humanities passages:

1. Keep track of facts and dates, as well as key ideas. Always mentally document the **sequence** of main arguments of the various viewpoints.

2. Expect to read about people who criticize certain viewpoints.
Understand why critics make certain claims. Humanities passages often include the ideas of critics.

3. Determine the strengths and weaknesses of arguments expressed by critics.
Who might agree or disagree with them? Critics typically appear in passages about art, drama, literature, and philosophy.

4. Be sure to understand how the opinions of the author compare to those of other experts mentioned in the passage.
Keep the opinions of the **critics** separate from those of the **author**. Many students confuse the two.

Some conclusions made by the author are omitted because the test expects you to figure them out. Identifying unspoken conclusions is known as making inferences.

5. Use Neuro-Visual Programming and do not speed-read.
If you are using NVP correctly and efficiently, then you will not need to rush through the passage. As you will read in Chapter 12, students who score very well on Verbal Reasoning do not need to speed-read.

6. Read for meaning, not just details.
While reading, always try to answer the *how* and *why* of ideas presented to you.

QUESTION STRATEGIES FOR THE HUMANITIES PASSAGE

The questions found on Humanities passages are usually straightforward. However, many Humanities questions will ask about the primary purpose of the author, as well as the inferences and conclusions that test for a deeper understanding of the content.

The following points serve as strategies for answering Humanities questions:

1. Many questions test your direct understanding of the various viewpoints found in the passage.
For these questions, use a process of elimination. Identify and eliminate answers that express the **opposite** to what the correct answer should be, and look for answers that express some **other viewpoint** than that found in the passage.

2. Some questions ask about how the author would *respond* to a concept in the passage.
Does the author find certain concepts to be flawed, of limited use, correct, inaccurate, deft, or a combination thereof? Keep an open mind as you look for the author's opinion.

3. Try to answer the question before reading the answer choices.
Humanities passages are very tricky in that **many answer choices are often slightly misleading.** Thinking of a possible answer before looking at the choices will help you identify the correct answer with greater accuracy, and in less time.

4. For each point that the author makes, determine why the author is making that point.
Some questions ask **why** the author made specific references in the passage. (These are often questions with roman numerals.) Again, first look for the answer choices that are obviously in contradiction to the material presented.

5. Humanities questions like to test your understanding of assumptions.

Each conclusion made by the author depends on certain assumptions. For these questions, test each answer choice. The correct assumption is one that must be true in order for the conclusion to stand. **Find the answer that must be true.** This is the assumption. Answers that **could** be true or **may** be true are considered **wrong**.

Many MCAT passages test your understanding of competing theories, and to what extent the author agrees or disagrees with them. You need to discern the theories of the author, as well as those of everyone else in the passage.

CHAPTER

5

The Questions Identified

Being able to **predict** the questions for each passage is **vital** to scoring well on the Verbal Reasoning section of the MCAT. Most students jump into a passage blindly, without having a set of questions at their fingertips. This comes from a lack of practice and familiarity. Those who achieve high scores are able to anticipate questions and identify wrong answers. **Mastering the skill of predicting questions begins by knowing what kinds of questions to expect on the exam.**

As a dedicated student who wants to increase his or her verbal score dramatically, you must get your hands on plenty of sample MCAT Verbal passages.

✓ You will find a plethora of sample passages offered by the AAMC, and by commercial MCAT preparatory courses. So get your hands on as many as you can!

In the final months of your reading training program (see Chapter 10), you should plan to go through on the order of 70, yes 70, or more sample passages before you take the MCAT. These passages can be from a combination of sources. After you complete the reading training program outlined in this book and go through 70 or more passages, you should see an improvement of two or more points in your VR score **at least**.

Let us now learn the eight question types of Verbal Reasoning:

I. MAIN IDEA QUESTION

Main Idea questions ask for the author's overall message. The main idea is the thesis of the passage that ties everything together; **it is never beyond the subject matter of the passage.** Wrong answer choices are either too narrow in focus, or are beyond the setting of the passage. The following is an example of a Main Idea question:

The main thesis of the passage is that:

A.   hedonism serves the pragmatist well.
B.   the principle of pragmatism allows psychologists to identify hedonism.
C.   pragmatism is the most important principle in the field of Greek psychology.
D.   the hedonist school of psychology is responsible for the rise of all of philosophy.

Key words in a question that signal a Main Idea question are:

primary message • *central thesis* • *main idea*

Examples of Main Idea questions:

> *The primary message of the passage is that one should:*

> *The central thesis of the passage is that:*

> *In the passage, the author is primarily concerned with*
> *expressing which of the following:*

Let us take a look at the following paragraph and its accompanying question. Keep in mind that the correct answer to a Main Idea question must include ideas from the entire passage.

Equally as important as the mechanical equipment used in direct connection with the ship, is the equipment on land. Modern practice in building ocean terminals differs radically from that of the past. Today the gantry crane is
5   the unit around which all else seems to revolve. We quote once more from the above mentioned article which appeared in The Americas: 'The crane has demonstrated itself to be the most economical, most flexible, and quickest of all machinery used in connection with the
10   handling of general cargo. When the United States was suddenly called upon to equip ports in France with machinery by which a potential army of 4,000,000 American soldiers could be fed and munitioned, a gantry crane was chosen for the major share of the work.'
(Zimmermann, 253)

The main point of this passage is that:

A.   the crane is the most economical of all machinery used in the handling of cargo.
B.   the modern methods of building ocean terminals depart from those of the past, especially when considering the gantry crane.
C.   the crane is a singular example of the importance of equipment on land, an importance which parallels that of equipment used directly with ships.
D.   the equipment for serving ships has changed over time.

The paragraph begins with the salient point that the equipment on land and those in direct connection with the ships are equally important. The discussion about the gantry crane highlights this idea and serves as the pinnacle example of the importance of the equipment used on land.

The main purpose of the paragraph is not simply to show the importance of the crane, so choice A is wrong. Answer B may fool some students because it is nearly a direct excerpt from the passage. But it is wrong since it is too specific and does not answer the question. The main thesis of this passage focuses on the evolution of equipment for ships, not on the methods of building ocean terminals. So while B is true, it does not provide the main idea of the paragraph.

Just because an answer is true does not make it correct!

Choice D is also true, but is too vague. Yes, the equipment for serving ships has indeed changed over time, but the main message of the paragraph requires more focus. The **main idea** of the passage is that the importance of the equipment used directly for ships parallels that of the equipment on land as exemplified by the gantry crane. Thus, the best answer is C.

Always remember that the correct answer to Main Idea questions must have the correct level of focus that is not too general, or too specific. Do not be fooled by answer choices that are true, but are too vague or too focused. Other wrong answer choices may include those that stray away from the focus of the passage. For example, if a passage were to cover volcanoes in Alaska, then an answer choice about volcanoes in Hawaii would be beyond the setting of the material, and incorrect. For more discussion on the topic and setting of a passage, see Chapter 6.

II. DIRECT COMPREHENSION QUESTION

Comprising the majority of Verbal Reasoning questions, the Direct Comprehension question asks the reader to draw a direct, non-implied conclusion based on passage material. These questions require straightforward analysis; they do not ask the reader to apply information to a new context, or draw inferences using an implied detail.

At least half of the questions in Verbal Reasoning ask you to make a direct evaluation of the information. Many questions ask you to evaluate the **effect** of an issue or activity presented in the passage. Other questions ask you **why** something in the passage is happening. These are simple questions that test your comprehension. Your best strategy is to use the Three Point analysis when reading the passage. Let us look at the Three Point approach:

(Before we proceed, let us be clear about the term *question stem*. The question stem is the sentence or phrase that precedes the answer choices - it is the part that actually poses the question.)

THREE POINT ANALYSIS

Whenever an event, argument, or phenomenon is discussed in the passage, you should answer three questions about it:

> **1.** What are the claims of this argument; what does it represent or what does it state?
>
> **2.** When does this argument succeed or fail; what weakens and strengthens it?
>
> **3.** Who supports and rejects this argument, and why?

Always make it a point to answer these three questions whenever you come across a key hypothesis, argument, or phenomenon in the passage. A good barometer is to expect one key argument to appear at least *once per paragraph*. There are exceptions to this of course, but this level of expectation will cover most situations.

Key words in the stem signaling a Direct Comprehension question:

can be concluded • which one best represents • are the reasons for • which would be the most/least effective

Examples of Direct Comprehension question stems:

> *According to the passage, how did the problem of viability change since the turn of the twentieth century?*

> *Which of the following best represents the relationship between hubris and jingoism, as it is described by the author?*

> *According to the passage, the introduction of iron solved the migratory problem in which of the following ways?*

Based on the information presented in the passage, the poupée most likely represents which of the following?

Which of the following types of film processing techniques would be the most effective for preservation, according to passage indications?

The practices of the Orange clan described in the passage most clearly agree with the ancient legal practice of:

The following is a good example of a straightforward Direct Comprehension question:

It can reasonably be concluded from the passage that modern archeology began when archeologists:

A.   accepted modern tools into their repertoire of methods and practices.
B.   rejected outmoded models of geological history.
C.   began to accept tenured positions in academia.
D.   developed more sophisticated instruments.

✔ As you read **each paragraph** of a Verbal Reasoning passage, you should make a **mental note about the main conclusion or idea of that paragraph**. Each paragraph has a special message and purpose. Each paragraph tells a story with a short, yet crucial point.

On the day of your MCAT, your mind should automatically understand and remember the main message of **each** paragraph within a passage. Taken together, the messages of all the paragraphs reveal the overall message, or thesis, of the passage. Being able to tackle Direct Comprehension questions means that you must perfect the art of finding and then comprehending the message of **each** paragraph.

Remember to look for themes and conclusions, and make an extra effort to remember the order in which they were presented.

✓ Early in your reading training, do not focus on details. Just read for ideas and points made by the author. Take note of them in your mind.

III. DIRECT REFERENCE QUESTION

Another type of question on the MCAT Verbal Reasoning section is the Direct Reference question. This type, in which the question stem makes a direct reference to the material, refers back to specific words in the passage. You do not need to look back at the passage to answer these questions necessarily. Just because the question quotes the material, you should resist the temptation to look back at the passage and *search* for the answer. Each time you refer back, you throw away valuable seconds. **Look back at the passage only to confirm your answer, not to search for it.**

The Direct Reference question is not only testing your direct comprehension of the material, but also your understanding of assumptions, implications, applications, function, and structure. The following is an example of the multi-faceted nature of a Direct Reference question:

> In the context of the arguments made by the author, the phrase "ultimate serendipity" refers to:
>
> **A.**   the author's view of Smith's astrological discovery.
> **B.**   a character from a novel by Smith.
> **C.**   a view of Smith's metaphysical interpretation of the universe that the author dismisses.
> **D.**   the discovery of the North Scrolls.

> Very rarely, a Verbal Reasoning passage may contain a chart or diagram. In the off chance that a diagram does appear, then you can expect to see questions asking what it represents and how it applies to specific contexts.

A Direct Reference question may be testing your ability to make a deduction, as in:

> The author states that "many Neolithic practices ensured the survival of migration." This proposition rests on which of the following characteristics about migration?
>
> **I.**   settlements are established year-round
> **II.**   villages are not permanent
> **III.** migration differs from nomadic behavior
>
> **A.**   I only
> **B.**   II only
> **C.**   I and II
> **D.**   I, II and III

Any **direct quote** from the passage found in the question stem indicates a Direct Reference question.

Examples of Direct Reference question stems:

> *According to the passage, people considering "veiled attempts" in the context of usury would:*
>
> *Which of the following would a "gracious interloper" regard as the funeral right that must not be abridged?*

The passage suggests that the attempt to impugn
"backwater hardened crooks" failed because:

The reader can conclude that a basic assumption of
"those in favor of using any means possible to dispose of
denigrating cloisters" is that:

One of the biggest traps of Direct Reference questions is the loss of time. Most students - in a knee-jerk response - look back at the passage to search for the quoted reference. **Do not suddenly look back at the passage; think about it first.**

Using Neuro-Visual Programming (see Chapter 9) with refined reading skills should enable you to answer these questions **without having to refer back to the passage.**

Furthermore, the computerized MCAT exam usually omits line or paragraph reference numbers. Therefore, searching for the quoted portion will most likely waste valuable time.

> . Many Direct Reference questions do **not** include
> a line reference number in the stem.
>
> You do not have time to search for the reference.
> Simply answer the question, and then look back to verify.

IV. INFERENCE QUESTION

Many questions in Verbal Reasoning test your understanding of concepts that are **not stated** in the passage. These include inferences, assumptions, and implications. These all fall under the category of Inference questions.

Inference questions require that you understand arguments, and how they are constructed. You must feel comfortable identifying:

> ✓ stated conclusions
> ✓ stated evidence
> ✓ implied conclusions
> ✓ implied evidence

If you are at all uneasy about logical argumentation, I suggest you visit your local library or bookstore and acquire a book on logic. In the meantime, here is a quick review.

LOGICAL ARGUMENT REVIEW

Understanding logical argumentation is very important on the MCAT. In the world of logic, the **premise** of an argument is the statement that presents reasons or evidence, and the **conclusion** is the statement that the evidence supports. Thus, forming an argument is the process of providing stated facts (called evidence) to support a statement (the conclusion). The conclusion is the proposition arrived at by logical reasoning. For example:

ALL DOGS ARE ANIMALS, ALL ANIMALS ARE BLUE   -   the *evidence*

ALL DOGS ARE BLUE   -   the *conclusion*

On the MCAT, the logical argument may be subtle and not clearly presented. The author may either state the evidence or conclusion, or leave them undisclosed:

1. *stated* evidence, as revealed through **facts**;

2. *stated* conclusions, as revealed through **opinions** or arguments;

3. *unstated* evidence, also known as **assumptions**;

4. *unstated* conclusions, also known as **inferences**.

✓ Always strive to identify unstated evidence and conclusions. This is absolutely crucial to your Verbal Reasoning success.

Let us look at the meanings of an inference and an assumption. Making an **inference** is the act or process of deriving a conclusion based solely on what one already knows. It is a determination arrived at by reasoning, using facts to arrive at a broader conclusion. **Making an inference is the act of drawing a conclusion from, or making a decision upon an analysis of data.** For the MCAT, you can think of an inference as an implied conclusion (one that is not stated). The following illustrates this:

Evidence:

ALL HAPPY ASTRONAUTS HAVE BLUE EYES, AND
MARY IS A HAPPY ASTRONAUT.

What inference can we make from the evidence? We can conclude that Mary has blue eyes. Since this conclusion was not stated, it is called an *inference*.

Let us look at the meaning of an assumption. **An assumption is a presupposition, or the basis of an assertion, required to be true for the assertion to be true.** Assumptions are often unstated, and nearly all thought processes and knowledge are based upon one assumption or another. On the MCAT, an assumption is an **unstated fact or evidence** that must be true for the particular conclusion to be true. On questions where the conclusion is presented to you in the question stem, you may need to identify the assumption. Let us look at the following example:

On Mt. Chambers, the number of ski lift tickets doubled in the month of January. Thus, skiing on Mt. Chambers became much more popular during January.

How do you find the assumption of an argument such as this? First, figure out various reasons that **could explain** what is happening in the statement, (think about a couple of reasons that would cause sales of ski lift tickets to double). Second, determine which of those reasons must be true in order for the conclusion to be true. This is the assumption.

So, ski lift tickets could double because more people are purchasing them, or the same number of people are purchasing more than one ticket. Or, perhaps, fewer people went skiing in January, but those who did purchased many ski lift tickets. You can see the possibilities.

After thinking of various explanations, we select the explanation that **must** be true for the conclusion (that more people decided to go skiing) to be true. The assumption, then, must be that **the rise in tickets occurred because more people bought them**, and not because the same number of (or fewer) skiers purchased multiple tickets.

When you encounter an MCAT question asking you to identify the assumption, the correct answer **must** be true in order for the conclusion to be true. **An answer that could be true, or is sometimes true, is wrong.** Understand the difference. Test each answer choice to see which one must be true to make the argument true.

> You can identify the assumption of a conclusion by asking what implied evidence **must** be true in order to make the conclusion true.

Some Inference questions may ask for conclusions, others may ask for assumptions, while others may look for what is implied. The following are two examples of Inference questions:

There are many assumptions in the scientific community about the Mountain of Vallarm. Which of the following conclusions about the Mountain of Vallarm can be most reasonably inferred from the passage?

A.   the Mountain of Vallarm is likely to be excavated for its rich mineral resources.
B.   mining for rare metals in the Vallarm Valley is prohibited which will prevent the erosion of the Mountain of Vallarm.
C.   the Mountain of Vallarm is taller than all other mountains in the valley.
D.   more vegetation covers the Mountain of Vallarm than any other mountain in the valley.

The passage suggests that which of the following is implicit in written documents concerning globalization?

A.   the larger the number of scientific breakthroughs, the greater the globalization.
B.   industrial activity correlates with the amount of globalization.
C.   higher pollution is an indicator of greater globalization.
D.   the fewer the number of plant species, the greater the globalization.

Key words signaling Inference questions:

imply • *the passage suggests* • *it can be inferred*

Examples of Inference question stems:

The passage suggests that an effective way for artists to improve their talent would be to:

In what way does the passage imply that The Salamander and Ulysses differ?

It can be inferred from the passage that the author would most likely agree with:

Which one of the following about venture capital can be inferred from the passage?

When you encounter an Inference question, first determine whether the question asks for an unstated *conclusion* or an unstated *piece of evidence*. **Since the answer to an Inference question is not stated explicitly, you should not need to look back at the passage to identify it.**

✓ Remember, you want to save as much time as possible. This means that you should look for the unstated conclusions and pieces of evidence during your initial reading of the passage.

V. STRUCTURE AND FUNCTION QUESTION

Questions on Verbal Reasoning will also test your understanding of the **structure** of the passage, as well as the **purpose** of key ideas or phrases within the passage. How arguments are presented can differ widely, and knowing why certain ideas or words are used is equally as important. Actually, you should expect to find a question asking for the purpose of a word or phrase on nearly every passage. Questions asking for the structure of the material, however, are not as common.

Many questions on the MCAT ask you to identify the purpose of a word, phrase, or idea in context of the entire passage. An author may state something for a number of reasons that may be apparent, or difficult to discern. Keep in mind that an author may use a certain word, phrase, or argument in order to:

1. provide an example

2. emphasize a point

3. support an argument

4. weaken an argument

5. demonstrate or illustrate an idea

6. define a concept.

Be aware that a Structure and Function question can sometimes resemble a Main Idea question, even though *they are not the same.*

Remember, the Main Idea question asks you to identify an overall **idea** or concept summarizing the entire material. The Structure and Function question asks the reader to identify either the **purpose** of certain material (the reason specific material was written), or the **construction** of the passage (how the material is presented). The two examples below help clarify the difference:

Main Idea question

The primary message of the passage is that one should:

A.   recognize the social aspects of sculpting.

B.   appreciate the religious history of sculpting.

C.   understand the tension between the sculptor and his invisible audience.

D.   distinguish between the labor and the celebration of sculpting

STRUCTURE AND FUNCTION QUESTION

The primary purpose of the passage is to:

A.   present two conflicting arguments, and find one
to be more acceptable then the other.

B.   discuss the many aspects of a single theory.

C.   convince the reader to side with one theory.

D.   compare the similarities between two theories.

Here we see that the first question asks for the main concept of the passage, the *what* of the overall material. The second question asks for the intention of the passage, or the *why* of the passage. **Pay close attention to these distinctions** as you figure out the meanings of passage material. Read each question carefully because many students miss points for not understanding the difference.

> Whenever you come across facts or evidence in a passage,
> always ask yourself why the author presents it.

Let us look at more examples of Structure and Function questions:

Asks for function

A probable reason for the use of the word "computerism"
is the author's:

A.   awareness of the differences between popular
technological advances and secret projects.

B.   opinion that the use of rare metals in computer
chips will pollute the planet.

C.   belief in a divine presence that occupies computer
motherboards.

D.   wish for all people to speak a common computer
language.

Asks for structure

Which of the following characterizes how the author's argument is presented?

A.   examples followed by a theoretical explanation.

B.   a critique followed by examples.

C.   a hypothesis, followed by examples, ending with logical arguments.

D.   descriptions of theories followed by examples.

Asks for function

The author quotes Neucomb in the third paragraph. His primary purpose in doing this is to:

A.   suggest that Hardy's theories were misconstrued by Neucomb.

B.   emphasize a flaw found in Hardy's isocentric model after the Great Fire.

C.   clarify a commonality between anthropology and astrology in the Silver Age.

D.   indicate the extent of Neucomb's influence over matters of luck and magic.

Questions that ask for the purpose of a word or phrase are really testing your understanding of the author's arguments and ideas. You must read below the surface of the text and understand the purpose and structure of each paragraph.

Key words in the stem signaling a Structure and Function question:

*the purpose of • probable reason for • in order to
• the structure of • what role*

Examples of Structure and Function question stems:

> *What role does the sentence "However, the poor man's philosophy should embrace the upper crust of society" play in the passage?*

> *The reference to the subliminal orchestra of plant life serves which of the following purposes?*

> *A probable reason for the use of the phrase "transient goodness" is to:*

> *The purpose of introducing the Bremmen theory after the introduction of the Verta theory is to:*

Structure and Function questions are not terribly common on the MCAT, but you should still be prepared for them. It is estimated that perhaps three or four Structure and Function questions will appear on the Verbal Reasoning section, which means that you have about a fifty-fifty chance of finding one on any given passage.

Always ask *why* and *how* given information is presented in the passage.

VI. STRENGTHEN AND WEAKEN QUESTION

A more common question on the MCAT is the Strengthen and Weaken question. The writers of the exam love to test your understanding of how concepts fail or succeed. This question takes many forms as we will see. Basically, **once an argument, process, or hypothesis appears in a passage, you are responsible for comprehending how to strengthen or weaken it.**

The good news about Strengthen and Weaken questions is that you can **quickly eliminate one or two of the answer choices** most of the time. How, you may ask? There appears to be a trend that one answer choice is the *opposite* to what the question asks. For example, if the question asks for you to find what strengthens the author's argument, then one answer choice will most likely weaken the author's argument. Another common wrong answer is the one that *neither strengthens nor weakens* a given argument. These answers that have no impact on the argument will occasionally trap students, so be careful.

The recommended strategy to tackling Strengthen and Weaken questions is to look quickly for the answers that are wrong: the answer that is **opposite** to what the question asks, or the answer that **neither strengthens nor weakens** it. By looking for those wrong answers, you become more aware of the correct answer.

> By looking for wrong answers, you engage your mind
> and eliminate choices. This will make identifying the correct answer
> much easier.

The following rudimentary example demonstrates the point:

> The author states that "people care more about sports than science." Which of the following would most *weaken* this assertion?
>
> **A.** People would rather attend baseball games than science fairs.
> **B.** Scientists fail to recognize the value of sports in their communities.
> **C.** People watch more science shows than sports events on TV.
> **D.** There is a great rise in science majors.

Looking at the answer choices, we can immediately throw out choice A because it presents the **opposite** to what we are looking for. We expected to find such a choice.

Choice B is wrong because it **neither strengthens nor weakens** the argument. The answer addresses only a subset of the population. Whether scientists care more or less about sports is not relevant. Thus, choice B is too narrow in focus.

Choice D neglects addressing the rise, or lack thereof, of sports enthusiasts, so we cannot surmise whether the rise in science majors is outpacing a supposed rise in sports enthusiasts. Thus, choice D is not the best answer.

Choice C correctly weakens the assertion that people are more interested in sports than science. From this we can infer that the people care more about science. We see that choice C is correct.

Key words in the stem signaling a Strengthen and Weaken question:

which would weaken • which would strengthen
• which would be most troublesome • which would most help to clarify
• which statement is inconsistent with

Examples of Strengthen and Weaken question stems:

> *Which of the following would most weaken the author's conclusion that Greek pottery incorporates Eastern symbolism?*

> *Which of the following findings about the Icelandic cliff formations would be most troublesome for the Erosion theory?*

> *The concept of reciprocal psychology most strongly supports:*

> *Suppose that all Muskeet birds migrated South before Summer. This statement would challenge which astrological myth?*

Let us look at a few other forms of the Strengthen and Weaken question. Sometimes, the strengthen and weaken aspects of a question appear in the answer choices. The following example is both an Inference question and Strengthen and Weaken question:

> It can be inferred that in relation to his theory of nebula refraction among binary systems, Gregory's "transient quark" experiments:
>
> **A.** strongly supported the theory.
> **B.** provided supporting evidence but not conclusive evidence for the theory.
> **C.** left many in doubt about the theory.
> **D.** disproved the theory convincingly.

This question is asking for the impact that Gregory's experiments had on his theory of nebula refraction among binary systems. The passage does not reveal the impact explicitly. You must infer it. Before looking at the answer choices, always try to answer Strengthen and Weaken questions by first thinking about them. Try to come up with the answer yourself (before looking at the answer choices).

Again, be suspicious of extreme language such as "disproved . . . convincingly" in choice D. In order for a claim like this to be correct, the author would need to make such sentiments very clear in the passage. If the author leaves any doubt about the extreme stance, then answers with such strong language cannot be justified (and are thus incorrect).

> Answer choices that use extreme language must be clearly supported in the passage. If they are not, eliminate them.

✔ Sometimes, a question is actually a combination of two question types. You may find an Inference question and Direct Reference question combined. Or, you my see a Direct Comprehension question combined with a Direct Reference question.

Shown on the next page is another form of the Strengthen and Weaken question. On occasion, a question stem includes a new concept that must be weighed against the information in the passage. This is called a New Information question (see page 73). The new information provided in the stem can take the form of an assumption, opinion, or fact.

The following example is both a Strengthen and Weaken question, and a New Information question:

Assume that Chioma's imaginary civilization could acquire synthetic polymers as easily as experimental ceramics, and recycle them at a lower cost. Would this information, if true, further the author's argument?

A.   Yes; it would make more impressive the fact that ten percent of global resources would help advance future societies.

B.   Yes; it would support the Geary theory.

C.   No; it would simply weaken the other civilizations of Chioma's futuristic world.

D.   No; it would reveal nothing about the future allocation of global resources.

As you have seen, Strengthen and Weaken questions test your understanding of how concepts or theories relate to each other. Pay attention to facts presented in the passage, and ask how those facts impact various arguments or theories.

VII. ABOUT THE AUTHOR QUESTION

A certain number of Verbal Reasoning questions will ask about the opinion, tone, and background of the author. These questions often catch the casual examinee off guard because they appear very subjective and arbitrary. But remember, **there is one best answer that cannot be disputed.** Do not fall for extreme choices. Select what sounds most reasonable to you. With plenty of reading practice, you will develop a good feel for the tone of an author. If you read most of the books in the suggested reading list in Chapter 11, you will gain enough experience to identify when an author is being sarcastic, serious, humorous, etc.

Keep a lookout for opinions expressed in the passage. These are very valuable for answering questions regarding the author.

REMEMBER THE AUTHOR

The temptation for most readers is to focus solely on the facts and ideas, on the concepts and details of the passage. But there is also an entirely deeper level to which we should pay attention - that of the author's perspective.

When we read, the author invites us into his or her world. We oblige by giving our full attention to the voice the author so kindly shares. The author wants us to hear more than mere ideas. We should listen to the author's **tone**, and read between the lines to make **inferences**. In an abstract sense, we become an author as well. We write the interpretive half of the written page, and we need to write it responsibly. (For more on the philosophical aspects of the author-reader relationship, read Terry Eagleton's book, *Literary Theory: An Introduction*.)

> Pay attention to the deeper levels of meaning, such as that of inferences and tone.
>
> And remember, try to answer the questions before you look at the answer choices.

As you read any book or article, you should pay attention to two elements: the concepts, and the author. You need to discern the *what*, the *how*, and the *why* of the various elements in the passage; not only what the author is saying, but how he is saying it. Why is he saying this? From what vantage point?

Let us look at some About the Author questions:

The author of the passage seems to hold the belief that:

A. psychosocial progress ignores the dangers of social anxiety and assimilation.
B. members of society who reject assimilation will triumph in a new land.
C. larger countries offer new freedoms.
D. social anxiety helps guide psychosocial progress.

The author's attitude toward monolithic business practices in third-world countries is most accurately described as:

A. optimistic.
B. neutral.
C. dubious.
D. worrisome.

Many About the Author questions are combined with Direct Comprehension questions. About the Author questions ask about the author, whether it be the tone or attitude, or the ideas supported or rejected by the author. The Direct Comprehension question evaluates concepts. The following is a combination of a Direct Comprehension question and an About the Author question:

According to the author, the general effect of seasonal foliage on farming land is:

A. a slight decrease in water levels.
B. discoloration across rocky terrain.
C. an increase in the wood beetle population.
D. a drop in the soil pH.

Key words in the stem signaling an About the Author question:

the author would most likely agree with
• opinion of the author • the tone of the author
• the author's point • the author's attitude

Examples of About the Author question stems:

Which of the following opinions would the author be most likely to endorse?

The author's apparent point in referring to the melting of the golden amulets is that:

Apparently, the author's preferred approach to the dismantling of sink vessels is to bring attention to:

The author's attitude towards lightening storms in the winter months is most accurately described as:

The tone of the author is best described as:

Always remember that the **content** of the passage and **beliefs** of the author are not always congruent. Many arguments in a passage may reflect opinions **not supported by the author**. Separate the two.

✔ **The author may write about views that he or she disagrees with.** Be prepared to encounter theories and ideas that run counter to those of the author. Questions on the MCAT will test whether or not you make these distinctions.

VIII. NEW INFORMATION QUESTION

Some of the more difficult Verbal Reasoning questions involve the application and incorporation of new concepts. The New Information question will provide new content that will ask for a specific inference or conclusion that requires you to incorporate ideas from the passage. Whether you are applying concepts in the passage to new information, or applying new information to concepts provided in the passage, the end result is the same.

The temptation, when tackling New Information questions, is to select the answer that looks most similar to the passage. This temptation is fraught with peril. One choice may even include a direct quote from the passage, which you should be wary of. Be cautious of selecting an answer choice that sounds very similar to specific wording in the passage.

✓ To stave off this temptation, first try to answer the question without looking at the answer choices. This is wise for two reasons: it prevents you from falling for attractive wrong answers, and it allows you to eliminate wrong choices more efficiently which saves you time.

Here are three examples of New Information questions:

Suppose it was demonstrated that blue light can pass through binary star systems in the vicinity of a black hole. What impact would this have on the author's claim?

A.   It would weaken it by suggesting that the Pulsar Phenomenon held true for all star systems.

B.   It would weaken it because the author does not support the Pulsar Phenomenon.

C.   It would strengthen it, by supporting the KP Stellar Theory.

D.   It would strengthen it, as the author believes all light passes through star systems.

In 1207, a foreign clan of leaders appointed a governor to write the new constitution for the East Valley. One could infer from the passage that the constitution included:

A.   the implementation of a taxation system.
B.   the elimination of stone masonry.
C.   an emphasis on free education.
D.   the division of land into fealties.

Before wooden statues were completely replaced by woven dolls, the Verasang Tribe made hybrid figurines made of both wood and wool. The most reasonable expectation on the basis of passage information is that customers valued:

A.   softer materials.
B.   more expensive materials.
C.   the wool, which proved costly for craftsmen.
D.   silk, which craftsmen replaced with wool.

Key words in the stem signaling a New Information question:

suppose it were demonstrated • *given the following were true* • *consider the following*

Examples of New Information question stems:

Consider the following statement: "The gross product of the European Union will increase faster than the GNP of South America under free trade agreements." How does this statement impact the ideas in the passage?

If the passage information is correct, what inference is justified if one were to learn that crop rotation existed twenty years after the Jade Period?

Elsewhere, the author of the passage states that the character Zora considered her ability to fly her best trait, but that such a trait proves nothing about the magical abilities of the Fairyfolk. This statement most directly weakens the passage assertion that:

Many New Information questions include other kinds of question types, the more common being the Strengthen and Weaken question and Inference question. **Whenever you see new content that is provided in a question stem, you are dealing with a New Information question.**

When you encounter a New Information question, recall in your mind the main points of each paragraph in **list fashion**. If you are using Neuro-Visual Programming, then you should track this information in your mental arena. Next, think about *how* the new information impacts each main point from the passage. Look for *who* or *what* is impacted, and in which manner. Then, predict your own answer to the question. Finally, look at the choices to see which one comes closest to your educated prediction.

THE FOUR-STEP METHOD FOR NEW INFORMATION QUESTIONS

1. Summarize **main points** of each paragraph.
2. Determine the **how, who** and **what for each point**.
3. Make a prediction of the answer in your own words.
4. Compare answer choices.

IX. ADVICE FOR ANSWERING QUESTIONS

In order to avoid attractive answer choices that are wrong, first try to answer the question on your own (always begin this way). Then, look for the two fairly common wrong choices: the answer that is **opposite** to what is being asked, and the answer that is **never mentioned in the passage.** Cross out these choices using the strikethrough feature, and select the best answer from the two remaining choices. If you have to guess, at least you have a 50% chance of success.

X. IDENTIFY THE QUESTION QUIZ

After you have memorized the eight question types of Verbal Reasoning and feel comfortable identifying each, you can try your hand at identifying these sample questions. You should be able to identify questions based solely on the stem (answer choices are not provided). Some questions are combinations of two different types. Answers to this exercise are found in the Appendix. The first one is done for you:

1. The author of the passage probably supports the use of red fireworks in lunar celebrations because the custom:

Question Type(s): Direct Comprehension

2. Given the author's statements, if a team of civic engineers found a number of rusted supports previously repaired using G30X Paint, the discovery would most likely strengthen the assumption that:

Question Type(s):

3. Which of the following, if true, would least weaken Josiah's assumption that "the Celtic religious ceremonies always occurred at dusk"?

Question Type(s):

4. The author's discussion regarding the broken bowls and ceramic relics is intended to illustrate that:

Question Type(s):

5. According to the Easton Theory of Lending, exponential growth plateaus every three years in exact multiples of the lender's interest rates. How does this new theory impact the argument that "people will face better times ahead"?

Question Type(s):

6. If the quotation from Professor Horvasky were to strengthen the author's argument that "submarine vectors mimic those of whales," then which of the following assumptions must be true?

Question Type(s):

7. According to the passage, the people of Norway:

Question Type(s):

8. Which of the following questions can best be answered by arguments implied in the passage?

Question Type(s):

9. Based on arguments about "ancient roller coasters for religious ceremonies," with which of the following statements would the author least likely agree?

Question Type(s):

10. The main thesis of the passage is that:

Question Type(s):

11. The passage suggests that complicated emotional responses are responses that can interfere with:

Question Type(s):

12. The author's tone towards Civic Nationalist legislators is most accurately described as:

Question Type(s):

13. Why does the author consider the impact of transitional housing to be "less understood" than the impact of vagrancy?

Question Type(s):

14. What inference is justified if one were to learn that brown lichen lives symbiotically with another organism?

Question Type(s):

15. According to the passage, recreation in the United States is like a bowl of cherries in all of the following ways EXCEPT:

Question Type(s):

16. It is reasonable to conclude that the author of this passage would accept the argument that:

Question Type(s):

17. The arguments of the anthropologists are presented in the passage in the following manner:

Question Type(s):

18. The author presents a critique of threaded baskets that appear to mimic those made by indigenous people. This critique serves to:

Question Type(s):

19. In this passage, the author's tone is one of:

Question Type(s):

20. The passage states that the blind concentric principle promotes the notion that:

Question Type(s):

21. The fact that Loran of the Fire represents a synergistic avatar of the many functions of the caste system would most directly cast doubt on an assumption that:

Question Type(s):

22. According to the author, the "fabulous finding" that the imaginary numbers of physics appear to have been influenced by Nature's Hand impacts biologists how?

Question Type(s):

23. One can most sensibly infer from the passage that "benevolent signs in the sky can influence agricultural practices":

Question Type(s):

PART III

Building the Foundation:
Developing Your
Comprehension, Memory,
and Active Reading Skills

CHAPTER

6

Essentials of Reading Comprehension

IN THIS CHAPTER

One of the most important goals of your training is to achieve excellent reading comprehension. There is a difference between reading comprehension that comes easily, and the comprehension that you must work hard to master.

Anyone can pick up a magazine and understand what it says. But can you read an MCAT passage in three minutes and understand what it says? Can you retain the main idea of each paragraph, the implied and non-stated conclusions, the supporting evidence, along with the sequence in which those ideas were presented, and apply all of this to new information and draw appropriate conclusions?

This high level of reading comprehension does not come easily. It requires an analytical mode of reading with diligent effort on a continual basis.

COMPREHENSION PART ONE:

I. IDENTIFYING TOPIC, SETTING, AND MAIN IDEA

The ability to comprehend material on the MCAT at an advanced level is absolutely essential. To comprehend written material means to fully understand both the **direct** and **implied** meanings, which the MCAT will test.

The MCAT draws material usually from expert writers that have published within the last half century, covering diverse topics like psychology, sociology, anthropology, natural sciences, literature, government, and humanities. While professional expository writers present their ideas in structured ways, the passages on the MCAT are often discontinuous paragraphs pieced together. This means that the topics, ideas, arguments, and tones may shift quickly from paragraph to paragraph, creating a potentially distressing experience for any untrained reader. Let us look at three basic elements of a passage that should be identified in the first steps towards full comprehension. They are: **topic**, **setting**, and **main idea.**

THE TOPIC

The subject matter of the passage, what the author is writing about (not the author's viewpoint), is the **topic**. There is a difference between the opinion, or argument, of an author and the subject which the author is writing about. You should identify the topic of any passage automatically. If the passage is about trees, then the topic is trees. **Be able to state the topic in a word or two in your mind.** The topic will help you answer questions about the **main idea**. Be careful to identify as the topic that which fully encompasses the **entire** passage.

> Erroneously, many students focus on the latter portions of a passage, mistakenly identifying the topic as that which summarizes only the second half of the material.

Let us take a look at the following excerpt from *Chemistry and Civilization*:

> Educated people are, of course, aware that fixed nitrogen
> in combination with carbon, hydrogen, and some few other
> minor elements is built up by vegetable life and is in turn
> assimilated into the bodies of animals, thus supplying our
> 5   food of almost every variety. It is also fairly well
> understood that in the process of digestion the complex
> nitrogenous bodies built up by plant life are broken down
> to simpler forms, in part supplying animal life energy and
> in part being voided by the animal, the manurial nitrogen
> 10   products going back to the soil, thus completing what is
> known as the nitrogen cycle, caught in the wheel of which
> all material life, including the much-vaunted culture and
> progress of modern civilization, hangs suspended.
>
> One thing that is not very generally apprehended by
> 15   educated people, however, is that without fixed nitrogen in
> great abundance mankind could not wage war upon one
> another under modern conditions. Ever since gunpowder
> replaced the bow and arrow, fixed nitrogen has been used
> by man to hurl destructive missiles at his adversaries. In
> 20   fact, it should be stated that no explosive substance has
> ever been used in peace or war, which did not depend for
> its activity on the extraordinary properties of the element
> nitrogen, which, as the major constituent of the air we
> breathe, could almost be said to content itself with the inert
> 25   and pacific role of toning down the activities of its restless
> neighbor, oxygen. (Cushman, 81)

What is the topic of this passage? Start by looking at the first paragraph.
We read that the first sentence talks about fixed nitrogen and its part in
food. This could be the topic. The rest of the first paragraph discusses
the nitrogen cycle and its central importance to civilization.

From this we feel led to believe that the topic of the entire passage may be
about fixed nitrogen, but we need to see **whether the second paragraph
supports or refutes this.**

The first sentence of the second paragraph (lines 14 - 17) shifts our focus to war, and the role of fixed nitrogen in battle. As we read further, we see that the rest of the paragraph is about the central role of fixed nitrogen in warfare once gunpowder replaced the bow and arrow. Thus, the topic of the second paragraph can be given as fixed nitrogen as well. Since the first and second paragraphs are in agreement, then we can thus conclude that the topic of the overall passage is *fixed nitrogen*.

THE SETTING

The setting of a passage describes the breadth of the topic, placing the topic in a specific context.

A passage may have more than one setting. For example, a passage comparing the manufacturing practices of the automobile industry to those of the textile industry will have two settings (automobiles and textiles). Many questions on the MCAT exam test for setting. For these questions, wrong answer choices look attractive because the topic will be correct but the setting will either not exist, or refer to the wrong portion of the passage.

If an answer is correct factually, it may still be the wrong answer. In order for an answer to be correct, it must provide the right information and refer to the **same place** in the passage as that referred to by the question.

Also, an answer may be correct factually, but may fail to answer the question. Watch out for these tempting, yet wrong answer choices.

Let us refer back to the excerpt from *Chemistry and Civilization*. We saw that the topic is fixed nitrogen. What is the setting of this entire passage? The setting of the first paragraph can be summarized as the nitrogen cycle. The setting of the second paragraph places the focus on nitrogen's importance in warfare. Thus, the setting of this entire passage can be given as nitrogen's role in both nature and modern warfare.

ANOTHER SIMPLE EXAMPLE

Imagine that you are given a passage about volcanoes. If the first half of a passage discusses volcanoes in Hawaii, and the second half presents volcanoes in Fiji, then the **topic** is *volcanoes* and the **setting** is *Hawaii and Fiji*.

To say that the setting is the Pacific Rim would be incorrect, because that answer would include Hawaii, Fiji, and many other locations never mentioned in the passage.

Consider a variation of this. If the first half of a passage were to discuss volcanic eruptions in Hawaii and the second half were to examine tsunamis in Jakarta, then the **topic** could be *volcanoes and tsunamis* while the **setting** would be *Hawaii and Jakarta*. Any answer choices involving other geographic regions would be beyond the setting of the passage. **On the MCAT, be on the lookout for answer choices that belong to a setting different from that of the passage.**

THE MAIN IDEA

The **main idea** of a passage is the author's thesis, or main point, which usually includes the *topic* and *setting*. **The skilled reader should be able to express the main idea in one concise sentence.** The main idea can be thought of as the overall goal of the passage. The main idea is the **reason** why the author wrote the passage, such as to argue for or against something. The main idea should reflect the message of the author, or the author's **opinion**. In addition, in order to comprehend the material fully, you must be able to identify the main idea **of each paragraph** as well.

Looking at the excerpt by Cushman on page 85, we can see that the author expresses a main idea for each paragraph.

In the first paragraph, the main idea is to show that all material life depends on the nitrogen cycle (or fixed nitrogen). The main idea of the next paragraph is to demonstrate that modern warfare would not have arisen without fixed nitrogen. Notice how each main idea **includes the topic and setting of the passage.**

> When you correctly identify the topic and setting, you comprehend the main idea much more readily.

Let us look at another example to practice identifying topic, setting, and main idea:

But it is not after all as a stimulant that alcohol will play its great role in the future history of mankind. Civilization needs power. The nineteenth century worked out its destiny with coal, the twentieth is working toward gasoline
5   and oil. The steam engine started as a coal burner, the internal combustion engine as an oil burner, but what is to come when the coal mines and the oil wells have been gutted? Coal and oil, though abundant, are not inexhaustible, but alcohol can be made while we sleep by
10 the tireless energy of countless billions of microorganisms. Wherever starch and sugar in any form can be made to grow, alcohol can be harvested to feed the engines of the future, as hay and oats were grown to feed the horses of the past. Herein, we may with some degree of confidence
15 predict, lies the future of alcohol in the service of man.

We all remember the part that the dirigible balloon played in the war, and that recently an English dirigible has crossed and re-crossed the Atlantic. It would seem that it

is now only a question of time before transatlantic aerial
20 passenger and mail transportation will be regularly carried
on, provided that the menace due to the extreme
inflammability and the explosiveness of the accidental
admixture of hydrogen gas with air can be overcome. The
answer seems to be helium which is not only
25 uninflammable in itself but when mixed with hydrogen in
sufficient quantity makes a perfectly safe, extremely
buoyant gas for balloons. During the war somebody
discovered that some of our natural gas from the
southwestern oil and gas fields contained notable
30 quantities of helium, probably derived from the
decomposition of radium contained in subterranean rocks.
(Cushman, 120, 125)

Can you determine the topic, setting, and main idea of this passage?

The topic of this passage is as follows: *sources of fuel*. Even though it is tempting to think there are two topics (i.e. alcohol and helium), it is usually best to identify one topic. What is the setting for the above passage? Now you can be more specific: *transportation fuel in the nineteenth and twentieth centuries*.

Next, consider the main idea. In finding the main concept, ask what the author is trying to tell you. Do not be too vague or too specific. The two beneficial substances that we read about are alcohol and helium. In this passage, these two concepts carry equal weight. Therefore, we can include alcohol and helium as central concepts in the main idea. The main idea of the above excerpt is that *alternative natural substances, namely alcohol and helium, can solve transportation needs*.

This was a relatively straightforward example. Practice finding the topic, setting, and main idea of every page of material that you read from this day onward. By the time you take the MCAT, finding the topic, setting, and main idea should be an automatic process.

COMPREHENSION PART TWO:

II. READING TRAINING

If you are determined to master the MCAT, you **must engage in plenty of reading**. Starting now, set aside approximately **two hours each day** for reading: one hour of reading in the morning and one hour in the evening.

Your MCAT study methods have just changed dramatically. **No longer will you study only the sciences.** You will study reading, so to speak. If you are a slow reader, do not be concerned. **The first step is to boost your reading volume.** We will worry about speed much later.

Starting today, you must make time for **at least two hours of reading a day.** Three hours would be better. Some students read for one-and-a-half hours in the morning, and again in the evening for a total of three hours a day. From now on, reading will be as important as eating and breathing.

If you do not read every day, then your chances of improving your VR score will be hampered. And remember, a low VR score could very well limit your medical school acceptances (and impact your future direction as a physician).

> Many examinees have to repeat the MCAT because they achieved impressively high science scores and a low VR score.
> Don't let this happen to you!

Serious students allocate at least two hours to reading every day, and maintain this for several months. If you are scoring around a 6 or 7 on Verbal Reasoning, and wish to achieve a 10 or better, then plan on reading for **two to three hours each day for six to eight months.**

Why is reading for at least six to eight months necessary? In the first month, your brain needs time to adjust to the process of reading so that your eyes stop skipping and misreading words. In the next two months, your eyes will start moving much more naturally over the page. Plan to set aside at least three months to turn the mechanics of reading into a fluid and effortless skill. **Only after you have fine-tuned your reading mechanics will your mind begin to understand material on a deeper level.** And we have not even considered speed, memory, or handling difficult material. This leaves three to five months to develop reading speed, improve comprehension of complex topics, and sharpen Neuro-Visual Programming for excellent retention of detail. See Chapter 11 for a complete list of reading sources, and begin today!

COMPREHENSION PART 3:

III. THREE LEVELS OF COMPREHENSION

Many students have never learned how to read properly. Fundamental to reading is knowing that **different words on the page carry different levels of importance.** The untrained reader considers every word on a page as equally important as every other word, not wanting to miss a single one. This untrained reader also considers every sentence as significant as any other, and every paragraph to be of equal weight. To the inexperienced eye, everything on a page sits at the same level. Such an approach is problematic.

CRUCIAL DIFFERENCES
Words carry different weight. Some words are more central to the meaning of a sentence or paragraph than others. Some sentences will tell you the main idea of the author's argument, while others serve to support the argument. As you read, be aware of these different levels of importance. You must develop a sensitivity to these various levels of emphasis within a sentence, and within a paragraph.

Eventually, you should be able to comprehend material at three different levels: the Literal Level, the Interpretive Level, and the Applied Level.

THE LITERAL LEVEL

This is the lowest level of comprehension. The Literal Level of comprehension refers to the ability to understand the primary, direct, surface-level meaning of a text. Many people read only at this level. It is a simple, uncritical understanding of what the author says. This can be understood as *reading the lines*. At this level a reader can usually identify, and memorize certain portions of what the author has said. However, this reader may have little understanding of the many meanings conveyed by the author.

THE INTERPRETIVE LEVEL

The next level of comprehension is the Interpretive Level in which a reader understands the Literal Level and is able to comprehend some deeper, unstated meanings as well. The following includes some of the skills necessary for understanding at the Interpretive Level:

1. drawing inferences

2. making generalizations

3. determining cause and effect

4. figuring out what happened between events

5. anticipating

6. understanding implied ideas

This level requires that the reader use his or her experience, background, knowledge, and reasoning ability to infer what is **not explicitly stated**. This is known as *reading between the lines*.

THE APPLIED LEVEL

To understand material at the Applied Level, the reader must first understand both the Literal and Interpretive Levels. Then, the reader uses analysis, reasoning, and judgment to reach a deeper level of comprehension. The following includes some of the skills used at the Applied Level:

1. organizing information
2. analyzing strengths and weaknesses of arguments
3. selecting and rejecting information
4. detecting opinions and bias

Also called *critical reading*, this level requires the reader to organize information, select and reject information, and detect bias and propaganda. This level of reading is also known as *reading beyond the lines*.

In order to reach the Applied Level of comprehension, every reader must master the Literal and Interpretive Levels. This is why your reading training dedicates five months to developing reading comprehension.

COMPREHENSION PART FOUR:

IV. BUILDING FOCUS

Maintaining complete, and I mean unbroken, focus for an hour is absolutely mandatory on Verbal Reasoning. But achieving this requires diligent practice.

When you take the MCAT, you must think of nothing else but the material on the screen. This may be easy to do on a single passage (surprisingly, some students struggle even with this), but to maintain focus in 60 to 70 minute intervals over the course of approximately five hours is much more challenging. **Achieving this high level of focus requires thorough preparation.**

Let us look at one exercise that can improve reading focus.

CLUTCH READING

The reading technique whereby the reader catches himself every time his focus drifts away from the page is called **clutch reading**. By practicing clutch reading, you will develop the ability to maintain focus for longer periods of time:

> ✓ **Clutch Reading**
>
> **1.** if your mind begins to wander
>
> **2.** stop reading
>
> **3.** clear your mind, regain focus, and continue.

Clutch reading is a process whereby the reader stops reading every time his mind begins to wander off the text. At the instant your mind begins to wander, *stop reading*. Nobody likes to break the flow of reading, but you must. Then, consciously bring your attention back to the text, and resume reading.

You must pay attention to moments when your mind begins to drift. Realize that your mind may drift and day-dream often in the beginning of your training. Whenever this happens, you must stop yourself. After you stop yourself, make a conscious effort to cease thinking about your distractions. Bring your mind back to the page - *clutch* the material - and continue reading.

Give extra effort to maintain a high degree of focus, and pay close attention to what your mind is doing while you read.

After the first week of practicing clutch reading, you will find that your mind daydreams less often. You should find that after a month or two, you can maintain focus for 15 to 20 minutes or more without interruption. Your goal is to maintain focus for 45 to 60 minutes without difficulty, so that you will never lose focus during the Verbal Reasoning section.

The more you catch and correct yourself, the more aware you will be of the temptation to daydream. **Soon, you will be able to catch your mind wanting to wander before it actually does.** By this point, you will be able to prevent your mind from wandering. Keeping a focused mind will greatly improve your reading comprehension.

By the time you take the MCAT, you should be able to stay focused for one solid hour. On Verbal Reasoning especially, you have no time to lose focus.

A BIT OF ADVICE

✓ **Become a curious reader.** Take interest in each passage. Find something fascinating about the material. Each passage has something very intriguing to share. By becoming a curious reader, you boost your ability to stay focused.

COMPREHENSION PART FIVE

V. ANTICIPATING THE MATERIAL

Excellent readers read with a sense of anticipation, always thinking ahead of the text. Anticipating the text means that the reader **understands the direction of the material**, and has an idea of what the author **might say next**.

You eventually need to read at a level that anticipates ideas. Of course, this comes with much practice which an extensive reading program will provide.

WHY ANTICIPATION IS IMPORTANT
Anticipation gives the reader a three-fold advantage by:

> 1. enabling the reader to make better sense of the information.
>
> 2. forcing the reader to stay focused on the material.
>
> 3. making the information more memorable.

As you read, your mind asks questions. You may not be aware of these questions since they are mostly subliminal, but as you become a better reader your mind will ask more questions.

There are several key questions which will help you anticipate as you read. Over time, these should begin to occur automatically. Let us start with a few basic ones to set you off on the right foot:

Key Questions

1. *What is the author saying here?*
2. *Is the author convincing? If not, what is missing?*
3. *What can I learn?*
4. *Does this example strengthen or weaken the argument?*
5. *What do I find interesting?*
6. *Why was this article published, or what makes it special?*
7. *Who would care to read this?*

These key questions are **forward-looking**. They beg the author to reveal what lies ahead. They also force us to think about **what comes next**, and in this sense we begin to **anticipate the information**.

✓ By the time you take the actual MCAT, you should automatically be thinking ahead of the text. In this manner, you are engaging in a dialogue with the author. This will prepare you for any unexpected shifts in tone or setting, which can sink many unprepared students.

COMPREHENSION PART SIX:

VI. ANTICIPATING THE QUESTIONS

Do we expect you to be prophetic? Are you responsible for predicting the future? You would hope to know every Verbal Reasoning question ahead of time. But, of course, you cannot. However, **you can anticipate the kind of questions that may appear.**

Anticipating a question means that you predict the most likely questions to appear based on the material in the passage. Here is one simple example of predicting questions based on passage content. Verbal Reasoning passages that present conflicting theories will most likely contain at least one Strengthen and Weaken question (see Chapter 5, Section VI). The MCAT seeks to evaluate your level of comprehension, and Strengthen and Weaken questions are a common way of doing this when discussing two or more conflicting hypotheses.

To develop this skill, let us look at a few passage constructions and the questions typically found associated with them as a place to start.

PASSAGE CONSTRUCT #1: THESIS DEVELOPMENT

Every passage contains an author's main idea. As you read any passage, always look for the author's **thesis**. When you identify and fully understand the main idea, you should prepare to answer several specific questions:

✓ What does the author believe to be true and why?
✓ What does the author believe to be false and why?

Popular types of questions that test your understanding of the author's thesis include the following:

- Main Idea
- Direct Comprehension
- Strengthen and Weaken

Of course, other kinds of questions are possible. These represent the more common ones related to the thesis of the author.

PASSAGE CONSTRUCT #2: COMPETING THEORIES

Certain passages present various arguments about a topic, usually as competing theories. Always keep your eyes open for two or more theories in any given passage. The author may present different viewpoints in order to support his own conclusions, or debunk competing theories.

Common questions that appear in relation to passages with competing theories include the following:

- Inference
- New Information
- Direct Comprehension
- Strengthen and Weaken
- Structure and Function

Other questions are possible, of course. These represent the more common questions related to competing theories.

PASSAGE CONSTRUCT #3: A PROCESS

Many times the author describes a process. A process occurs whenever something undergoes a change in stages. Typical examples of passages with processes are those that describe experiments. The term process can apply to nearly anything, such as a physical system or a theoretical idea. Everything from natural phenomenon, like volcanic eruptions, to social systems, like elections, describe processes. The key is for you to recognize a process in the passage, and understand how it functions. When you encounter a process, you might consider these questions:

      ✓ When does the process work, and when does it fail?

      ✓ Who supports, and who refutes the process?

Common questions that appear in relation to material describing processes include the following:

- Inference
- Direct Comprehension
- New Information

Other questions regarding processes are possible, of course, but these represent the questions that are more likely to appear.

PASSAGE CONSTRUCT #4: OPINIONS

The opinions of the author may be made explicit, or they may be difficult to discern. **If a passage discusses two or more competing theories or arguments, be careful to correctly identify which one the author supports.** In passages where the opinions of the author are present, be prepared to answer the following kinds of questions:

- About the Author
- Strengthen and Weaken
- Inference

Again, other types of questions may appear in relation to the author's opinions. But the three listed above are quite common.

You must take many practice tests and go through a large volume of questions for a good month or so. Again, go through as many passages as you can. Turn to the AAMC, or to commercial MCAT preparatory companies for a good supply. The goal is for you to develop a feel of what questions seem most probable given certain logical constructions of the passage.

> Anticipating questions is an extremely useful skill which comes after much reading and passage practice.

IN SUMMARY

These four passage constructs are not exhaustive. You could make a list of additional passage constructs, and watch for common question types for those constructs. In time, you will develop an uncanny ability to anticipate questions once you spend several months reading challenging material and going through dozens of practice Verbal Reasoning passages.

Your brain is learning a new skill, so you must give it ample time and practice to develop that skill. Remember, six to eight months of reading two or three hours a day is step one. Step two is doing two or more practice passages each day during the last two months of your reading training program. Step three is analyzing why you miss questions. We will discuss this in more detail later.

✓ Remember, each MCAT passage will most likely present two or three major theories, critiques, or interpretations about a subject. Identify each, and be sure to comprehend how each relates to the other. Figure out how they differ and agree.

VII. SUMMARY OF COMPREHENSION SKILLS AND METHODS

This is a complete summary of reading comprehension development skills and methods explained in various chapters of this book. The list below also appears as a reference in the Appendix.

FOR PRACTICE:

- ☐ read challenging academic material - see book list (Chapter 11)
- ☐ read two to three hours daily for six to eight months

AS YOU READ, BE SURE TO USE:

- ✓ **Clutch Reading** - improve focus (use always)
- ✓ **Sentence Recall** - improve memory (15 min/day)
- ✓ **Paragraph Summary** - boost comprehension (30 min/day)
- ✓ **Anticipation** - improve comprehension (always)
- ✓ **Three Point Analysis** - improve comprehension (always)
- ✓ **TSM Analysis** - improve comprehension (always)
- ✓ **Neuro-Visual Programming** - retain all details (always)

KEEP AT THE FOREFRONT OF YOUR MIND:

- • key questions about the material - see list (page 96)
- • topic, setting, and main idea (TSM analysis)
- • the Interpretive and Applied Levels of reading
- • your mental dialogue with the author
- • interest in the material
- • awareness of your thoughts and focus level

CHAPTER 7

Do You Have These Reading Symptoms?

For many students, critical reading is akin to doing the laundry. It is avoided at all costs until the last possible moment. Often times, students complain of all sorts of things happening to them when they read critically. Some get consumed by distracting thoughts, some forget what they read, while others succumb to a yawning spell. This chapter is devoted to diagnosing several symptoms that hinder people from reading effectively, which must be addressed before moving further. Do not feel discouraged should you identify with a troublesome manifestation. Remember, all great readers were, at one time, amateur readers.

I. DO YOU READ THE SAME THING OVER AND OVER?

Have you ever caught yourself reading the same thing again and again while your brain was turned off? We all have. The problem occurs when your mind and eyes are not in agreement. While your eyes may be reading line after line, your mind can be thinking about tomorrow's baseball game. Your mind is a very independent creature, and it can exist in its own little world in spite of what your body is doing. When you allow your mind to wander, you become a passive reader. Letting your mind slip into passive reading spells disaster on Verbal Reasoning.

How do you know if you are a passive reader? The passive reader is not very interested in the material. He or she **does not ask questions** about the text. The passive reader retains very little, and usually misses all of the arguments and ideas. In other words, when you let your mind wander, do not expect to remember what you have read.

TWO STEPS TO ACTIVE READING

1. CLEAR YOUR MIND
One way to avoid reading passively requires **conditioning your mind to think actively even before you read**. Placing your mind in the right state is a two-step process. First, you must clear your mind of distractions and focus on the page before you. Stop thinking about anything else, and become interested in the material that you are about to read.

2. ASK QUESTIONS
Second, ask what the material is about. Become curious. What journey will this author send you on? By asking these questions you begin to anticipate the material. This is key. Once your mind is free from distractions and can anticipate ideas, then comprehension can occur.

✓ As you read, you are responsible for **staying focused and involved** in the material. Ask questions to stay engaged. If your seatbelt unbuckles, so to speak, you will fall off the rollercoaster. Staying focused and interested in the material will keep your seatbelt fastened for the entire reading ride.

> Practice clearing your mind and asking questions about the text every time you read.

If the material does not seem interesting, you may want to ask these key questions that we saw in Chapter 6:

1. *What is the author saying here?*
2. *Is the author convincing? If not, what is missing?*
3. *What can I learn?*
4. *Does this example strengthen or weaken the argument?*
5. *What do I find interesting?*
6. *Why was this article published, or what makes it special?*
7. *Who would care to read this?*

By asking key questions, you are forcing your mind to understand the material (whether you are interested in it or not). This is a great way to boost your understanding as you read.

During your months of reading training, if you catch yourself reading a sentence while paying attention to something else in your mind, stop reading! Go back a few sentences, clear your head, turn up the curiosity meter, and begin reading again. This technique is called **clutch reading** (see Chapter 6). By asking simple questions about the text, you force your mind to engage the material. Questioning the text can rescue a wandering mind, and with practice your mind will stop wandering.

II. DO YOU FORGET WHAT YOU HAVE JUST READ?

Forgetting material is a common problem. **Many students forget what they read as soon as they finish the passage.** In order to remember the material, you have to comprehend it first. Most examinees that score in the range of 11 and above on Verbal Reasoning have the ability to remember most of the ideas and details of the passage, which we will read more about later. **Interestingly, these high-scoring examinees do not need to look back at the passage for answers.**

✓ Forgetting what you read can be a symptom of a weak memory, a distracted mind, or a lack of interest in the material (passive reading).

We have already addressed how to overcome distractions and passive reading, so let us look at how to improve memory. You can improve short term memory by performing memory-enhancing exercises, and taking interest in the material that you are reading. Fortunately, the MCAT presents passages about topics that are unusual and interesting (for the most part). Unusual material is often intriguing, which will pique your curiosity. **Develop your ability to become interested in the text. Do yourself a favor and always build up a sense of anticipation before you read a passage.**

The following are two exercises that can help readers at any level:

TWO EXERCISES TO IMPROVE READING MEMORY

1. SENTENCE RECALL

One very effective method to improving reading memory is to practice **sentence recall**. Sentence recall is the process in which the reader pauses after a sentence or group of sentences, recalls as much as possible word-for-word, summarizes the meaning, and moves to the next sentence or two. This is a very laborious process, but very helpful. It will improve your short-term memory dramatically:

> ✓ **Sentence Recall - 15 to 30 minutes each day**
>
> **1.** read a sentence, then try to restate it word-for-word
>
> **2.** look back at the sentence and compare
>
> **3.** then move on to the next sentence

After a few months of practicing sentence recall, your ability to remember passage material will improve greatly. Every time you read a book or journal, start each session with fifteen to thirty minutes of sentence recall. You should notice a small improvement even as early as the second week of daily practice.

2. PARAGRAPH SUMMARY

Another exercise is called **paragraph summary**. This exercise requires the reader to recall the main ideas of each paragraph.

> ✓ **Paragraph Summary - 30 minutes each day**
>
>   **1.** stop after each paragraph and summarize its main ideas
>
>   **2.** look back to catch any ideas that you missed
>
>   **3.** continue to the next paragraph and repeat

Whether the paragraph is short or long, the reader is to stop after **each paragraph** and summarize its key ideas. Here is an example:

> The three great divisions of Philosophy - Metaphysics, Physics, and Ethics - now begin to assume their peculiar English form and name, being known to us all through school and college as Mental, Natural, and Moral
> 5   Philosophy, which have a tendency to develop separately in the separative Eighteenth Century, particularly in England. After this spirit they are taught still today, little or no attention is paid to their connection, "all three being toto coelo different, three provinces wholly separate and
> 10 distinct," according to Locke. (Snider, 423)

A proper summary of the main ideas in this paragraph could be the following: "The three great divisions of philosophy take on English forms and names, and these forms develop separately in Eighteenth Century England. They were, and still are, taught in a manner that disregards their connections."

Notice that this summary does not include details. The point of paragraph summary is to focus on the main ideas without worrying about details. **However, on the MCAT, you will need to absorb both the main thoughts, and the details of each paragraph.** The technique called Neuro-Visual Programming allows you to capture the details for greater comprehension (see Chapter 9).

III. DO YOUR EYES MOVE TOO SLOWLY?

When you read, your mind should never fall behind what your eyes are doing. There is a difference between reading speed and eye speed. Reading speed is the speed at which your mind is accustom to comprehending text. Eye speed is the speed at which your eyes move comfortably across text. If you are a slow reader, then your eyes and mind both need to speed up.

One of the major reasons people read slowly is because their eyes are not accustomed to moving rapidly. To improve eye speed, you should make a conscious effort to make them move across the page faster.

The untrained reader has a troublesome temptation to look at each word. This reader usually moves his or her eyes across the printed page in a series of short movements, stopping for a fraction of a second on nearly every word. To advance beyond this poor habit to a more efficient and productive reading mode, the number of visual stops made per line must be reduced. Even a slight reduction in the number of visual stops will accelerate your reading rate.

When you begin to read, your eyes have a tendency to fixate on the first word, then on the next word, and so on. The untrained reader makes many unconscious eye stops as he reads the entire line. What follows is a comparison of underlined words that the eyes of the untrained reader and expert reader unconsciously look for.

Aim for reading at **250 words per minute** comfortably with full comprehension by the time you take the MCAT.

Use a stopwatch to time yourself when you practice. Then, approximate how many words you cover to determine your words-per-minute reading rate.

Untrained reader:
<u>Untrained</u> <u>eyes</u> <u>read</u> <u>the words</u> <u>on a page</u> <u>by</u> <u>making</u> <u>frequent</u> <u>stops</u> <u>across a</u>
<u>printed</u> <u>line</u>. <u>The</u> <u>goal</u> <u>is to reduce</u> <u>the</u> <u>number</u> <u>of words</u> <u>your eyes</u> <u>stop to</u>
<u>look</u> <u>at</u>. <u>Your</u> <u>eyes</u> <u>will see</u> <u>more</u> <u>words</u> <u>than</u> <u>you</u> <u>realize</u>.

Expert reader:
Expert <u>eyes</u> read the <u>words</u> on a page by <u>making</u> infrequent <u>stops</u> across a
printed <u>line</u>. The <u>goal</u> is to <u>reduce</u> the number of <u>words</u> your eyes <u>stop</u> to
<u>look</u> at. Your <u>eyes</u> will see more <u>words</u> than you <u>realize</u>.

As you can see, the untrained reader **looks for every word** and **tries to
hear each one in his mind**. By having to hear the words, the untrained
reader slows down even further. What the untrained reader does not
understand is that he does not need to hear the words at all in order to
understand them.

The expert reader makes fewer stops with his eyes, and does not need to
hear the words. Thus, he registers what he sees much faster. The expert is
also able to spend a **very short amount of time on each stop while
seeing the neighboring words**. In addition, the superb reader does not
travel back to previous material, and is able to read without any break in
focus.

By changing how your eyes behave and your mind works, you can make
great strides in your reading speed and comprehension. **For now, try to
look at every second or third word, instead of every word.** Practice
doing this for the first two weeks of your reading training. In time, your
eyes will learn to see the neighboring words automatically. Your goal is to
see groups of words as you read. As you improve the flow of your
reading, you will improve your understanding of the passage. With time,
you will learn to look at only four or five words per line, while your eyes
see all of the neighboring words.

IV. DO YOU DAYDREAM?

Daydreamers end up in the clouds with low Verbal scores. Daydreamers come in two flavors. The first is not interested in what he is reading about and would rather think of more exciting things. The second becomes overly wrapped up in the written material which inspires the reader to think of all sorts of fanciful events.

Daydreaming is really a problem of maintaining a **proper level of focus**, no matter which version of daydreamer you are or to what degree. At some point, everybody struggles with maintaining proper focus while reading. The mind naturally wants to think of many things, and sometimes all at once. Early in your reading training you must make a conscious effort to stop thinking about anything other than the text, which requires discipline. Techniques such as **clutch reading** will help greatly.

> Reading forces our minds to think along one track, and it takes practice to stay on that track. Use **clutch reading** (see Chapter 6) to improve your ability to focus.

V. DO YOU LOSE INTEREST IN THE MATERIAL?

You do not have a choice in the matter. Everything you read on the MCAT needs to be interesting to you. If you cannot develop a sense of interest in the material, then achieving a high level of focus and comprehension will prove quite challenging.

The books and journals that you decide to read for practice may not be very interesting to the average reader. However, they will be interesting to you. Or rather, **you should force yourself to find them interesting.** Learning to see uninteresting material with genuine interest is a necessary step towards a high VR score. So, practice taking interest in all sorts of subjects by forcing yourself to read books on subjects that you normally find uninspiring.

Please note that you should **put away any leisure reading material**. If you prefer reading fashion or sports magazines, then do not read them during the months of your MCAT preparation. Deprive yourself of the glitz and glamour of your reading life. The books you will read for MCAT preparation will gradually seem more interesting the more you read them. For a suggested reading list, see Chapter 11.

There are plenty of challenging, yet fascinating books of MCAT caliber in almost any library. Look for any one of a host of books written by professors from respectable universities.

Why Do You Miss Questions?

There are several recurring reasons for making mistakes on Verbal Reasoning. They include the following:

- ✓ reading inefficiently
- ✓ failing to understand material
- ✓ failing to understand the questions
- ✓ skipping key information
- ✓ making incorrect assumptions
- ✓ overanalyzing answers
- ✓ feeling uncomfortable reading a computer screen
- ✓ losing control of time
- ✓ becoming distracted

The difference between a good student and a successful one is a matter of self-analysis. A good student may answer many questions correctly, but does not bother to understand why he is making mistakes. For this student, scores will vary almost by chance. There will be no clear steady progression of improvement. On the other hand, **the successful student goes out of his way to pinpoint exactly why he missed particular questions.** By becoming a detective of wrong answers, the good student will correct poor habits to become a successful reader.

I. DO YOU MISREAD THE PASSAGE?

Have you ever looked for something and not seen it, even though the object was in front of you? Sure you have. Plenty of times your eyes may see what your mind pays no attention to. Other times, your mind misremembers what your eyes have just seen. Both phenomena can happen while you read, and are deadly on Verbal Reasoning. **Let us look at various strategies that will help train you to catch everything on the page accurately.**

There are several ways you can misread a passage. You may miss a simple word, like *not*, in a sentence which would drastically change its meaning. Other times, you may miss the overall theme or idea of the passage. So how can you prevent these accidents from happening?

The first step is to slow down your reading speed. You need to read at a pace at which your eyes and mind feel comfortable seeing everything in a sentence (preferably without having to look at each word). The next chapter will provide more details about ways for readers to move their eyes across a page efficiently. For now, **read slowly enough to register each word.** Later, you can work on speed without overlooking any words. Efficient readers can almost skim each line and still catch all of the words.

The next step is to become an active participatory reader. The active reader takes interest in the material and asks questions about the main ideas. By asking yourself, "What is the author's message in this paragraph?" you will force your mind to read more closely. This, in turn, will force your eyes to read more carefully and pick up more words. For a more complete list of key questions, see Chapter 6. By transforming your mind into an interested participant, you can help avoid misreading or overlooking words on the printed page.

II. DO YOU RUN OUT OF TIME?

Having time expire before finishing a section is one of the leading causes of poor scores on the Verbal Reasoning portion of the MCAT. For most examinees, the Verbal Reasoning section seems like a daunting race to the finish line. Indeed, most examinees feel as if they are caught in a Catch-22: if they read too slowly, then they will run out of time, but if they read too quickly, then they will not answer enough questions correctly. How do thousands of students attempt to resolve this dilemma? They mistakenly assume that reading at the speed of light will save the day. Many take this approach, and face much disappointment upon receipt of their scores. **What these students need to realize is that their brains need a chance to absorb the material.**

The day of your MCAT is not the time to push your reading speed beyond what is comfortable for you.

Practice pushing your speed months prior to the MCAT, so that a faster pace will become comfortable for you.

✓ Realize this: **absorbing all of the material for each of the seven passages can be done within the time limits using proper pacing.** Please do not underestimate the importance of pacing yourself and staying on time for this section. You have an advantage over examinees who took the paper test because the computer gives you a clock, your immediate feedback assistant. Should you fall behind, the clock on the screen will reveal that fact if you have your time points memorized. Let the clock be your guide (but do not stare at it as some students have done out of stress).

PROPER PACING

Let us look at the proper pacing for Verbal Reasoning. Because there are seven passages, you will have about eight-and-a-half minutes to complete each passage. You probably have figured out that some passages are more difficult than others. You can expect about two relatively easy passages, three moderately challenging passages, and two difficult passages. These numbers will vary depending on the test, and on your level of skill. Undoubtedly, one passage will stand out as being very challenging. **For this most difficult passage, plan on spending nine to ten minutes for reading and answering questions. For the two or so easy passages, plan on spending about six to seven minutes on each.** All in all, you should find yourself finishing on time by spending about eight to nine minutes on the rest of the passages. Here is the schedule that you should try to follow. You might deviate from these time points a bit. Just return to set time points after getting through the difficult and easy passages:

Table 6.1 Time points during Verbal Reasoning

Time on clock (counts down)	Begin this VR Passage
60:00	I
51:00	II
43:00	III
34:00	IV
26:00	V
17:00	VI
9:00	VII

✔ Remember, whether you spend more or less time on a passage, you should average 8.5 minutes per passage.

Commit the pacing in Table 6.1 to memory. Notice that the above schedule provides nine minutes for the first passage, eight minutes for the second, nine for the third, and so forth and so on to give you an average of 8.5 minutes. All you need to memorize are these numbers in the following order: 60, 51, 43, 34, 26, 17, and 9. **These time points will act as your pacing guide.**

What happens should you deviate from this pacing? Well, **everything will be alright as long as you get back on track.** When you encounter the most difficult passage (which may occur at any point), you will deviate from this schedule and be off by about two minutes or so. On the other hand, you will encounter an easy passage which will bring you back on track to the correct time points. The tradeoff should work in your favor.

Since you only have eight or nine minutes on average per passage, then read for three to four minutes, and answer questions in four to five minutes. **Remember to never spend more than a minute or so on any one question.**

3 MINUTES READING
5 MINUTES ANSWERING QUESTIONS PER PASSAGE

If you are stuck on a Verbal Reasoning question, mark it and move on. Come back to it if you have extra time.

On the computerized MCAT, you have a 'MARK' feature. For every question there is a small box in which you can place a check using the mouse pointer. Once a question has a check in this box, it is considered

'MARKED' and will appear on your question grid as a marked question. Marking questions is a quick and easy way to keep track of troublesome questions in order to review them later. If you need more than a minute-and-a-half to answer a particular question, then mark it and move on. **Do not waste precious time on any one question.**

PACING OF A SAMPLE STUDENT

The following example demonstrates the pacing of an actual student, Jane, during her Verbal Reasoning section:

> Jane began Passage I at 60:00 minutes
>> Passage II at 52:00
>> Passage III at 43:00
>> Passage IV at 31:00
>> Passage V at 24:00
>> Passage VI at 17:00
>> Passage VII at 9:00

QUESTION:
Which passage was the most difficult for Jane, and which passages were relatively easy?

Analyze her pacing above. She covered passages I and II in eight and nine minutes, respectfully. She encountered her most challenging passage next, spending twelve minutes on it, and then caught up on passages IV and V. She completed passages IV and V in seven minutes each, thus bringing her back on track by starting passage VI with the standard 17 minutes left on the clock. If you answered numbers IV and V as the easy passages, and number III as the challenging passage, then you are correct. Impressively, this student remained right on course. This is a good sample schedule, which demonstrates that spending even twelve minutes on one passage is manageable. **This student did not panic or fall off track.** She stayed calm through her most difficult passage and finished on time. This is excellent pacing performance.

Resist the temptation of reading a question more than once. Much time is wasted by reading a question, searching for answers in the passage, and then reading the question again. Practice reading the **question stem only once**. As you will see later in the chapter, reading **each question once, and each answer choice twice,** is advisable.

✓ Having to re-read material is the number one killer of the clock. In Chapter 9, you will learn how to visualize the text in your mind which will greatly boost your recollection and comprehension. By applying the process called Neuro-Visual Programming to Verbal Reasoning, you will minimize the need to re-read material.

III. DO YOU MISREAD THE QUESTION STEM?

Maybe you fall into this category of examinees: you missed a question because you thought it was asking for something else. Afterward, when you checked your answers, you discovered that you had misread the question. Don't feel too bad. This mistake is quite common. In the hurry to finish on time under enormous pressure, a student often rushes through the questions.

A student may subconsciously try to make a question easier by reinterpreting what the questions ask. If you change the question subconsciously to meet your own needs, then, obviously, the outcome cannot be valid. No wishful reading is allowed.

There are two ways to misread a question: either you skip key words and do not realize it, or you read all of the words but forget a few in the rush of things. If you are having trouble seeing the words for what they are, then **slow down**. By the time you finish reading the passage, you should have a good four to five minutes to answer questions. This translates to approximately 45 to 55 seconds per question, which is a decent amount of time to tackle even difficult questions.

When you reach the first question, slow down and read it very carefully. Pretend that you are inspecting diamonds. Each word is a sparkling diamond that you want to examine carefully. Fully grasp each word in the question stem and comprehend its meaning. You should be able to read and fully comprehend the question stem in five to ten seconds without any trouble.

The time to apply speed to your reading is during the **passage**, not during the questions.

If you have trouble remembering all of the words of the question, then you may need to improve your understanding of it. Forgetting what the question is asking may be a sign that you do not understand it fully. As you practice, make sure that you read the questions stem slowly enough. In order to improve your understanding of the question, actively read the stem using the Three Question Test.

THE THREE-QUESTION TEST
After you read the stem, ask yourself:

> ✓ **1. What is this question really asking?**
>
>   Put it into your own words.
> ✓ **2. Where did I read about this in the passage?**
> ✓ **3. Why is this question interesting?**

When you restate the question and find something interesting about it, **you force yourself to comprehend and remember the question.** How do you find something interesting about a question? You might discover a new way of seeing the world, or gain insight about the author.

Questions can make you think in new ways. As strange as it may sound, try to admire the thought that went into composing each question. Questions are mini puzzles, and your job is to solve the puzzle. Each question is very fascinating because, as a puzzle, it contains traps and clues. Try to enjoy the process of working through every question and discovering its true solution.

IV. DO YOU MISREAD THE ANSWER CHOICES?

You may be surprised to know that many students finish reading the passage on time, understand the questions, but fail at comprehending the answer choices because they did not take the time to understand them completely. Their eyes **miss key words in the answer choices**, or their **minds reinterpret the concepts.**

One approach to overcoming this poor habit is to read the answer choices once, and then **scan them again as a check**. You can do this in one of two recommended ways. As you progress through answers A, B, C and D, you may want to read choice A, and then skim A again, then read B carefully and skim it again, then C, and so on. Or, a more surefire approach is to read A through D once, and then go back and skim answers A through D to confirm your understanding.

Whatever you do, never lose track of time, and never misread the answer choices. This means that **you may need to slow down** when reading the answers. Realize that by simply improving how carefully you read answer choices, you can improve your Verbal score dramatically.

✓ Be sure to read the answer choices slowly and carefully. Never underestimate the specter of MCAT pressure. It can cause an examinee to read too fast and gloss over key words. **Do not rush through the answer choices.** Read them slowly enough to catch everything, and then read them once again as a quick check (twice total).

V. DO YOU MISINTERPRET THE PASSAGE?

Understanding the passage requires a **mental dialogue** with the author. For expert readers, this mental dialogue occurs naturally. What you must develop is the **habit of asking the right questions as you read.** You should always ask about the author, the critics, and the passage. Here is a series of possible questions that you can ask during and after you read the passage:

Author

1. *What is the overall message of the author?*

2. *Do I find the author convincing? Why or why not?*

3. *What support does the author provide?*

4. *How would I describe the author's attitude?*

Critics

5. *Who else agrees with the author and why?*

6. *Who disagrees with the author and why?*

7. *What supports or weakens the author's main argument?*

8. *What facts or ideas would strengthen the author's point?*

9. *How can I apply the message of the author to a different scenario?*

Passage

10. *How is the passage constructed? In which order do theories, evidence, experiments, and counterexamples appear?*

11. *What is the main idea of the first paragraph?*

12. *What are the second and subsequent paragraphs about?*

As you can see, there are plenty of questions that should be firing off in your brain as you read. You must practice this mental dialogue for many months, so that you naturally look for the answers to such questions by the time you sit for the MCAT.

This is why students preparing for the MCAT should follow a six to eight month reading schedule. **Trying to master this mental dialogue in two months is just not enough time, and it should not be forced on the day of the test.**

✓ Remember that your goal is to fully comprehend the material. Anyone can pick up an article and understand the words. But to fully understand and comprehend the text means that you must recognize its main points, supporting evidence, conclusions, and assumption, as well as how they relate with each other (while remembering them). Do not be satisfied with a cursory understanding of the passage. Many students fall into this trap. They read only for detail and facts, and ignore other layers of meaning. **These readers mistakenly conclude that they understand the passage because they understand the words.** Anyone can understand the words. The MCAT is not testing for a regurgitation of simple meaning.

VI. DO YOU MISINTERPRET THE QUESTION?

Understanding the passage is a different experience from understanding the question. Questions often contain words with distinct connotations that can be missed easily. Each word is important. Strangely, many students drop their guard once the passage is behind them. Their minds take a break from the rigorous critical reading that they employ on the passage, and lapse into a casual mode of reading on the questions. Do not do this. **Just because the questions are shorter than the passage, you do not have the license to treat them with greater laxity.** Maintain your critical reading skills for the questions, just as you would for the passage.

Here is an example of a verbal question that could be misleading for some:

> If asked, the author of this passage would probably give his greatest support to which of the following hypothetical actions by the Red Square movement?

Many students gloss over two very important modifiers, "greatest" and "hypothetical," and fail to fully understand the question.

To the student who hurries through and is not very careful, this question may appear as:

> If asked, the author of this passage would probably give
> his support to which of the following hypothetical
> actions by the Red Square movement?

This version ignores the word *greatest*. Notice the difference in meaning. The first question asks for the author's greatest support. The second question asks for the action that the author simply supports. Wrong answer choices would include actions that the author supports, but not to the greatest extent. The rushed or lazy examinee may also interpret the question as follows:

> If asked, the author of this passage would probably give
> his greatest support to which of the following actions
> by the Red Square movement?

This version leaves out the word *hypothetical*. Wrong answer choices would include actions that the author supports the most, but that are not hypothetical. The difference between hypothetical and non-hypothetical actions would elude many students. From the above example, you can see the necessity of **reading every word very carefully in the question**.

If you overlook even a single word in the question,
then you will most likely miss the question.

✔ Verbal Reasoning is unforgiving and exacting. To achieve a high score, you must read and comprehend carefully and accurately. Never assume anything.

If you find that you do not understand questions on a regular basis, then your best plan is to practice *ad nauseam*. Sign up for an MCAT preparatory class and get your hands on as many Verbal Reasoning passages as you can. The more questions you tackle, the better you will become at answering them. **The key is to analyze your mistakes so that you catch bad habits.** Go over each question that you miss and see whether you fully understand the question or not.

VII. DO YOU LOSE FOCUS?

Maintaining your focus is one of the most fundamental steps toward succeeding on Verbal Reasoning. Your task is to maintain focus during an entire hour of steady analysis and comprehension. This takes practice and time to develop. Work into your daily reading practice exercises to build your focus, such as **clutch reading** that was introduced in Chapter 6.

VIII. DO YOU HAVE LOW READING CONFIDENCE?

You should know that your level of confidence impacts your performance on not only Verbal Reasoning, but also on all other sections. Do not underestimate the importance of having high confidence during the MCAT. Wrong answers can result from not only test-taking mistakes and weaknesses, but also low confidence.

Let us walk through the experience of the insecure student. Since the student is insecure, he walks into the testing center with self-doubt. He doubts his reasoning skills, and second guesses his answers. Why is this a serious problem? **The insecure student will display poor pacing skills, and fall for wrong answers.** He feels tempted to read the passage either too quickly to finish on time, or too slowly to catch all the concepts. Since he is not confident in his reading abilities, he gives in to the temptation to speed-read and rush through the questions. Many insecure students take too much time to read because they are not confident in their abilities to pick up all the important information.

In addition to having poor reading skills, the insecure reader falls for wrong answers. Insecure students admit to choosing an answer simply because, ironically, it sounds sophisticated, complicated, and way over their heads. When asked whether they remember reading about their sophisticated choice, they admit to having never read anything about it. So why does the insecure reader jump for the most complex, but obviously wrong answer choice? Here are three reasons:

1. THE INSECURE READER DOUBTS HIS READING SKILLS

On the MCAT, many answer choices refer to concepts that are beyond the setting of the passage. To the expert reader, these answers are clearly wrong because the passage never made mention of them. But for the insecure reader, irrelevant answer choices are tempting because the insecure reader figures he must have missed key information.

When the insecure reader is unsure of an answer, often he will lean towards the choice that seems radical to him. The insecure reader figures that the radical answer is probably correct for two reasons: he doubts that he can remember everything in the passage, and he thinks that test-makers would not be so dumb as to include an obviously wrong answer choice. Well, test-makers do include answers on the MCAT that are obviously wrong for precisely this reason. By choosing the radical answer choice, the insecure reader falls into the psychology trap of the test by having low confidence.

2. THE INSECURE READER COMPREHENDS POORLY

Since the insecure reader has trouble comprehending material under pressure, he figures that the complicated "I-don't-recall-reading-this" choice will be correct more often than not. After all, the questions seem difficult, so why should the answers be any different? The first step to building confidence is to fix poor comprehension skills, which this book covers in Chapter 6.

3. THE INSECURE READER DOUBTS CORRECT ANSWERS

Lastly, the student who is insecure about reading and comprehension will second-guess correct answers that occur readily to him. When the reader does identify a correct answer without much struggle, he will most likely change his mind about it. "Because I am a poor reader, finding the right answer must be very difficult. So an answer that occurs quickly to me, even though it seems correct, must be wrong!"

He will select, instead, the answer that seems very advanced or complicated because he is trying to compensate for a weakness in his reading abilities. Since he has low confidence, he assumes that an answer cannot possibly be correct if he arrives at it too easily.

> Never select an answer simply because it sounds complex. Every correct answer on Verbal Reasoning is direct and appropriate to the question. With proper comprehension, the correct answer should be clear. Do not jump for the complex answer simply because it sounds advanced and beyond what you recall reading.
>
> **Having low confidence on Verbal Reasoning spells disaster.**

IX. DO YOU BRING OUTSIDE IDEAS INTO YOUR ANSWERS?

Many students may not be aware of how easily they can bring their own ideas into the questions. Some students may even assume that doing so is correct, especially since the other two MCAT sections - Physical Sciences and Biological Sciences - require outside knowledge. Contrary to this temptation, you should **never** bring outside knowledge into any Verbal Reasoning passage. Your outside knowledge should stay outside. Correct answers on Verbal Reasoning reflect information provided by the accompanying passage only, and inferences made from it. For instance, even if you happen to know everything about card games, your knowledge must never influence your reading of a passage about card games.

Since most passages cover unusual and uncommon subjects, you will probably not be fully knowledgeable about any one topic. Questions that ask for facts about common topics are very rare on Verbal Reasoning. Nevertheless, if you do happen to come across a subject that is familiar to you, then keep your knowledge to yourself. Bringing outside information to the passage will only hurt you because authors often take unusual stances that are unexpected to the traditional reader (you).

> Do not let outside knowledge influence the content of what you read.

CHAPTER 9

Neuro-Visual Programming

IN THIS CHAPTER

We all wish that we could remember everything in a given passage. Remembering the material is more than half of the challenge, because most examinees waste time looking back at the passage. Unfortunately, many students cannot remember important details and concepts. If examinees could preserve everything on the page, then their verbal scores would definitely improve.

Let me introduce to you a powerful technique that I developed for enhancing reading memory. I call it *Neuro-Visual Programming*.

I. INTRODUCING NEURO-VISUAL PROGRAMMING

The human brain has the amazing ability to think about an object in both an abstract way, and a direct, tangible way. For many, we can look at an object, close our eyes, and remember its appearance in dramatic detail. Neuro-Visual Programming (NVP) is a methodology centered on mental imagery. Used correctly, NVP can enhance how we think critically as we read. We can improve how our mind understands words by transforming them into mental images.

Let us look at the components of NVP:

Neuro is about our nervous system and its processes. NVP works because our brain experiences the world through our senses and translates that information into meaning and perception. Our eyes see an image and our mind interprets that image in order to identify it. Our skin is touched and our mind interprets that touch as pleasurable, painful, rough, smooth, or whatever the feeling may be. The nervous system is the nexus of all environmental input, and the mass interpreter of that information.

Visual concerns the way humans use sight and mental imagery to understand the world. Through images, we capture dimensional information about our environment. Images can tell a story, and a collection of images can convey a rather complex story. By capturing a series of images, the obvious and non-obvious details of any narrative can be recalled. In the world of NVP, visualization is the method by which our minds generate a series of images that reflect the words on the page. This makes those images, and therefore our understanding of thoughts, available to our conscious mind.

Programming is a process of learning that capitalizes on the plasticity of our neuronal connections. How we program our minds to make new connections as we read information depends on our thinking patterns and mental rehearsals. The programming component of NVP requires that we practice mental visualization **as we read**. We program a series of carefully created images in a certain sequence that expresses the **meaning** of the words on the page. The more we practice the programming aspect of NVP, the better it can serve us.

If you would like to get a sense of how NVP works, take a moment to think about an animal, any animal. Notice how your mind responds. What are you thinking about? Most people first bring up a mental **picture** of that animal. Your mind is accustomed to thinking in terms of pictures.

Many of us think **visually** much of the time. When you think about going to the store, you probably conjure a quick picture of that particular store. NVP draws from this natural way of visual thinking and applies it to reading.

HOW NVP WORKS

Specifically, Neuro-Visual Programming is a **method** of training the brain to **visualize** in great detail the meaning of what the eyes read on the page (or computer screen in our case). The ultimate goal is for the reader to transform ideas of each sentence into a collection of pictures and movies that interact with each other to reflect the entire meaning of the passage.

✓ By retaining details and seeing how those details interact with each other, you will actually force your mind to comprehend the material and make inferences.

Since mental images remain much longer in your mind than do random facts, you can retain this visual panorama while answering questions. Your mind will become very effective at creating visual representations of the arguments of the author. By thoroughly practicing this method a reader can greatly enhance his memory, retention, and interpretation of the material.

As the author of this book, I can attest to the great efficacy of NVP because I used it on all practice exams and on the actual MCAT. My verbal score stayed at or above an 11 on all tests.

> The ultimate goal is for the reader to translate each sentence into a collection of pictures and movies that interact with each other to reflect the entire meaning of the passage.

Be warned - NVP requires significant practice to master. Perfecting NVP requires about six months of reading difficult books for two to three hours each and every day. If you skip a day, you will fall two days behind. Skip two days, and you fall a week behind. This is not for the faint-hearted. Those who succeed will think and read at a much higher level. This training requires significant time because it literally demands that your brain process information in a new way.

✓ Before proceeding, you should first spend a month or so perfecting your reading mechanics before attempting Neuro-Visual Programming. You may even want to skip this chapter and return to it once your reading mechanics have vastly improved.

When you take the MCAT, **your NVP skills will save you from wasting valuable time jumping back and forth between the passage and the answers.** You will refer back to the passage only to confirm an answer (not search for it). The high-scoring examinees who experience very little trouble with Verbal Reasoning are able to absorb most of the passage information on the first read-through and remember it. These expert examinees refer back to a passage sparingly, much less often than do the average test-takers. Excellent students remember details quite accurately, and are able to recall the exact place in the passage that contains necessary information. NVP allows you to do this.

At this point, take a moment to stop and evaluate your reading ability. You should have no trouble with the mechanics of reading if you wish to learn NVP. Your eyes should not skip over words or miss key punctuation. Instead, your eyes should flow effortlessly from line to line as your mind picks up each and every word. If you are not at this point, then stop here. Take more time to master your reading skills. Dedicate three or more weeks to reading two to three hours a day until you have no difficulty with the mechanics of reading. When you understand all the material you read, and can do so smoothly at a steady pace without skipping words, then you can begin learning Neuro-Visual Programming.

II. USING NVP FOR THE FIRST TIME

BEGIN WITH A FAMILIAR PLACE

Let us start by first thinking about a very familiar object that is a flat surface, an object that you might see every day that has no distracting pictures or other things on it.

Suppose we choose the mirror in your bathroom — a wide, plain surface that you see every morning or evening typically. (The idea is to think of a surface that you have no trouble imagining. Later, you can, if you prefer, choose a different surface.)

On this mirror in our mind we will draw very simple cartoons in red marker so that the pictures are bright, vivid, and easy to remember. Now, let us read the following sentence:

The dog ran to the castle.

Our task is to create a drawing of this sentence using our marker and mirror. So how is this achieved? (Read what follows and then try the exercise with your eyes closed.) Imagine using the red marker to draw a simple stick figure of a dog somewhere on the far left side of the mirror. Make every stroke clear. Your picture should be as simple as possible.

After you have drawn the dog, imagine moving to the right side of the mirror and drawing a basic outline of a castle. This can be a simple square with a large door in the middle and a flag on top. Remember, keep your pictures simple.

Can you go back to the left side of the mirror and see your dog precisely how you drew it? Can you see in your mind the red castle sitting on the right? Practice doing this about five times until you can see both objects exactly how you drew them without any loss of detail. This is your first exercise in visualization.

Are we finished? No, because we cannot ignore the action of the sentence. The dog ran to the castle. How will we draw this? We want to keep things simple so that we can recall them with ease - drawing the dog in several running positions across the mirror would be a waste of time and brain power.

Do we have a better solution? Yes. With your marker draw a long arrow from the dog all the way across the mirror pointing to the castle. This arrow shows motion and intent, the dog running, which brings us to our next point.

The use of simple signs and symbols to represent meaning and motion is one of the key elements of transforming what we read into images we can remember.

III. SYMBOLS BECOME MENTAL GUIDES

A few common symbols (lines, arrows, circles, etc.) will add important meaning to our images:

THE LINE

The line is one of the simplest items to draw and remember in our minds. It should be used clearly and carefully. A horizontal line can be drawn between two or more objects to show connection or agreement. A vertical line can be drawn between two or more objects to also divide and show a separation in a relationship.

Taking this a step further, different colored lines can represent different meanings in the relationship. A blue line joining two objects can indicate a very stable harmonious connection, whereas a red line can indicate a harsh or negative interdependence. What each color conveys is up to you to decide.

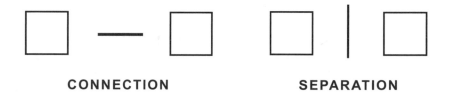

CONNECTION   **SEPARATION**

THE ARROW

The arrow is used to represent direction, motion, and intention. Curved arrows are especially useful for indicating more complex action, such as *moving over* or *leaping over*, or more sophisticated meanings, such as *to overcome* or *to surpass*.

THE CIRCLE

A circle that surrounds an object can indicate completeness, importance, or self-sufficiency. A broken circle can indicate insufficiency. Use different colored circles creatively. A green circle can show, for example, healthy growth. An orange circle can represent caution or hazard. There are many possibilities.

THE X

The X represents an important location, or a crossed-out item when used on top of a given object.

THE BOX

The box is especially useful around an object to indicate containment, protection, or impermeability. An empty box with an arrow pointing at its top can mean something will fill the box or something will be contained in the future. A box containing an object with an arrow pointing out of it can mean the object will leave, or is leaving.

CONTAIN   **FILL, PLACE INSIDE**

NUMBERS

Numbers convey order, priority, and identification. Numbers can be placed on, or near objects in your mind. For example, if theories A, B and C occur in a specific order, then numbers can represent this order:

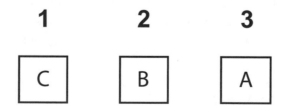

> This list of shapes is simply the beginning of many possible symbols,
> and you should think of more for your own reading needs.
>
> Your ability to handle more complex reading material will grow
> as you develop your ability to represent complex sentences
> using images and symbols.

IV. YOUR MENTAL ARENA

NVP utilizes the power of visualization in which the reader transforms written words into graphic mental images. The pictures that the reader creates are made of symbols, words, and numbers that the mind's eye can see. The goal is to place those words and images in an imaginary three-dimensional space that will be easy to remember. These locations are called **mental arenas**.

Now that you are familiar with several basic symbols, you can move to the next stage of your NVP introduction: selecting a mental arena in which to place your images. This arena will contain the images that represent the details of the passage. The aim here is to select a place that you can easily think about and remember, a place that is not distracting in which you can easily navigate mentally. You can use a place that is extremely familiar to you, such as your living room or apartment, or you can create an entirely new space, such as a white room. **Any space will do, as long as you can remember exactly what and where you place things within it.**

✓ You should know that, eventually, your mental arena will have to accommodate many images and symbols. Due to the complexity of MCAT passages, using a single room for your mental arena may prove too limiting. You may not be able to fit every image and symbol into one room. Instead, you may try using a vary large space, such as an imaginary gymnasium or warehouse. The walls of these large spaces are tall and wide, providing great surface space on which to draw symbols and images. However, other spaces may prove more useful. Let us look at several common mental arenas:

THE FAMILIAR ROOM

Any familiar room, such as a bedroom or living room, is a good place to begin practicing NVP as your mental arena. Try to close your eyes and imagine the space in great detail. Your bedroom, or any other familiar room, will work well because your mind already knows the space clearly. When using the familiar room, be sure to make use of all the space.

You can draw images and symbols on not only the walls, but also the floor and ceiling. You can also use the furniture in the room on which to place three-dimensional symbols and objects. Or, you can imagine your room completely empty. In either case, do remember to make full use of the space. Feel free to place objects in the middle of your room as needed.

The pros and cons of the Familiar Room arena:

Pros - a familiar area; simple dimensions; relatively easy to keep track of everything inside; easy to navigate and look around at pictures and symbols; good for simple passages.

Cons - relatively small shape and size so the number of objects inside is limited; a monotonous space (the walls probably look the same, so keeping track of locations of objects may prove challenging).

THE IMAGINARY ROOM

What we mean by an imaginary room is one that does not exist in reality. This is a space that you can create, with the dimensions and characteristics of your choice. You can create a room that has four white walls about ten feet tall, or green walls that are three stories tall. This room can hang in space, or you can place it in a more traditional location. The choice is yours. The goal is to customize the room to your own reading requirements in order to maximize retention and memory. Create whatever best suits your mind, but once you create a room, be sure to use it often.

The pros and cons of the Imaginary Room arena:

Pros - a space customized to your needs; greater wall size and color freedom; can change the room size to accommodate many images and objects generated by the text.

Cons - unfamiliar space; may forget key dimensions or artifacts placed inside; difficult to replicate the same space every time.

THE HOUSE

Most MCAT passages contain many ideas and details presented in a somewhat complex fashion. Transforming each sentence into visual cues can quickly fill the mental space of a single room. Rooms can only hold a limited number of symbols and images on its walls. Furthermore, remembering which object belongs to which paragraph can be difficult with only four walls, a floor, and a ceiling on which to work. While some students dedicate each wall of their mental room to each paragraph of the passage, others find this cumbersome and too limiting. A single wall may be unable to accommodate longer and more complicated passages. To overcome the spatial limitations of a **room**, you can try using a **house** or **apartment** in which you live.

Using a house as your mental arena has two strong advantages: familiarity, and usable space. In using your own house, you gain the advantage of having several familiar rooms in close proximity to each other. **You can dedicate each room to a paragraph, or dedicate each room to represent a specific meaning.** Images in your living room could represent, say, the opinions of the author, while those in your bathroom could represent the opinions of the author's critics. In this way you no longer have to remember whether certain images represent the author or the critics. Just remember in which room the images appear. You could take this a step further, and place images outside of the home. You could have the outside represent the people or theories that oppose the author's ideas, since they now sit *outside*.

In this manner, a house offers much more flexibility for representing relationships. You can connect rooms with colored lines to indicate certain meanings. Plus, the walls and mirrors of the house can provide clean surfaces on which to draw symbols and pictures. Be creative, and practice using every room of your house.

If you do use a home, be sure to take advantage of the outside areas. The backyard can represent special information, as well as the front yard. The roof can also be used for certain ideas, such as main themes of the passage.

The pros and cons of the House arena:

Pros - a space with many dimensions for complex thoughts and relationships; easy to keep track of various ideas in different rooms and outside spaces; very familiar (if you choose your own house).

Cons - none, as long as you empty the house of all familiar objects before using NVP.

THE HOME STREET

Whether you actually live on a cul-de-sac or a long street, you can choose to assign each house on the street to a paragraph of your passage. This works remarkably well for many students. In this arena, you imagine yourself standing in the middle of the street looking at each house. Pick a house for your first paragraph and designate that to be house number one. The idea here is to place all the details of the first paragraph on the first house, those of the second paragraph on the second house, and so forth. Specifically, as you read the first paragraph, transform all the ideas into pictures and place them on the front yard of house number one. Then, as you read the next paragraph, move to the next house and start building images on its front yard. Continue this for each paragraph, and soon you will have a sequential record of all passage details, paragraph-by-paragraph (in this case, house-by-house).

The sequential placement of paragraph details is a remarkable tool. Imagine that you encounter a question regarding the details of the third paragraph of the passage; you can quickly see everything you placed on the third house and answer the question without ever having to look back at the third paragraph. **Instead of looking at the passage, you simply look at your mental image.** In an instant, you can actually see the correct answers in your mind. This is what makes NVP very powerful.

The pros and cons of the Home Street arena:

Pros - easy to keep track of each paragraph in sequence; very familiar area;

Cons - some front yards may not be amenable for use as a mental space.

Learn to look at your NVP mental images when answering questions.
You should not have to look back at the passage to find answers.
Just look at the images in your mind.

ON THE MCAT

Since you will encounter seven passages on Verbal Reasoning, you should consider alternate starting locations in your mental space to help avoid overlapping images. Does this mean that you should use seven different streets as mental arenas for the seven paragraphs? Not necessarily.

✓ Try using one street only. You can start at one end of the street and apply the ideas of each paragraph to each house sequentially. Then, for the next passage, start at the house at the other end of the street. In this manner, you will avoid having to use multiple arenas. Use the homes at the ends of your street and alternate between them as you move from one passage to the next.

Problems arise if you always start at the same house for the first paragraph of each passage. **You run the risk of confusing images from one passage with the next.** You may see images that you placed on a front yard and not realize that they are left over from a former passage.

RECAP OF MENTAL ARENAS

We have introduced four mental arenas, or spaces, for you to try as you practice Neuro-Visual Programming. Use the arena that works best for you. When you first begin using NVP, you may want to try different arenas to see which one proves most comfortable and useful. Be sure to use the arena that also best suits the needs of the text.

In my personal experience, the mental space that worked best for me on the MCAT was the street where I grew up. I lived on a cul-de-sac, which worked perfectly because the location was so familiar. During the test, I assigned each paragraph to a neighboring house, and could place images and symbols without any loss of detail. I refined this technique by designating special areas of each house to have special meaning. For instance, the *garage door* represented the attitude of the author for that particular paragraph. So, if the author happened to express an argument that attacked another idea in a certain paragraph, I would make the garage door appear red. I utilized the backyard to represent ideas contrary to those of the author. For instance, if the author mentioned a critic, then I would place the ideas of the critic in the *backyard*. Everything that supported the author I placed in the *front yard* and on the *driveway*. In this manner, I was able to allocate special meanings to apecial places.

✓ By assigning meanings to specific places in your arena, you can keep track of many complex details. For example, you may not remember whether John Doe agreed or disagreed with the author. But, because you remember placing him in the backyard of a house, you automatically know that he was in disagreement (since you had already assigned the backyard to contain people or things that disagree with the author). **This is how you can use your mental space in a creative and specific manner.**

V. EXAMPLES OF NVP IN ACTION

Now that we have discussed several useful mental arenas, let us work through a few examples where we can apply NVP. Let us start with a single paragraph and work our way to more lengthy material.

NVP EXERCISE #1:
LEARNING TO TRANSFORM WORDS INTO IMAGES

Our first example will give you a feel for the density and complexity of material that is of medium difficulty on the MCAT. For your mental arena in this exercise, try using the front driveway of a familiar house.

Begin by clearing your mind of any distractions. As you read the following paragraph, try to transform the words into objects and symbols that represent the meaning of the text. Place these objects on your imaginary front driveway in a manner that is easy to remember. Give it a try:

The implicit separation between the transcendent and the immanent spheres, which runs through the Seventeenth Century, and which were held together by Leibniz with great difficulty and doubtful success, becomes an explicit
5   acknowledged separation in the Eighteenth Century, and is expressly formulated as that between the unknowable and the knowable. It is still the modern problem of the Ego knowing the object. (Snider, 367)

At first glance, this paragraph looks complicated and perhaps intimidating. However, using NVP will help you easily comprehend this material. The first sentence reveals a separation between two spheres, the *transcendent* and *immanent*. Try to translate this image into mental pictures in a straightforward manner. Create two spheres hovering above the driveway, on your left and right, separated by a certain distance. The spheres should hover at equal heights above the ground since, so far, they carry equal importance. (If one were to carry greater importance, you could elevate that more important sphere in your mind.) Next, place a big letter T on one sphere, and a big letter I on the other, to represent the transcendent and immanent.

We next read that the separation runs through the Seventeenth Century (line 2). To handle this **quickly and with little effort**, imagine that the driveway itself represents the Seventeenth Century. You can place a big 17 on it if you wish. Down the middle of the driveway, place a long black piece of tape to represent the separation that runs through the Seventeenth Century. Your two spheres should sit on opposite sides of the divided driveway.

The next part of the sentence reveals that these two spheres were held together by Leibniz with great difficulty and doubtful success (lines 3 - 4):

> . . . and which were held together by Leibniz with great difficulty and doubtful success . . .

On your driveway, place a man standing with one hand on one sphere and his other hand on the other sphere. Imagine this man struggling to keep the two spheres close to each other, as if there were a force keeping them apart. **Such a simple image conveys the meaning of this excerpt succinctly, which should be your goal always.**

As we read further, we see that this separation becomes overtly explicit in the following century:

> ... becomes an explicit
> 5   acknowledged separation in the Eighteenth Century ...

How can we represent this in our mental space? One approach is to use the logic that something explicit is more obvious than that which is implicit. Since we are talking about a chronologically subsequent time period, then its representation should somehow connect with the surface of the driveway which we designated to be the Seventeenth Century. If we let the garage door represent the Eighteenth Century (place a large number 18 on it) then we have two surfaces in our arena that represent two consecutive centuries. To handle the explicit nature of the Eighteenth Century separation, place a large deep gash down the middle of the garage door. This deep gash is much more explicit than the black tape running down the middle of the driveway.

Already, we have created with relative ease a vivid series of images that represent the text. Let us continue. The end of the sentence indicates that the separation of these spheres in the Eighteenth Century is defined as that between the unknowable and the knowable (line 6 - 7):

> expressly formulated as that between the unknowable and
> the knowable ...

Here are two suggested ways to transform these words into images. You can place a large letter U on one side of the gash in the garage door, and a large letter K on the other side to represent the unknowable and the knowable separated. Or, a better approach perhaps, is to use vivid symbols. On one side of the gash you can place the outline of a brain to represent the knowable. On the other side, you can place the outline of a large question mark to indicate the unknowable. **Feel free to use simple,**

yet effective symbols to convey meaning. Combining symbols with images is a fundamental aspect of NVP.

The final sentence of our passage is almost a passing comment, but quite important nonetheless. Remember, every sentence on Verbal Reasoning is crucial to understand and remember. Do not skip over any sentence. **Students who do well on Verbal Reasoning have the extraordinary ability to remember most of what they read the first time through.** The last sentence of our example reveals that the preceding material still persists as the problem of the Ego knowing the object (lines 7 - 8):

> . . . It is still the modern problem of the Ego knowing the object.

Since the action of recognition is fairly human in character, this sentence may be handled best by letting a **person** represent the Ego. Off to the side of the garage door and driveway, you can place a person standing dressed in very modern clothes. On this person's shirt, you can place the word 'EGO.' This person represents the Ego in a modern setting. You can have this person holding some object in his hand and looking at it with confusion, not knowing what he is looking at. In this way, you can represent the modern problem of the Ego knowing the object.

ADDITIONAL POINTS

This concludes our first analysis of text using NVP. Our example demonstrates how to begin with a mental arena (such as the driveway of a house in our example), create objects and symbols to capture every detail, and position those objects to convey the correct meaning of the text.

✓ The same steps of this exercise should take place as you read each passage on the MCAT. However, generating images and symbols quickly as you read requires many months of practice. In the first few weeks of using NVP, you will sense that transforming words into images slows down your reading rate. This is normal, but temporary. You must work through this slow period until the process occurs quickly and naturally.

You will begin using NVP in the third month of your reading training. As you will see in Chapter 10, reading for two to three hours each day using NVP for at least three months. This high level of preparation will allow NVP to happen naturally on the MCAT, or when you read anything else.

When you become an expert at using NVP, you will create panoramas of objects and symbols that capture every detail of what you read automatically. This will help you greatly on not only Verbal Reasoning, but also Biological Sciences.

NVP EXERCISE #2:
REPRESENTING HUMAN CHARACTERISTICS

This next exercise will examine how to visualize the characteristics of a person or thing that are somewhat abstract and difficult to imagine. For human actions and emotions, begin by using a person for your model. When in doubt, use images of people that are bizarre or strange. **Our minds will remember more vibrant pictures for a longer period of time.** Here is the paragraph for our second exercise:

> Similarly we have a record of Chopin's outer life. We know his sensitive, melancholy temperament, his struggles and disappointments, something of his love-affairs and the story of his social and artistic success; but how much
> 5   deeper is the revelation of the man through his music. When we listen to those strangely moving melodies, those harmonics pushed almost to discord, those appeals to sad and tender sentiment till the very heart strings ache, we come to know the soul of Chopin with its burden of
> 10   revelation, its painful struggles, far-reaching hungers and aspirations. (Griggs, 101)

This excerpt from *The Philosophy of Art* is a very descriptive paragraph, one that most MCAT readers might gloss over because of its numerous descriptive details. You must resist the temptation to rush through material, even if it is laden with such details. Going back and searching for facts that you glossed over initially wastes significant time. Using NVP will allow us to remember most, if not all, of the details the first time through.

So let us begin our analysis of the excerpt. Let us start with a fresh new mental arena of a house with a front yard. Remember to clear the house and front yard of any clutter. The excerpt above begins by revealing that a record of Chopin's outer life exists. Let us stop here and account for this in a simple and direct manner. We can picture a large, say, six-foot tall, notebook with the image of a man drawn on it. This is the written record of Chopin. Let us place this six-foot tall notebook *outside*, on the driveway of the house, which shows us that it is a record of his *outer* life (a record of his inner life would belong inside our house).

Following the first sentence, we see a list of characteristics regarding this outer life (lines 1 - 4):

> Similarly we have a record of Chopin's outer life. We
> know his sensitive, melancholy temperament, his struggles
> and disappointments, something of his love-affairs and the
> story of his social and artistic success . . .

Since symbols and objects do a poor job conveying complex emotion, we are better off using people to represent emotion. The sentence above describes Chopin's sensitive and melancholy temperament. In your mental arena, imagine a man made out of glass standing on the driveway of the house. He is looking down with a sad facial expression to convey melancholy. The fact that he is made of glass shows that he is fragile and sensitive. **Remember that the materials of objects you create will convey important meaning as well.**

Use people or faces in your arena to represent complex emotions
or attitudes expressed in the passage.

Specifically, we can use facial expressions and two-person interactions to show emotion. What do we mean by two-person interaction? If I tell you that a man hugs a woman, you immediately think of affection, care, or a farewell. By showing how two people interact with each other, we can convey human emotion and conduct.

We read that Chopin experienced struggles and disappointments (lines 2 - 3). Imagine, somewhere else on your driveway, two children arm-wrestling with each other. One wins at the other's expense. Make the child who lost begin to cry. Now draw a large red circle around the sad child to emphasize frustration. This scene conveys both struggle and disappointment. Sometimes it is necessary to highlight one component of an image to draw attention and prevent confusion. We would not want to accidentally focus on the winning child, and then assume that Chopin's record represented moments of victory. Next, imagine in some other location on the front yard a bed with two people on it. This quickly captures his love-affairs. Finally, on the garage door place a painting, as well as two men talking to each other. These convey both his social and artistic dimensions of his life record.

Let us move on to the rest of the paragraph. The focus shifts to his music, and the characteristics of it. Here the passage dives into even more complex emotion and human sensitivity (lines 4 - 8):

> . . . but how much
> 5   deeper is the revelation of the man through his music.
> When we listen to those strangely moving melodies, those
> harmonics pushed almost to discord, those appeals to sad
> and tender sentiment till the very heart strings ache . . .

The passage here tells us that Chopin's music reveals deeper elements about the man. To prepare our minds for this, we can make a distinction between the front yard of our house and the side and back yards. Everything in the front yard we can consider to be obvious revelations, characteristics about Chopin that are more readily apparent. **As we move into the side and back yards, we enter deeper territory which**

contains more hidden revelations about the man. In this manner, we use a physical dimension to represent an abstract concept. (Use this strategy often on the MCAT.)

Now that we understand where to put the rest of the deeper revelations, let us continue. First, we read about strangely moving melodies (line 6). Place a ten-foot tall black musical note in the side yard of the house, and try imagining the note wobbling in a strange fashion.

Second, we read about harmonics pushed to discord (line 7). Behind the strangely moving note, place an upright piano with a man pushing it over. This represents the harmonics pushed almost to discord.

Third, we read about appeals to sad and tender sentiment which cause heart strings to ache (line 8). If you wish, behind the upright piano with the man pushing it over, place a very sad woman in the side yard playing a violin. Imagine her heart beating outside her body, and make the bow that she holds connected to her beating heart via thin strings. She represents the appeal to sad and tender sentiment that causes heart strings to ache.

The decision to use a woman instead of a man is, in this case, strategic. Since we already used a man in the neighboring image (pushing over the piano), using another man may cause confusion. By using a woman, say, in a white dress, we make the two images very clear and separate. Furthermore, a woman more readily represents "tender sentiment." Having a woman represent a characteristic about Chopin presents no problem because our discussion of a man, namely Chopin, is obvious. These three images - the oversized wobbling note, the man pushing over the piano, and the female violinist - are created nearly instantly in our minds. They are **unforgettable, and convey vivid meanings that match those of the text**.

As we move to the end of the paragraph, we are moving into the back yard of our imaginary house. Remember, it is wise to **dedicate one house to one paragraph - no more, no less.** There is plenty of room around the house and inside of it to contain every image and symbol mandated by the complexity of a single paragraph on the MCAT. Let us look at the final section of our paragraph (lines 8 - 11):

> and tender sentiment till the very heart strings ache, we
> come to know the soul of Chopin with its burden of
> 10   revelation, its painful struggles, far-reaching hungers and
> aspirations.

We are now in the back yard where we can place images that reveal the most intimate characteristics of a person or thing. So, let us place a large red balloon in the form of a beating heart in the backyard. Make the balloon float at eye level, about six feet off the ground since we need to represent its burdens underneath it.

On the bottom of our heart-shaped balloon, connect a long black cable with a glowing light bulb on the other end. The light bulb is acting to weigh down the balloon, keeping it from floating up. This is the burden of revelation (a light bulb can symbolize intelligence and thought).

Connect another cable to the bottom of our heart-shaped balloon, and have it suspend a puppet of the boy we saw earlier (who lost in the arm-wrestling match). Fasten a third cable with a plastic stomach dangling on its other end, and finally a fourth cable with an asp on its end.

This very bizarre image represents the soul of Chopin, burdened by revelation, painful struggles, far-reaching hungers, and aspirations. For this last symbol, we used an object (asp) that has a name that corresponds to the first three letters of a complex concept (aspirations).

✔ Feel free to use objects with names similar to concepts that are otherwise difficult to represent.

NVP EXERCISE #3:
HANDLING COMPLEX MATERIAL

Let us look at a longer excerpt that better approximates the length of a short MCAT passage. The following text from *Zimmerman on Ocean Shipping* about steamships covers four paragraphs. In this exercise, you should read the passage and then work through your own NVP analysis. When you are finished, go ahead and read the analysis presented in the book.

Try to use the full extent of your mental arena, and be creative in how you transform concepts into images. As a rule of thumb, **the more creative and exaggerated your mental images, the more memorable they become.** Try to use the mental arena of a street as you read, and use each house for each paragraph. Take your time, and enjoy the process.

It is interesting to study how the different steamship companies have arrived at different speed, size, passenger and cargo accommodations, cabin and steerage accommodations, etc. Contenting ourselves with a rough
5   characterization of the most important steamship companies serving the North Atlantic route, one may say that the Cunard Line has emphasized speed; and the White Star Line comfort and luxury. In their latest bids for the leadership in North Atlantic travel, the Hamburg-American
10 Line tried to combine the speed of the Cunard with the comfort and luxury of the White Star Line, without at the same time sacrificing the chance of earning a fair sum from the transportation of cargo.

Different considerations determine the policy regarding
15 passenger accommodation on different routes. Thus, the almost extravagant display of luxury which marks the latest products of the marine architect, created for the North Atlantic route, might prove a doubtful asset to a company catering to the Australian or South African
20 traveling public. It is an interesting speculation whether, in the future, the North Atlantic route will hold first rank as regards luxury and display. Reports are current that passenger ships are to ply between Pacific ports of the United States and Hawaii, whose luxury and comfort will
25 outdo anything previously offered.

30   While the outstanding consideration controlling the
construction of cargo-carrying vessels is maximum
economy, safety is the prime desideratum in the case of
passenger ships, with speed and comfort - or luxury - as
secondary factors. The main aim of safety devices is the
prevention of disaster. In so far, however, as all human
handiwork is imperfect, the possibility of disaster must be
included in the calculation of the ship-builder, and devices
must be installed which reduce to the minimum the
35   consequences of a disaster, should such occur.

Accordingly, safety devices fall into two groups. Among
the preventive types, the submarine bell and wireless
telegraphy, allowing constant conversation between
steamers approaching each other in a fog, and permitting
40   the transmission of warnings from ship to ship or from
land to ship, have reduced the danger of collision to a
minimum. Double bottoms reduce the danger from
grounding, and automatic sprinklers and the substitution of
electricity for gas or oil reduce the danger from fire. The
45   greatest safety is achieved by scientifically devised ocean
lanes, careful patrolling of the ocean, improved weather
reports and better knowledge of currents, winds, etc.
(Zimmerman, 327-329)

NVP ANALYSIS

The first sentence reveals that it is interesting to study how various
steamship companies have arrived at various accommodations:

It is interesting to study how the different steamship
companies have arrived at different speed, size, passenger
and cargo accommodations, cabin and steerage
accommodations, etc . . .

Beginning at the first house in your mind, imagine a student standing on
the sidewalk looking with great interest at the driveway. He is studying it.
Maybe you can have him holding a magnifying glass looking through it to

emphasize the act of studying. What does he study? He watches three or four gentlemen in business attire wearing hats in the shape of ships on their heads walking onto the driveway. They represent the steamship companies arriving. You can make each gentleman have a different speed of arrival, and a different waist size. You can have each one hold a different size box and steering wheel in each hand, to represent different cargo and steerage accommodations.

The rest of the paragraph compares the various steamship lines. When you encounter similar examples, try using different regions outside the house (the two side yards and the back yard) to represent each one. Apply this approach to the following paragraph (lines 4 - 11):

> ... Contenting ourselves with a rough
> 5   characterization of the most important steamship
> companies serving the North Atlantic route, one may say
> that the Cunard Line has emphasized speed; and the White
> Star Line comfort and luxury. In their latest bids for the
> leadership in North Atlantic travel, the Hamburg-American
> 10   Line tried to combine the speed of the Cunard with the
> comfort and luxury of the White Star Line ...

The first sentence here reveals that we are dealing with the North Atlantic route. On the garage door, you can simply place the letters NA. **With practice, you will remember meanings of single letters that you place at various locations in your mental space.**

Now, let us handle the steamship lines. The first one is the Cunard Line, which emphasizes speed. Imagine that each side yard of your house contains a pool. Place a ship with a big letter C in one of the pools. Can you see the ship with a large C floating in the pool? If not, try making the ship bright green or pink to help your memory. **Extreme colors can make an image more memorable.** Now, imagine this ship moving in the pool - make it move extremely fast to exaggerate the concept of speed. The fact that a ship is moving rapidly should make its speed easier to remember.

In the pool, on the other side of the house, we want to convey the White Star Line. One easy visual cue is to place a big white star floating in the pool. On one of the large arms of the star, place a woman reclining in a bathing suit. This relaxing woman represents the comfort and luxury of the White Star Line.

Lastly, we read that a third line is attempting to become the leader of North Atlantic travel by combining the speed of the Cunard Line with the comfort of the White Star Line (lines 9 - 11):

> . . . the Hamburg-American
> 10   Line tried to combine the speed of the Cunard with the
> comfort and luxury of the White Star Line . . .

Here we need to be creative. How should we place the third cruise line so that it includes the attributes of the other two lines, and conveys a bid for leadership? We read in lines 8 through 10 that the Hamburg-American Line attempted to combine these attributes and take primacy over North Atlantic travel. We do not know whether the Hamburg-American Line actually succeeded in doing so, however. One very effective mental image is to utilize the pool in the backyard by placing a large floating hamburger in it. Imagine two cables coming out of this oversized hamburger towards the ships in the other pools on the sides of the house. One cable will connect to ship C, and the other cable to the star ship. Finally, imagine that this hamburger is slowly rising up out of the water towards the sky. It is attempting to surpass the ships in the other two pools.

The last part of the paragraph conveys the goal of making a profit from transporting cargo (lines 11 - 13):

> . . . without at the
> same time sacrificing the chance of earning a fair sum
> from the transportation of cargo.

We can interpret this to mean that the Hamburg-American Line must find a balance between luxury and profitability. Thus, we can imagine a large see-saw next to the hamburger. On one end of the see-saw sits a letter 'L', for luxury, and on the other sits several cargo crates overflowing with gold coins. This image symbolizes the balance between luxury and profitability.

Moving to the second paragraph, we advance to the next house on our imaginary street. (Make sure that this new property is clear of any objects, so that you have an undisturbed arena in which to create your visual images.) Here is the first sentence of the second paragraph (lines 14 - 15):

> Different considerations determine the policy regarding
> 15 passenger accommodation on different routes.

Since this is a somewhat complex statement, it deserves simplification. **Whenever you encounter concepts that are difficult to convey with images, first summarize the ideas in your own words.**

> NVP is customizable. You can select the mental arena and symbols that work best for you. In addition, you can translate complex ideas into your own words and images.

The excerpt above most closely means that passengers of different routes have different interests, and these determine the accommodation policies. So, to represent the routes, imagine two small rivers running through the front yard of your second house. In one river stands a scientist with a white lab coat reaching for a wood table. In the other river stands a banker in a business suit reaching for a golden table. In this way, passengers of different routes have various interests, which dictate their accommodations. Let us keep reading (lines 15 - 20):

> 15 passenger accommodation on different routes. Thus, the
>   almost extravagant display of luxury which marks the
>   latest products of the marine architect, created for the
>   North Atlantic route, might prove a doubtful asset to a
>   company catering to the Australian or South African
> 20 traveling public . . .

At this point in our mental arena, we have a golden table on one side of the front yard, and a wood table on the other. Notice that the choice of materials establishes a contrast between luxurious and normal accommodations. Next to the golden table (representing luxury), put a sailor standing with a protractor in his hands. The letters NA (in bright colors) appear on his white shirt. This image represents the marine architect preferring the extravagant display of luxury, which is characteristic of the North Atlantic route.

When using NVP, you can **use groups of letters to represent longer words and concepts**. The more you practice this, the more easily you will be able to remember abbreviations. Now, place a group of people standing around the wood table. On the table place a flag with the letters AU, and a flag with the letters SA. These people represent the Australian and South African traveling public who do not prefer the luxury of the North Atlantic travelers. By having them huddle around the wood table, you have them show preference (for non-luxury).

The next part of the paragraph raises an interesting question as to whether the North Atlantic route will maintain supremacy of luxury over other routes in the future:

20   . . . It is an interesting speculation whether, in
            the future, the North Atlantic route will hold first rank as
            regards luxury and display. Reports are current that
            passenger ships are to ply between Pacific ports of the
            United States and Hawaii, whose luxury and comfort will
25   outdo anything previously offered.

There are three concepts that we cannot ignore in the statement above: the idea of the *speculation*, the *future*, and the *rank*. How do we represent these in our mind? For the idea of speculation, let us use a ten-foot tall question mark. We will place this in our mental arena momentarily. For the **idea of time**, let us use the surface of the driveway in the following manner: the garage door represents the **far future**, and the street represents the **present**, so that objects on the driveway closer to the garage door are farther into the future than objects closer to the street. In this manner, the length of the driveway can represent time.

Notice how we use a physical dimension to represent an abstract idea. That which is placed closer to the street occurs before that which is placed closer to the garage. Be creative with your use of space as you practice NVP.

Let us look again at the first sentence of the excerpt above (lines 20 - 22). To capture the speculation of whether or not the North Atlantic route will hold first rank for luxury in the future, let us place a golden table with a large Olympic gold medal (first rank) on it near the garage door on the driveway.

We are repeating an object (golden table) to represent the same meaning (luxury). Above this table, floating in air, place your ten-foot tall question mark. If you have forgotten that this table represents the North Atlantic route, then stamp "NA" on its surface.

To represent the second sentence (lines 22 - 25), imagine that the sidewalk touching the street is made of paper and is one long notebook (reports). On the left side of this long paper sidewalk, write a large PA for Pacific ports. On the right side, draw a pineapple to symbolize Hawaii. We see the letters PA and the pineapple on opposite sides, which triggers in our mind the ships traveling from the Pacific coast of the USA to Hawaii.

Lastly, let us place a pile of gold coins ten-feet tall on the notebook to convey the meaning of unparalleled luxury on this Pacific-Hawaii route.

✓ The better you become at using symbols to represent ideas, the less you will have to depict every single detail. You will rely more on your memory with a few symbols to recall the full meaning of the passage.

NVP becomes visual shorthand for your brain.

This takes us to the third paragraph, which means that we need to shift to the third house in our mental arena. **Remember to dedicate one paragraph to one property to keep ideas well organized and uncluttered**. Some questions on the MCAT pertain to certain paragraphs. The third paragraph reveals a comparison between the key considerations of cargo-carrying vessels and those of passenger ships (lines 26 - 30):

> While the outstanding consideration controlling the
> construction of cargo-carrying vessels is maximum
> economy, safety is the prime desideratum in the case of
> passenger ships, with speed and comfort - or luxury - as
> 30   secondary factors . . .

On our third property, we need to represent a division of ideas. When we encounter a comparison between two entities, in this case *economy* and *safety*, we can use the left and right sides of the front yard to represent the divided concepts. Between the left and right sides of the front yard is the driveway, which is a good surface on which to place symbols that compare and contrast the two ideas to the right and left of the driveway.

So, on the left side of the front yard let us place four large crates fitting neatly inside a large box. The neat packaging of the four crates should trigger the concept of economy in your mind. If it does not, then you need a more vivid symbol for economy. You could try placing an oversized dollar bill floating above the crates, but remember that the meaning of economy most nearly means efficiency in this passage. **Be careful to recognize the correct connotation of ideas when using symbols.**

Now let us compare the priority of cargo-carrying vessels to that of passenger ships. On the right side of the front yard, place a group of people standing around a large orange life raft. The crowd of people represents passengers (hence, a passenger ship), and the life raft in the middle represents the priority of safety. Behind this crowd of people, you can place a Ferrari and a sofa next to each other with a large letter L floating above them. Immediately, this picture tells us that speed and comfort comprise luxury, which is secondary to safety due to the nature of its background position. You can show priority by placing one set of objects behind or underneath another. **Do not be afraid to use current modern objects that are vivid and descriptive.**

The rest of the third paragraph discusses disaster prevention:

30 . . . The main aim of safety devices is the prevention of disaster. In so far, however, as all human handiwork is imperfect, the possibility of disaster must be included in the calculation of the ship-builder, and devices must be installed which reduce to the minimum the
35 consequences of a disaster, should such occur.

Since we are still reading the same paragraph, we will continue using the same property in our mental arena. So, let us build the next series of images in the backyard where we have plenty of room.

How do we represent the idea of a safety device, the concept of purpose, and the act of disaster avoidance? Again, we must be creative in a very quick fashion. Use any images or symbols that first come to mind which correctly convey meaning.

The following is one suggested way of handling the above excerpt. Place a **man whose surface is made of metal** standing in the backyard. He holds a bow and arrow, aiming. On the far end of the backyard, place a mini-tornado that is moving towards the house (a very vivid image that is difficult to forget). When the metal man **fires the arrow** at the mini-tornado, the tornado vanishes. In this manner, we **implement human action to convey more complex meaning**.

> You must be extremely efficient at choosing a location in your arena, whether outside or inside your imaginary house, to place images and symbols. Selecting a region for placing images must happen almost instantaneously.

Here, the metal man represents a safety device that aims to prevent disasters. **The use of a person to represent an object is more appropriate because the object is performing a task that is more human in character.** In the above example, we use a sequence of actions to capture the full meaning of a device aiming to dispel disaster. Let us continue with lines 31 through 35:

> . . . In so far, however, as all human
> handiwork is imperfect, the possibility of disaster must be
> included in the calculation of the ship-builder, and devices
> must be installed which reduce to the minimum the
> 35   consequences of a disaster, should such occur.

The above excerpt reveals more about the process of building ships. Here we read that all human handiwork is imperfect, and the ship-builder is responsible for including the possibility of disaster in his calculations. Furthermore, we read that devices must be installed to minimize the consequences of a disaster, should one occur.

In our backyard, let us place a ship-builder who is making calculations with a five-foot long calculator. We **exaggerate the size** of the calculator to emphasize the fact that he is making calculations. Next, imagine the builder grabbing hold of disasters, like tornadoes and fire, and throwing these into the calculator. In addition, you can imagine this ship-builder wearing a plaster cast on his arm to represent his imperfect handiwork. This overall picture represents the imperfect ship-builder factoring disasters into his calculations. The picture is very clean and simple. Finally, imagine the ship-builder putting a metal box over the mini-tornado so that the box contains it. In this way we represent installed devices that help minimize disasters.

> When you use NVP, you want to work with very simple and straightforward images since time is of the essence on the MCAT.

✓ Creating images may now seem like a burden as you read. However, by the time you practice NVP for a few months you will create these images very quickly.

Let us now recap the images that we created for this paragraph. There are three main moving pictures in the backyard. First, we have the metal man aiming and firing at the mini-tornado, causing it to disappear. This is the main aim of safety devices diverting disasters. Second, we have the imprecise ship-builder throwing disasters into his calculator. This is the imperfect builder factoring the possibility of disasters into his calculations. Third, we have the builder putting a metal box over the mini-tornado. This represents the installation of devices that reduce the consequence of disasters when they occur.

Let us proceed with the fourth and final paragraph of this excerpt:

Accordingly, safety devices fall into two groups. Among the preventive types, the submarine bell and wireless telegraphy, allowing constant conversation between steamers approaching each other in a fog, and permitting
40   the transmission of warnings from ship to ship or from land to ship, have reduced the danger of collision to a minimum. Double bottoms reduce the danger from grounding, and automatic sprinklers and the substitution of electricity for gas or oil reduce the danger from fire. The
45   greatest safety is achieved by scientifically devised ocean lanes, careful patrolling of the ocean, improved weather reports and better knowledge of currents, winds, etc.

Since this is a new paragraph, we move to a new home in our mind that is neighboring the previous home that we just filled with images. **By keeping the homes adjacent to each other, we can more readily keep track of the details of each paragraph in a sequential manner.** This is a powerful tool on the MCAT, because certain questions test your understanding of the sequence in which facts were presented in the passage. This final paragraph discusses safety devices in some detail.

The first sentence reveals that there are two groups of devices (line 36):

> Accordingly, safety devices fall into two groups.

Let us again imagine a **left** and **right** portion of the front yard of our fourth house. What are the two groups? The lead-in word *Accordingly* suggests a close continuation of thought from the previous paragraph. Recall the final sentence of the previous paragraph:

> included in the calculation of the ship-builder, and devices
> must be installed which reduce to the minimum the
> 35 consequences of a disaster, should such occur.

Thus, we understand that one group must be *the devices that reduce the effects of a disaster*. Now we have an interesting situation. Our current paragraph makes reference to a previous one. So how do we handle this visually in our mental arena? Let us choose the right side of our front yard to represent the devices that reduce the effects of a disaster. Since we already created images for these devices on the previous house, we do not need to re-create them.

We can simply place a large arrow that points from the right side of our current house to the backyard of the previous house (with the metal box that covered the mini-tornadoes). Arrows are effective symbols for making connections from one location to another.

So, given that the first group reduces the effects of a disaster, what does the second group do? Let us keep reading:

> Accordingly, safety devices fall into two groups. Among
> the preventive types, the submarine bell and wireless
> telegraphy, allowing constant conversation between
> steamers approaching each other in a fog, and permitting
> 40   the transmission of warnings from ship to ship or from
> land to ship, have reduced the danger of collision to a
> minimum.

We learn that the second group is of the *preventive* type, so this conjures up the image of, say, a red stop sign as a symbol of prevention. Thus, we can place a stop sign on the left side of our imaginary front yard. Next, place a ten-foot tall metal bell and a ten-foot tall cell phone behind it. These represent the submarine bell and wireless telegraphy, respectively. (If you have other symbols that you prefer, then use those instead as long as they are clear and effective.)

Lines 37 to 41 explain how these devices reduce the danger of collision. Wireless telegraphy allows for constant conversation in fog. We can imagine a dense cloud of fog surrounding the oversized cell phone. This picture should be adequate to trigger the rest of the explanation, which is that wireless telegraphy permits constant conversation (line 38).

Regarding the bell, such a device permits warning transmissions from ship to ship, or land to ship. Such a function seems obvious since we are dealing with a large bell. You may want to place a large mound of dirt next to your bell to remind yourself that transmission is not solely between ships. Note that we do not need to show two ships avoiding a collision, because such meaning is understood. Intrinsic to the function of wireless telegraphy and the submarine bell is the prevention of disasters, namely collisions.

We next read about additional safety measures. We need to determine whether these belong to the group of devices mentioned previously, or to a new group (lines 42 - 44):

> . . . Double bottoms reduce the danger from
> grounding, and automatic sprinklers and the substitution of
> electricity for gas or oil reduce the danger from fire . . .

Since the double bottoms, sprinklers, and the substitution of electricity for gas or oil all prevent disasters, we can add these to the group of *preventive* safety measures already on the left side of our front yard.

Once again, we are faced with a concept, namely, *double bottoms*, that seems difficult to symbolize. What would be a good representation for double bottoms? Again, let us use an object that is **very vivid and conveys the meaning directly**. If we imagine an aluminum pot placed inside a second, larger aluminum pot, then we have a picture that can represent the double bottoms of a ship. This may seem bizarre, but **bizarre is effective because we enjoy remembering unusual things**.

> The mind more easily remembers strange and vivid images.
> So do not be afraid to create bizarre pictures.

As for the sprinklers, we can picture grass sprinklers spraying our front lawn. With regards to the substitution of electricity for gas or oil to reduce fire, imagine a car battery sitting atop a large oil drum and white foam coming out of the drum. The fact that the battery sits atop the drum shows priority, that the battery has greater importance than the drum. This positioning is symbolic of electricity replacing oil and gas, and the white foam reminds us of the foam from a fire extinguisher that minimizes the occurrence of fire. What do we do with the rest of the excerpt?

45   greatest safety is achieved by scientifically devised ocean
      lanes, careful patrolling of the ocean, improved weather
      reports and better knowledge of currents, winds, etc.

The author reveals in lines 45 to 47 that the greatest safety comes from a list of measures that act to prevent disasters. These include ocean lanes, patrols, weather reports, and better knowledge. For this list, let us move to the backyard to represent each concept. Since we are dealing with the ocean here, let us use a pool as its representation.

The first item listed above is *scientifically devised ocean lanes*. In our backyard, imagine three long narrow pools that run the length of the yard. At the head of each narrow pool, place a tall chemistry beaker made of glass. The beaker is a convenient symbol for science. The proximity of the beakers to the head of the pools represents the ocean lanes that are derived scientifically.

The next concept is the *careful patrolling of the ocean*. Simply placing a toy boat in one of these pools will convey the concept of a patrol. If you want to convey the idea of a patrol in the entire ocean, beyond the ocean lanes as represented by our narrow pools, then you can imagine a large moat around the entire backyard with a toy boat in it.

The next concept is *weather reports*. Near our three narrow pools, imagine a ten-foot tall book with the picture of a cloud on its cover. The cloud conveys weather, and the book reminds us of a report.

The last concept is *better knowledge of currents, winds, etc.* A useful symbol for knowledge is a human brain. **To show that something has improved, you can surround that object with rays of light** to emphasize brilliance. Above one of our narrow pools we can place a brain floating in space with rays of light emanating from it. In the pool below this levitating brain are large waves splashing about, with gusts of wind. Even the howling of the wind can be heard. This strange, yet memorable picture conveys *improved knowledge about currents and wind*.

At this point, if someone were to ask you about this maritime passage, then you could recall, with a good degree of accuracy, its salient points. This is the value of NVP. This is the power of a programmable visual memory.

✔ In the third month of your reading program, you should begin using NVP on all material.

VI. KEY POINTS OF NEURO-VISUAL PROGRAMMING

1. Neuro-Visual Programming is a process of remembering and comprehending written words by creating images and symbols of the text in your mind. Since NVP places new demands on your brain, mastering NVP requires much practice and patience.

2. Since every sentence in each passage of Verbal Reasoning is crucial to understand and remember, use NVP for the full 60 minutes during the MCAT. Be extremely efficient and quick at transforming text into visual representations.

3. Identify a mental arena that works best for you. If you use a street for your arena, then dedicate each neighboring house to each consecutive paragraph. Certain questions on the MCAT test your understanding of where facts are presented in the passage.

4. As you read, transform words into objects and symbols that represent the meaning of the text as quickly, vividly, and accurately as possible.

5. Try using strange or bizarre objects and symbols when appropriate.

6. You may use abbreviations or single letters to represent longer words and concepts. Sometimes it is more useful to place letters or numbers on objects to convey further meaning. Abbreviations and letters are best used to represent names or titles, not objects.

7. At first, you may sense that transforming words into images slows your reading speed. This is to be expected. You must work through this slow period until the process occurs quickly and naturally. NVP may take a few months to master.

8. Since symbols and objects do a limited job of conveying complex emotion, use facial expressions and two-person interactions to represent human characteristics. Do not hesitate using a person to represent an object.

9. The material out of which an object is made, such as glass or metal, helps to convey important meaning as well. Use materials to your advantage.

10. Use a physical dimension to represent an abstract concept. In the first and third exercises, the length of our imaginary driveway represented time. In the second exercise, the deeper spaces of our imaginary backyard represents the deeper revelations about a person (Chopin).

11. If you are having trouble remembering an image in your mind, exaggerate its size, color, or motion. You can make objects appear larger, brighter, move faster, etc. If you still have difficulty, then quickly switch to another image.

12. Many times, you may encounter a challenging sentence of complex ideas. Try restating the sentence in your own words to help transform the concepts into understandable pictures.

13. The physical placement of one object relative to another can convey important meaning. An object positioned above another object conveys a hierarchy of importance. Objects at the same height reveal that there is no difference in importance between them, as was seen in the first passage (the two levitating spheres).

14. You may find that a sequence of actions is needed to capture the full meaning of the text, resulting in a series of still frames.

15. Practice NVP until you can automatically create a panorama of objects and symbols that capture every detail of what you read. When you reach this point, then use NVP all the time up to the day of the MCAT.

PART IV

The Journey of
a Thousand Miles Begins
with a Single Word:
Reading

Launching Pad:
Your Reading Program

In This Chapter

If you thought that this book would offer a collection of fast tricks to boost your Verbal score by five points, then you were overly optimistic. There is no magical sleight of hand that might improve your comprehension overnight. Students who improve dramatically are those who revolutionize their reading habits through daily practice. Improving how you read takes time - your brain has to develop new critical thinking skills at a high level of proficiency.

The concepts presented in this chapter are essential to your development. The ideas discussed are based on the success of students who have put in the hard work to become great readers. Be sure to follow this chapter carefully.

> If you want to improve your VR score dramatically, then plan
> to read challenging material daily for six to eight months.

Reading is a skill that improves or fades, like a **muscle** that requires daily exercise. The more you practice, the better you read. If you stop reading for a while, then your reading skills will suffer. So right now, think about setting aside an hour in your morning and an hour in your evening to read **without any interruptions** . . . no small talk, phone calls, or snack breaks.

I. YOUR OWN READING PROGRAM

Six to eight months sounds like a long time, and it is. But for some students who commit to this program, changing a low Verbal score (7 or below) to a 10 or higher is well worth the effort. While there is no guarantee that you will make this leap in score, you should see a decent improvement in your performance.

Many students who follow this program also discover a love for reading which serves them well throughout their medical careers and beyond. Hopefully, you will commit to this training program from which you will emerge an excellent reader, and an improved thinker.

Your reading program begins with improving reading mechanics. After mastering reading mechanics, you will work on improving comprehension and memory. Finally, you will improve reading speed, and familiarity with Verbal Reasoning material and testing psychology. You will use techniques such as **force-reading** and **start-stop reading**, as well as **Neuro-Visual Programming**.

The table in the next page gives an overview of the training schedule.

> You will notice that reading becomes more fluid and relaxing as you progress.

Table 10.1 Reading Program Outline

Reading Month	Focusing On	Addressing These Problems
1st	**Mechanics**: reading a large quantity of material at a normal pace; improving eye movement; minimizing word skips.	Misreading Words, Skipping Words, Skipping Lines, Choppy Eye Movement
2nd	**Memory and Comprehension**: using **sentence recall** and **paragraph summary**. Looking for the *topic*, *setting*, and *main idea* of every paragraph.	Faulty Memory and Comprehension
3rd through 6th	**Memory and Comprehension**: practicing **Neuro-Visual Programming** during your entire reading session daily.	Faulty Memory and Comprehension
7th and 8th	**Speed and MCAT Familiarity**: pushing your reading speed to 250 words a minute; going through 70 MCAT VR passages minimum.	Slow Speed and MCAT Cold Feet

READING MONTH 1:
Cleaning Up Reading Mechanics

If reading difficult material is not now a daily habit of yours, chances are your eyes are not accustom to steady and focused reading. Most likely, the first few times you sit down to read, your eyes will skip over words here and there. Your eyes may also miss the correct beginnings of lines, by starting at the line you have just read.

These are problems with reading mechanics, which you must remedy before progressing in your training. **Bottom line - you cannot improve your reading comprehension, speed, or reading memory until you have cleaned up your reading mechanics.**

High Volume

The best fix for poor mechanics is to read a large quantity of material. In this process during your first month of practice, your brain will adapt to your eyes reading large amounts of text. During this time, your brain will automatically learn to follow the words more efficiently. This will improve how your eyes detect words and sentences.

✔ Do not worry about speed at this point. Only focus on **reading as much material every day as you can**. One hour in the morning and again in the evening will give you strong results if done on a daily basis. This program actually encourages two to tree hours of reading every day.

Force Reading

Force reading is a technique where the eyes of the reader do not stop moving until the allotted time has expired. People normally read in a casual manner, taking pauses to reflect on the material. Force reading excludes any such pauses. If you set aside, say, one hour to read a book, then your eyes should read for those 60 minutes without stopping.

You cannot stop to reflect on an interesting sentence, or an abstract idea. You must keep your eyes moving. This is force reading in action.

☐ **Force Reading - 30 minutes every day minimum**

   1. if you feel tempted to stop reading,

   2. then resist, and keep reading,

   3. never allowing your eyes to stop moving.

At minimum, you should engage in force reading for 30 minutes each day. This means that you must block out 30 minutes with no interruptions. **Your eyes cannot leave the page** for that duration. After some practice, you will notice that you can actually think about the material as you read. Your mind will begin to think at a higher level, and your ability to focus will also improve greatly.

DURING MONTH 1, EACH DAY DO THE FOLLOWING:

* **30 minutes** of force reading, followed by
* **1 hour** of normal reading in the morning
* **1 hour** of normal reading in the evening

   Total reading time per day = ***2.5 hrs***

✔ When you sit down to read every day, do not take any breaks during your reading sessions. Do not stop reading until your time is up. On the MCAT, you will have to read continually for 60 minutes, so start practicing now.

For the first four weeks of your program, you should engage in **force reading** for at least 30 minutes every day.

READING MONTH 2:
Developing Memory and Comprehension - Hunting for the Topic, Setting, and Main Idea

Unfortunately, many students throughout their college careers never learn how to read properly. As we discussed in Chapter 6, fundamental to reading is realizing that different words on the page carry different levels of importance. The inexperienced reader considers every word on the page with equal importance, as well as every sentence.

The experienced reader realizes that everything on the page does not sit at the same level. Words have different degrees of importance. Some words are more central to the meaning of a sentence than others. Certain sentences reveal the central argument of the author, while others merely emphasize supporting concepts. The experienced reader realizes two or three levels of emphasis within the text.

The second month of your reading training is dedicated to improving your memory and comprehension. You will use three novel exercises called **TSM analysis**, **sentence recall**, and **paragraph summary** on a regular basis. Let us discuss each of these exercises:

TSM Analysis

This book introduces a new exercise designed to improve reading comprehension, called **Topic, Setting, and Main idea (TSM) analysis**. There are three important points a reader should identify as he or she reads material: the **topic** of the entire passage, the **setting** of the passage and each paragraph, and the **main idea** of the passage and each paragraph. TSM analysis works in the following manner:

> 1. Read the text, identify the topic of the entire excerpt.
>
> 2. As you read each paragraph, identify each setting.
>
> 3. Identify the main idea of the passage, and of each paragraph.

Recall from Chapter 6 that the **topic** is the subject matter of the *entire* text, what the author is writing about. There is a difference between the opinion of an author, and the subject about which the author is writing. Your goal is to first identify the overall subject of anything you read, which you should have no problem identifying. Usually, the topic can be stated in one or two words. If the paragraph is about boats, then the topic is boats.

The **setting** of a passage describes the breadth of the topic, placing the topic in a specific context. **The setting of a passage changes often from paragraph to paragraph, so you need to follow any such changes and mentally keep track of each.**

The **main idea** of any text is the author's thesis, or main point, which is closely related to the topic and setting. The main idea of a paragraph can be thought of as the goal, or message, of the paragraph, such as to argue for or against something. The skilled reader should be able to express the main idea of each paragraph in one concise sentence. **You can readily identify the main idea by identifying the message of the author, or the author's opinion, for a particular paragraph.**

SENTENCE RECALL AND PARAGRAPH SUMMARY

In the second month of your training program, the demands on your reading will become more challenging, yet more beneficial. One very useful exercise for improving memory and comprehension will be to engage in **sentence recall** (introduced in Chapter 7). As was discussed, sentence recall works in the following manner:

1. Read a sentence
2. Pause
3. Repeat the sentence, trying to restate it word-for-word
4. Read the next sentence and repeat.

This process is painstaking and slow. But remember, you are only concerned with improving your memory and comprehension at this point. The goal is to identify the central point of *every sentence*, and remember as much detail as possible. Can you restate the sentence? Practice sentence recall for at least 30 minutes daily during the second month of your training program.

After the first two weeks of sentence recall, you should apply the technique to groups of three or four sentences. Read three sentences at a time, pause, recall as much as possible word-for-word, and continue to the next several sentences. Can you recall the details of those sentences? Do you remember the main ideas?

Soon, you should be able to recapitulate from memory the main ideas of entire paragraphs (see **paragraph summary** in Chapter 7). Read one paragraph, stop, do not look at the text, summarize in your own words its main ideas, and move on. Try to recall the arguments, and the order in which they appeared. Handle everything in this manner in your second month. Your mind will soon comprehend at a much higher level.

DURING MONTH 2, EACH DAY DO THE FOLLOWING:

- **30 minutes** of sentence recall and paragraph summary
- **30 minutes** of force reading
- **1 hour** of reading with TSM analysis in the morning
- **1 hour** of reading with TSM analysis in the evening

Total reading time per day = 3 hrs

✓ Three hours of daily reading probably seems like an excessive amount of time to spend on one activity. You must realize, however, that becoming an expert reader requires significant practice and dedication. If you must quit your day job and take a part-time job to carve out three hours in your day, then strongly consider doing so. Your future as a physician might well depend on it.

READING MONTHS 3 THROUGH 6:
USING NEURO-VISUAL PROGRAMMING

As we covered in Chapter 9, Neuro-Visual Programming is a very powerful tool for remembering and comprehending material in a visual manner. This technique takes time to develop due to its challenging nature, which is why we begin practicing it in the third month of training.

To recap, Neuro-Visual Programming is the process of reading material and simultaneously creating images and symbols in your mind that capture a complete meaning. Advanced users of NVP are also able to manipulate those images to comprehend the material on a higher level. They can construct mental images that reveal the inferences and assumptions of the text visually in their minds.

When you begin using NVP, please be patient with yourself. NVP demands a dramatic change in how your brain reads text, which takes significant effort and time. The good news is that, as the days go by, you will notice a steady improvement in your ability to use NVP. By month six, you should find that NVP happens almost automatically for even the most challenging material. Please note that you are not to stop using NVP after month six of your training program. You should continue using NVP with everything you read up to the day of your MCAT (and beyond if you like). Hopefully, you will continue using this system throughout your life as it provides an efficient way to remember and comprehend anything you read or hear. Also realize that you can use NVP quite effectively on the Biological Sciences section of the MCAT as a means of remembering and processing complex information.

DURING MONTHS 3 THROUGH 6, EACH DAY DO THE FOLLOWING:

- **1.5 hours** of force reading using NVP in the morning
- **1.5 hours** of force reading using NVP in the evening

Total reading time per day = 3 hrs

READING MONTHS 7 AND 8:
Pushing Your Speed and Practicing Passages

During the final months of training, you should build your reading speed and complete as many practice MCAT Verbal passages as possible. The best way to build your reading speed is to time yourself with specific benchmarks over a two-month period. We also recommend that you register for a speed-reading course at a local college.

How fast should you read when you practice? For the last two months of training you should practice at two reading rates: **steadily** at **200** words per minute, and **rapidly** at **400** words per minute. In these final two months, you should dedicate a **third of your daily reading time to rapid reading.** This means that if you read for 1.5 hours in the morning, then for 30 minutes you should use rapid reading.

> How fast should you read on the actual MCAT? You should spend no more than 3.5 minutes reading each passage.
> Given that passages run 600 to 700 words in length, **you should read at 250 words per minute on test day.**

Calculating Your Reading Speed

There are two ways to evaluate your reading speed: either by using computer software that generates text on the screen in a timed format, or by using a stopwatch and counting how many words you cover. Actually, we recommend you use *both* methods. Consider making a small investment by purchasing computer speed-reading software (we are not recommending any particular program for speed development - this is for you to find). We also strongly recommend that you purchase a stopwatch and track how many words you cover in a given time period.

When reading books or journals, estimate the number of words per page and use your stopwatch to find your total reading time. From this you can calculate how many words per minute you cover. If you are reading articles on a computer screen, then you can simply highlight and paste the text into a word processing program which will count the number of words for you.

You can calculate your reading rate thusly:

Words per minute =

$$(total\ number\ of\ words)\Big/(total\ minutes)$$

✔ Two months prior to the MCAT, you should also **begin going through sample VR passages.** This is absolutely crucial to your training. Both the AAMC, and various test preparation companies offer excellent sample passages. You should use both sources in order to **acquire as many as possible**. The minimum number of VR passages that you should go through is 70. Try to do as many as 100 before your test.

DURING MONTHS 7 AND 8, EACH DAY DO THE FOLLOWING:

- **30 minutes** reading at 400 wpm in the morning
- **1 hour** reading at 200 wpm in the morning
- **30 minutes** reading at 400 wpm in the evening
- **1 hour** reading at 200 wpm in the evening
- **2** sample Verbal Reasoning passages

*Total reading time per day = **3.3 hrs approx.***

II. SAMPLE TRAINING SCHEDULES

Eight-month sample schedule for examinees taking a summer MCAT, starting in October of the year prior to the test:

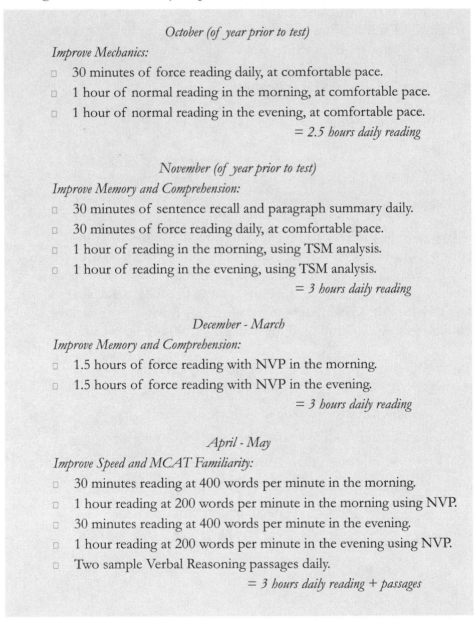

October (of year prior to test)

Improve Mechanics:

- ☐ 30 minutes of force reading daily, at comfortable pace.
- ☐ 1 hour of normal reading in the morning, at comfortable pace.
- ☐ 1 hour of normal reading in the evening, at comfortable pace.

= 2.5 hours daily reading

November (of year prior to test)

Improve Memory and Comprehension:

- ☐ 30 minutes of sentence recall and paragraph summary daily.
- ☐ 30 minutes of force reading daily, at comfortable pace.
- ☐ 1 hour of reading in the morning, using TSM analysis.
- ☐ 1 hour of reading in the evening, using TSM analysis.

= 3 hours daily reading

December - March

Improve Memory and Comprehension:

- ☐ 1.5 hours of force reading with NVP in the morning.
- ☐ 1.5 hours of force reading with NVP in the evening.

= 3 hours daily reading

April - May

Improve Speed and MCAT Familiarity:

- ☐ 30 minutes reading at 400 words per minute in the morning.
- ☐ 1 hour reading at 200 words per minute in the morning using NVP.
- ☐ 30 minutes reading at 400 words per minute in the evening.
- ☐ 1 hour reading at 200 words per minute in the evening using NVP.
- ☐ Two sample Verbal Reasoning passages daily.

= 3 hours daily reading + passages

Six-month schedule for examinees taking a summer MCAT, starting in January of the year of the test. For those better adept at using NVP:

January

Improve Mechanics:

- ☐   30 minutes of force reading daily, at comfortable pace.
- ☐   1 hour of normal reading in the morning, at comfortable pace.
- ☐   1 hour of normal reading in the evening, at comfortable pace.

= 2.5 hours daily reading

February

Improve Memory and Comprehension:

- ☐   30 minutes of sentence recall and paragraph summary daily.
- ☐   30 minutes of force reading daily, at comfortable pace.
- ☐   1 hour of reading in the morning, using TSM analysis.
- ☐   1 hour of reading in the evening, using TSM analysis.

= 3 hours daily reading

March - April

Improve Memory and Comprehension:

- ☐   1.5 hours of force reading with NVP in the morning.
- ☐   1.5 hours of force reading with NVP in the evening.

= 3 hours daily reading

May - June

Improve Speed and MCAT Familiarity:

- ☐   30 minutes reading at 400 words per minute in the morning.
- ☐   1 hour reading at 200 words per minute in the morning using NVP.
- ☐   30 minutes reading at 400 words per minute in the evening.
- ☐   1 hour reading at 200 words per minute in the evening using NVP.
- ☐   Two sample Verbal Reasoning passages daily.

= 3 hours daily reading + passages

III. SIGN THE CONTRACT

Simply put, the MCAT presents the opportunity of a lifetime. You either rise to the occasion and dedicate 110% of your effort to success, or miss a great chance by giving anything less than your best. While a high score may lead you to the path of becoming a physician, a mediocre score may deny you that opportunity. The bottom line is this: how you perform on the Verbal Reasoning section of the MCAT will impact your immediate and long-term future.

As we mentioned before, if you need to quit your full-time job in order to read for three hours a day to pull up a low verbal score, then it might be adventageous to find a part-time job. Many students make huge sacrifices to carve out enough time each day to study diligently for the MCAT.

✓ If you are scoring a **7 or below** on Verbal Reasoning, then you should consider dedicating **eight months** of your life to reading for two to three hours every day. There are no tricks or shortcuts to improving your VR score.

Reading should become your new best friend, your favorite occupation and most important hobby. So take the time now to figure out how you will read for two to three hours a day for the next several months. You will thank yourself in the end. Once you committ to this task and think carefully about how to isolate a few hours each day, sign your Personal Reading Program Contract below. It's your future, so take charge of it.

> Figure out when you should take the MCAT.
> Since applying **early** to medical schools is strongly recommended,
> you should take the MCAT no later than June of the year
> that you plan to file your AMCAS application.

PERSONAL READING PROGRAM CONTRACT

I, _____, hereby commit myself to reading EACH DAY for the next SIX to EIGHT MONTHS in the morning

from _____AM/PM   to _____AM/PM

and in the evening of the same day

from _____AM/PM   to _____AM/PM

starting   _____(mm/dd/yy),

ending   _____(mm/dd/yy).

This represents SIX to EIGHT MONTHS of reading training. I plan to take the MCAT on

_____ (mm/dd/yy)

Signature: _____

Date: _____

What Should You Read for Practice?

IN THIS CHAPTER

As with any endeavor, everything depends on how you prepare. For mastering MCAT Verbal Reasoning, good preparation depends on daily reading. This means that your success comes down to what you select to read, which is often difficult to determine. Many students wonder what kinds of material will be featured on Verbal Reasoning. While this book does not claim to know the exact sources used by the MCAT, it does provide guidance based on extensive studies of MCAT sample content.

Basically, you must go out of your way to find the types of books and journals that contain MCAT-level material. Ignore common newspapers and most office journals. **Every passage that appears on Verbal Reasoning has an elevated analytical quality which ranges from fairly straightforward to quite complex.** The typical MCAT passage contains two or three theories, arguments, or hypotheses that present many facts and details that you are responsible for not only remembering, but also analyzing and applying. Certainly, the level of a VR passage goes well beyond the level of a typical newspaper article.

Material that simply recounts facts in a single narrative format generally does not appear on the MCAT. So feel free to avoid books on history in general (however, do read the Will Durant book in our book list to practice handling passages with large quantities of detail). You can also put aside any fiction. **You want material that is full of theories, arguments, and experimental facts that support or refute hypotheses.**

I. TOPICS TO LOOK THROUGH IN A LARGE LIBRARY

Many students are unclear about which sources to read or where to look for them. A good place to begin is to visit one of the larger public or university libraries in your area and register for a library card (if you have not done so already). This will save you lots of time and money, and keep you from having to sit in bookstores for hours on end for all of your reading practice. Keep in mind that you should look for books that are difficult to read. When browsing for that perfect source, turn to a few pages and look for elevated language and high concept density. You want a book that compares many ideas on a single page in great detail with intelligence and depth.

Here are ten topics that appear often on Verbal Reasoning:

- Anthropology
- Art Criticism
- Economic Theory
- Humanities
- Literary Theory
- Natural Science
- Philosophy of Science
- Political Science
- Psychology
- Sociology

Many libraries use these same classifications, or combinations of the above classifications, to organize their books. In the library catalogs, you may find the above categories combined in various ways, such as Philosophy of Politics, Philosophical Anthropology, and Economics of Politics. Other topics that you should add to your reading arsenal include:

- Conservation
- Cosmology
- Ecology & Evolutionary Biology
- Human Nature
- Law and Legislation
- Linguistics
- Natural Theology
- Philosophy of Nature
- Planetary Science
- Religion and Science
- Social Ecology

To help you find the right books, you may want to search for qualified authors in these subjects. One suggestion is to visit the websites of prestigious universities, browse the departments that correspond to your subject of interest, and document the names of leading professors. Give their books a good read. This will prove to be excellent preparation for Verbal Reasoning.

Shortly, we will review the quantity of reading that you should cover on a daily basis leading up to the exam.

Do not rely on everyday reading material for practice. Books and journals that are easily accessible do not, in general, possess the complexity found in most VR passages.

Table 11.1 Summary of topics suggested for reading practice.

Topics to Read for MCAT Verbal Reasoning Practice

Anthropology	Economics of Politics	Philosophy of Science
Economic Theory	Ecology & Evolution	Political Science
Humanities	Philosophy of Nature	Psychology
Literary Theory	Conservation	Art Criticism
Natural Science	Linguistics	Sociology
Philosophy of Politics	Planetary Science	Anthropology
Cosmology	Natural Theology	Human Nature
Law & Legislation	Social Ecology	Religion & Science

II. MY PERSONAL READING LIST

Turning a VR score of 6 into an 11 required tremendous reading and passage practice. I began as an average reader, but ended as an expert reader. Students always ask how I achieved such a feat. My response is, "Read more than you ever imagined." The question that follows is, "What did you read?" Since you already asked, here are the titles that I completed in eight months prior to the day of the exam. To get through these sixteen books **demanded a very rigorous schedule that averaged two to three hours of reading daily.**

Read for two to three hours every day.

RECOMMENDED BOOK LIST

Agonito, Rosemary. <u>History of Ideas on Women: a Source Book</u>. New York: Putnam, c1977.

Arendt, Hannah. <u>Between Past and Future: Six Exercises in Political Thought</u>. New York: Viking Press, 1961.

Bloom, Harold. <u>William Faulkner</u>. New York: Chelsea House Publishers, 1986.

Daly, Herman, John B. Cobb, and Clifford W. Cobb. <u>For the Common Good: Redirecting the Economy toward Community, the Environment, and a Sustainable Future</u>. Boston: Beacon Press, c1989.

Durant, Will, and Ariel Durant. "Caesar and Christ." Story of Civilization. Vol. 3. New York: Simon and Schuster, 1950.

Eagleton, Terry. Literary Theory: an Introduction. Minneapolis: University of Minnesota Press, c1983.

Ewen, Robert. An Introduction to Theories of Personality. Hillsdale, NJ: Lawrence Erlbaum Associates, c1988.

Fish, Stanley. The Trouble with Principle. Cambridge, MA: Harvard University Press, 1999.

Malthus, Thomas Robert. On Population. Ed. G. Himmelfarb. New York: Modern Library,1960.

Margulis, Lynn, and Dorion Sagan. What is Life? Berkeley, CA: University of California Press, 2000, c1995.

Mayr, Ernst. Toward a New Philosophy of Biology: Observations of an Evolutionist. Cambridge, MA: Belknap Press of Harvard University Press, 1988.

Phillips, Ruth. Trading Identities: the Souvenir in Native North American Art from the Northeast, 1700-1900. Seattle: University of Washington Press; Montreal, Quebec: McGill-Queen's University Press, c1998.

Ridley, Matt. <u>Nature Via Nurture: Genes, Experience, and What Makes Us Human</u>. New York: HarperCollins, 2003.

Rudwick, Martin. <u>Bursting the Limits of Time: the Reconstruction of Geohistory in the Age of Revolution</u>. Chicago: University of Chicago Press, c2005.

Smith, Rogers. <u>Civic Ideals: Conflicting Visions of Citizenship in U.S. History</u>. New Haven: Yale University Press, c1997.

Smith, Thomas. <u>Revaluing Ethics: Aristotle's Dialectical Pedagogy</u>. Albany: State University of New York Press, c2001.

I happened to have selected these books for their diverse content and superb authorship. I have no other reasons for endorsing them. Hopefully, most of you will actually select books from this list for your eight-month training. These books should help you tremendously. Perhaps you wish to keep life simple and select books only from this list. If so, then please realize that many are long and rather challenging. But they are well worth your effort and time. Do read as many as possible, if for no other reason than your own enlightenment.

To achieve a solid VR score, you must be committed to a challenging reading list for many months. Make reading a daily obsession. One hour and a half of reading in the morning and again in the evening is highly recommended.

✔ I had to resign from my day job to find enough time to read for three hours a day (plus study the sciences), but the rewards were great. When I sat down to take the real MCAT, most of the VR passages seemed very straightforward. I was even familiar with many of the passage topics, and could predict the questions.

III. READING BEYOND BOOKS
THE ONLINE READING EXPERIENCE

The only drawback to reading books is that you do not practice reading material on a computer screen. Does this mean that you should stop reading books? Absolutely not.

But it does mean that you should include in your reading resources an online subscription to a scholarly journal (and read it daily).

> Reading passages critically on a computer screen is a skill that you must develop. Subscribe to an online journal and read articles for at least 30 minutes **daily**.

Surprisingly, some students wonder whether they should avoid reading journals altogether. By no means. There are many journals written with the same depth as the scholarly passages on the MCAT. Journals offer material that is generally more timely and relevant than books on a shelf, and cover a more diverse selection of topics in fewer pages. However, the selection of journals should be carefully considered. Put aside easy-to-read popular journals until after you take the MCAT, and turn to academic-based journals that feature articles written by recognized faculty.

Many students dread the MCAT for the sole reason of having to read critically on a computer screen, an uncomfortable task indeed. After a few months of reading articles on a computer screen, this fear should vanish. Many journals provide discounted subscription rates to students, so keep an eye out for them.

IV. MY SUGGESTED JOURNALS LIST

The following journals publish articles on par with the complexity and difficulty of the Verbal Reasoning portion of the MCAT. These journals are also highly interesting to read, and I expect that you will find them quite engaging and enjoyable. Like my book list, I used this journal list for its scholarly authorship and diverse content. Here is the list of suggested journals in no particular order:

American Scientist

Journal for Early Modern Cultural Studies

Foreign Affairs

New England Journal of Medicine

Shakespeare Quarterly

Common Knowledge

differences: A Journal of Feminist Cultural Studies

For a comprehensive selection of prestigious journals covering the humanities, arts, and social sciences, I recommend perusing the selection provided by Project MUSE® (http://muse.jhu.edu) at Johns Hopkins University. MUSE is the sole source of complete, full-text versions of titles from many of the world's leading university presses and scholarly societies, and every journal is heavily indexed and peer-reviewed with critically acclaimed articles by respected scholars in their fields. Note, however, that MUSE subscriptions are available **only to institutions**.

This should not prevent you from finding a few journals that are of interest and asking your local university library for availability. **University libraries will most likely carry a journal from the MUSE list, or one similar to it**. **Be sure to ask**.

V. ADDITIONAL READING SOURCES

In addition to my personal book list, I recommend selecting titles that have appeared on previous MCAT practice tests. Below is a collection of titles that have appeared on practice MCAT exams released by the AAMC and other groups.

NATURAL SCIENCES - SAMPLE JOURNALS

Scientific American

The American Journal of Psychiatry

Discover Magazine

NATURAL SCIENCES - SAMPLE BOOKS

Hawking, Stephen. <u>A Brief History of Time</u>. London; New York: Bantam Books, 1998.

Gould, Stephen Jay. <u>The Panda's Thumb: More Reflections in Natural History</u>. New York: Norton, 1992, c1980.

Lewis, Thomas. <u>The Lives of a Cell; Notes of a Biology Watcher</u>. New York: Viking Press 1974.

SOCIAL SCIENCES – SAMPLE JOURNALS

The Atlantic Monthly

The Kenyon Review

Anthropology Today

SOCIAL SCIENCES – SAMPLE BOOKS

Baym, Nina. <u>Novels, Readers, and Reviewers: Responses to Fiction in Antebellum America</u>. Ithaca: Cornell University Press, 1984.

Brewster, Lawrence, et al. <u>The Public Agenda: Issues in American Politics</u>. New York: St. Martin's Press, 1987.

Shepard, Jon. <u>Sociology</u>. Minneapolis/St. Paul: West, c1993.

Kanellos, Nicolás. <u>A History of Hispanic Theatre in the United States: Origins to 1940</u>. Austin, TX: University of Texas Press, 1990.

Bronowski, Jacob, and Bruce Mazlish. <u>The Western Intellectual Tradition, from Leonardo to Hegel</u>. New York: Harper, 1960.

Novak, Michael. <u>The Joy of Sports: End Zones, Bases, Baskets, Balls, and the Consecration of the American Spirit</u>. New York: Basic Books, c1976.

Churchill, Winston, Sir. <u>A History of the English-Speaking Peoples</u>. New York: Dodd, Mead, 1958-62.

Illich, Ivan. <u>Deschooling Society</u>. New York: Harper & Row, 1971.

Postman, Neil. <u>Amusing Ourselves to Death: Public Discourse in the Age of Show Business</u>. New York: Penguin Books, 1986, c1985.

HUMANITIES — SAMPLE JOURNALS

The Modern Language Journal

Women and Music: A Journal of Gender and Culture

The Henry James Review

Literature and Medicine

HUMANITIES — SAMPLE BOOKS

Wellek, Rene. <u>Theory of Literature</u>. New York: Harcourt Brace Jovanovich, c1977.

Russell, Bertrand. <u>The Problems of Philosophy</u>. New York, Oxford University Press, 1959.

Baker, Carlos. <u>Hemingway, the Writer as Artist</u>. Princeton, NJ: Princeton University Press 1972.

CHAPTER 12

Student Perspectives: Q&A with Top Performers

IN THIS CHAPTER

I. Q&A with Students
II. Gems of Wisdom

Over the years I have learned that success leaves clues. By studying how other people have achieved certain levels of success, I have saved myself much time and energy in various endeavors. Preparing to take the MCAT is a significant undertaking that involves mastering multiple subjects and skills, and the clues for succeeding on Verbal Reasoning, unfortunately, are few and far between.

Thus, I thought it quite beneficial to include the perspectives of several students who achieved scores of 11 or higher on Verbal Reasoning. Their scores are impressive, and their advice is quite helpful. These students appear specifically because of their high scores and willingness to share their valuable thoughts. They do not have any vested interest in this book. We heartily thank them for being so frank and willing to participate.

✓ The following answers are from real students. Their responses are largely unedited for the sake of capturing tone and sincerity. Each responded to the same set of questions in a very honest and straightforward manner. We hope you enjoy their gems of wisdom.

I. Q&A WITH STUDENTS

Jessica Murphy

VERBAL SCORE - 12
MCAT DATE - MAY 2007

Background
Jessica graduated in 2005 with a BA in Anthropology from Rice University, and most recently with an MPH in Global Communicable Diseases from the University of South Florida. During college, she spent the majority of her time balancing theater, public health research, and volunteer work at local hospitals. She began studying for the MCAT in January of 2007, and sat for the test in May of that same year.

1. HOW DID YOU STUDY FOR VERBAL REASONING?

JM: I've never struggled with the Verbal section on anything, from SATs, to GREs, to the MCAT. I was always very strong in English in high school and college. When I started preparing for the MCAT (in 2007), I took Kaplan's online prep course, which I found very helpful. Taking an online prep course really helped me work on my stamina with sitting and working at a computer for so long. I found that eye strain was a big problem during the verbal passages, especially after dealing with the Physical Sciences section, so practicing using a computer for extended periods of time was helpful.

Outside of the Kaplan class, I practiced with the AAMC practice tests, and with Kaplan's QBank [an online database of exam-style questions]. I only took one Kaplan practice exam, because my time was constrained, and I felt that it would be better to take exams from the test-makers themselves.

What I found most useful was using the Kaplan test, as well as the in-class work as diagnostics to see what types of questions I was missing more frequently than others. Kaplan classifies questions into categories, and then gives specific strategies for tackling those questions.

Being able to recognize the kind of question when I encountered it on the real exam was useful, as it helped me better predict the correct answer. To practice, I would create quizzes of only those types of questions that I missed most using QBank.

2. How did you approach each passage during the MCAT?

JM: I just read through each passage normally. I'm a fast reader, but I consciously forced myself to slow down and pay attention. I was confident with my timing, because I would do practice passages and time myself until I was averaging between 7-8 minutes per passage. I figured that would give me enough time to answer most questions, and then spend those extra few minutes on the really tough questions.

I didn't use my scratch paper at all during the verbal section, but I did take advantage of the highlighting function. After practicing for awhile, I was able to predict where, in a passage, there would definitely be a question. So that's usually what I marked, for quick reference.

After reading the passage, I would skim over all the questions, and then go in order, skipping any that I couldn't immediately get. I always, always, crossed out definite wrong answers as I went, even if I couldn't pick the correct answer right away. And in some cases, to save time I would mark an answer (even if I wasn't sure of my choice), flag the question, and then move on to the next passage. I came back at the end and gave those marked questions extra consideration. That used up my extra time that I had saved from using less time on each passage.

3. DURING THE MCAT, WHAT WAS YOUR MENTAL PROCESS?

JM: My mind worked a little differently on each passage. If I was at all interested in the passage itself, then it was easier for me to absorb the information which meant I didn't have to refer to the passage too much. But if it was something boring or more difficult, I referred to the passage nonstop for each question.

In the end though, I always went back over the passage and made sure my answers were reasonably supported by information from the passage. That strategy works really well for most questions (just not inference questions like "The author would most likely agree with . . ."). By checking to make sure my answers were supported by the passage, I eliminated a lot of error.

4. HOW DID YOUR PRACTICE EXAM SCORES COMPARE TO YOUR ACTUAL SCORE?

JM: During my test prep, all of my practice scores were right on par with the score I got on the actual MCAT. I was routinely scoring in the 11-13 range on my practice exams. When I took my MCAT, I scored a 12, which was kind of disappointing (because I've always considered Verbal my strong suit, and my secret goal was a 14).

But I found, in general, that the pressure of reading on the real MCAT versus my own practice at home was much higher, and that probably contributed to the slightly lower score.

I took several AAMC practice tests and my Verbal scores were as follows: 11 on AAMC Test 3R, 13 on Test 4, 11 on Test 5, 11 on Test 6, and 15 on Test 7. I stopped after Test 7, partly because I freaked myself out with that 15, and partly because it was two days before the real exam. I didn't want to psych myself out by doing more, when my score could only come down.

5. WHAT ADVICE WOULD YOU GIVE STUDENTS?

JM:

1. Time yourself. Practice reading and answering questions until you can read no more. Timing is everything for verbal, because there is no outside knowledge or background that you can fall back on. Consider it a race against the clock.

2. Look over your practice tests. See what you got wrong, and figure out why. Is there a pattern? Are you missing more of one kind of question than another? If so, practice that question type until you've got it down cold.

3. Start early and practice often. If you haven't been a big reader your whole life, the three months before the MCAT are not going to make you one. So, just practice your materials, and if you'd like, practice reading really boring political and art history articles. Pick out the main information. There definitely will be really boring political and art history articles on that test.

4. Peanut M&Ms. Eat them between each section; they're a perfect little package of sugar, fat, and protein that will give you energy (and frankly, cheer you up in a really stressful test). I also chugged an energy drink right before the verbal section, for a little pick-me-up. But, that has the downside of all that caffeine stimulating your body.

Lisa Harrison

VERBAL SCORE - 14
MCAT DATE - MAY 2007

Background
Lisa graduated in 2003 with a B.S. in Biochemistry from Washington State University. She also graduated with a Master's degree in Physiology and Biophysics at the University of Southern California in 2008. Her extracurricular activities include hiking and backpacking, cooking, and reading. Her favorite kinds of books are character novels, travel novels, and health and nutrition books. Lisa sat for the MCAT in May of 2007.

1. HOW DID YOU STUDY FOR VERBAL REASONING?

LH: My study for the verbal portion of the MCAT was pretty limited. I read through Kaplan's material on the subject, and took several of their online practice tests. I also took several AAMC practice tests. I can't say that I spent a set number of hours each day or week reading and studying, and I don't consider myself a speed-reader. I read a good deal for pleasure and for work, however.

2. HOW DID YOU APPROACH EACH PASSAGE DURING THE MCAT?

LH: I would read each passage carefully, with speed as a second priority. For most questions, I checked the passage to confirm my answer if the question was direct and content-related. I usually didn't return to the passage if the question required an inference; I just worked with what I remembered and my impressions.

3. DURING THE MCAT, WHAT WAS YOUR MENTAL PROCESS?

LH: I didn't pause and recap, or write a whole lot during the MCAT. I'd jot down some key numbers or facts if I felt it was needed. I generally had good visual recall for where information was presented in a passage, so I could return to it pretty quickly if needed for a question.

What was my mental process? I'd read the passages, try to figure out what the information was, and get a grasp for what kind of problems and questions I'd be asked to solve. I think my mind just naturally starts to postulate questions from the information given, so I am already thinking about and predicting the questions. I would then go right to the questions and start working through them, returning to the passage as needed. Stopping to summarize a passage on paper felt like a waste of time to me. The point is to answer the questions, right?

4. HOW DID YOUR PRACTICE EXAM SCORES COMPARE TO YOUR ACTUAL SCORE?

LH: I don't have a chronological list of my VR practice scores. I remember averaging about a 12, which I was happy with. I think I got a 13 once. So my score of 14 on the actual MCAT came as a surprise. My experience was that the Kaplan practice VR exams were harder than the actual MCAT VR portion.

5. WHAT ADVICE WOULD YOU GIVE STUDENTS?

LH: Do what works for you to maximize your speed and efficiency. Everyone reads and comprehends differently. Following the Kaplan method strictly did not work for me, so I modified it a bit. Take some time to try a few things and see what works for you, and what improves your score.

For me, I had to make sure I went slow enough to get what I was reading correctly. Several times during class exercises I got the wrong answer because I interpreted the passage oppositely. That was enough to show me that I needed to slow down and really pay attention. Find your weak points.

Lastly, in hindsight, I think my experience in graduate school was probably the main factor in my score. I didn't have the time to do more reading on the side that was suggested through my Kaplan course, and so I doubted I would score really high. But looking back, I realize that I have spent countless hours over the last three years struggling through hundreds of scientific journal articles for my graduate work. This was far from a pleasant experience for the most part, but it provided a consistent (almost daily) challenge to my reading comprehension that I believe is responsible for my high score. So I think there is something to what they say about reading a lot, and reading 'hard' material. So if you haven't spent a lot of time reading, and you are worried about your score, or want to do better, I think that reading in general will definitely help out.

Cecilia MacNeilson (alias)

VERBAL SCORE - 12
MCAT DATE - AUGUST 2007

Background
Cecilia graduated in 2008 with a B.S. in Biological Sciences and a Minor in Psychology from the University of Southern California. In college she spent much of her time in various organizations, including the Community Health Involvement Project, Alpha Lambda Delta, and Trojan Health Volunteers. As a hobby she enjoys playing classical piano. Her favorite reading materials include historical fiction, historical non-fiction, short stories, memoirs, and news-related magazines. She is especially drawn to Hemingway and Steinbeck. She sat for the MCAT in August of 2007.

1. How did you study for Verbal Reasoning?

CM: I studied all summer long in 2007, from May until my test date in August. In fact, I started my MCAT preparation knowing that I would need to work on Verbal more so than the sciences. I took a Kaplan classroom course, which provided me with a verbal review book along with other materials. It also gave me access to their online verbal section tests and online verbal exercises, as well as the AAMC practice tests.

I bought an Examkrackers verbal book that offered 101 verbal passages. Also, I read articles from *The Economist* and *The Wall Street Journal* (the former was more useful than the latter). I tried to spend an hour completing a verbal section test every other day, and I would read articles and complete Kaplan's exercises on the days in-between.

2. How did you approach each passage during the MCAT?

CM: I read faster than normal, without looking at the questions first. I did not use the highlighting or notes feature, because that would slow me down. I would just note in my head what the general gist of the passage was, as well as the layout of the passage (the main idea of each paragraph). I went through the questions from first to last, and skipped questions that I couldn't answer right away. After I finished the last question of the passage, I went back to the ones I skipped. If I still thought they would take too much time, I moved on to the next passage.

Usually, I looked back at the passage for every question to make sure I found evidence for my answer; this was easier when I had a general outline of the passage in my head.

3. DURING THE MCAT, WHAT WAS YOUR MENTAL PROCESS?

CM: I recalled where specific information was in the passage, because I was able to keep in my head an outline of the main ideas and where I could find examples and description of those ideas. At the beginning when I practiced, I forced myself to write down the main idea of each paragraph, in a word or a phrase, as well as the main idea of the entire passage. After I practiced that for a while, I was able to do that in my mind (which is still really useful!). I referred back to the passage for almost every question as a quick check for my answer.

4. HOW DID YOUR PRACTICE EXAM SCORES COMPARE TO YOUR ACTUAL SCORE?

CM: The practice AAMC tests were the most accurate in predicting my final score. I do not have a list of my practice test scores, but I remember that I improved generally.

5. WHAT ADVICE WOULD YOU GIVE STUDENTS?

CM: Start preparing for this section as early as possible, even before you begin your formal regimen of MCAT preparation. Get in the habit of reading articles from news magazines, such as the *Economist*, and summarizing (paragraphs and the entire article).

Ask yourself, "What is the author's motive? What is the author's purpose in writing that paragraph, in writing that work? What does the author think about this, that, and the other?" Start out answering these questions as best as you can, even if that means you label the tone of the article as "good" or "bad" towards the main topic. Eventually, you will be able to be more specific – and more successful in tackling any reading, MCAT Verbal passage or not!

Brian Lee

VERBAL SCORE - 11
MCAT DATE - APRIL 2007

Background

Brian graduated in 2006 with a B.S. in Mechanical Engineering from an Ivy League university (he wishes to keep his school private). During his college years, he served on the executive board of The Engineering Honor Society, Tau Beta Pi, and conducted research in various laboratories. He enjoys playing soccer and tennis in his spare time. His favorite reading materials include science magazines and history books. Brian sat for the MCAT in April of 2007.

1. HOW DID YOU STUDY FOR VERBAL REASONING?

BL: Well, I knew that Verbal Reasoning was my weakest subject, being an engineer and all. I never read anything other than text books full of math and engineering concepts. I had taken the MCAT a year prior, and scored really low on VR. I applied to medical schools and did not get even an interview. So I decided to fully commit myself to bringing up my really low VR score (I wish this book existed back then).

The way I studied for VR was I spent seven months reading as many books as I could. I also enrolled in a speed-reading course, as well as a Kaplan MCAT course. My friend gave me her Verbal Reasoning book from the Princeton Review MCAT class, so in terms of material I was well covered. The speed-reading class that I took at a community college really helped. They had us use computer software in a reading lab that improved my comprehension, eye movement, visual memory, and reading speed. Everything was done on computer so it gave me great practice reading on a screen. This was excellent preparation.

I read for about two hours, five to six days a week. In the last two months I started going through lots of practice passages. About twice a week, I would go through a full Verbal Reasoning section test (7 passages) using Kaplan's online resources, and then go through two or three passages from the Princeton Review book. I also subscribed to an online science magazine and read archives of articles at home on my computer. For engineers and science folk, I recommend doing all of these things.

2. How did you approach each passage during the MCAT?

BL: My approach was to read each passage extremely carefully the first time through, picking up on every detail and implied idea. I did not look at the questions until after I finished reading the passage. I did not read slowly, and I did not speed-read, but I read at a comfortable rate (which most people would consider rapid). By the time I took the MCAT my reading skills were advanced enough where I could read at a fast pace and remember everything. When I answered questions I did not have to look back at the passage. I only looked back at the passage to verify my answer choice when needed. I did not use the highlight feature, and I did not need to write anything down.

Basically, I paid attention to each paragraph, and how each one worked together. I figured out the main ideas and the message of the author for each paragraph, and remembered these in sequence. Also, I used the strikethrough feature on every question. I could always strike out two of the four choices, which helped a lot.

3. During the MCAT, what was your mental process?

BL: I'm a very visual person, so I was able to remember where information was contained in the passage. I could pinpoint a detail almost to the line, but only after tons of practice. I think seven months of reading difficult books helped me develop this skill. Also, I anticipated the kinds of questions that would be asked. After doing so many practice passages, I developed a sixth sense about great questions to ask regarding the passage. In fact, as I read I was asking questions in my mind. Some of them showed up, in one form or another, as an actual question! When I encountered a really hard question, I marked it and came back to it later. I had about 2 minutes to spare in the end to work on marked questions.

4. How did your practice exam scores compare to your actual score?

BL: The AAMC practice tests did a very good job of predicting my score, as well as the Kaplan Verbal Reasoning subject tests. Princeton Review passages were excellent too. On my first practice test I scored a 6 on VR. After four months of reading, I started scoring 9s. I then ramped up to 11s two months before my MCAT which was a dream come true. So when I got an 11 on my MCAT, I was thrilled, but not entirely surprised.

5. What advice would you give students?

BL: Read! I found that reading critically takes a really long time to improve, so I think anyone taking the test should start reading as early as possible. I had very little reading experience, so I knew I had to become a really great reader. There are no shortcuts to achieving a high score. Just pick up very challenging books and journals and read as much as possible. This takes lots of discipline, so I recommend working on that. But once it becomes habit, it sticks.

Other advice is to get plenty of sleep. I can't comprehend anything if I'm really tired. Also, be patient because this stuff takes time. It's not like physics where you spend a few hours learning about pulleys and then you can do any pulley problem. Every passage is different, and reading analytically is challenging. But also know that it's possible to pull up a low VR score. There's hope, you just have to do the hard work!

II. GEMS OF WISDOM

We have heard from students of all reading backgrounds explain their approaches and studying methods that have guided them to success on Verbal Reasoning. Coincidentally, many of their ideas agree with the training concepts outlined in this book.

We can safely conclude that an effective method to prepare for Verbal Reasoning does exist, and this method produces results for traditional readers and non-readers alike (who have the potential to become great readers). All in all, following a long-term reading program with winning strategies and plenty of exercises.

So, let us summarize some of the more important lessons that we have learned from these top performers:

PREPARING FOR THE TEST:

1. Recognize that the process of boosting reading comprehension takes time. In all likelihood, three months or less of reading practice will not be enough for someone who is an inexperienced reader. As one top performer indicated, seven months was necessary to make significant improvement in reading ability.

2. Read as often as possible, and read very difficult material. The top performer who scored a 14 on VR had read very challenging material for three years. (So the eight-month reading program described in this book should come as no surprise to you.)

3. Diagnose and make a list of the kinds of questions you get wrong. Always go through your practice tests, find the questions you miss, and understand why you miss them. Make a list and look for trends.

4. Practice reading on a computer screen. Fighting eye strain can be a significant challenge. Plenty of reading on a computer screen, in addition to doing passages on a computer, will help greatly.

5. Go through as many sample Verbal Reasoning passages as you can. Try to enroll in a commercial MCAT preparatory class as it will provide a great source of VR passages. The scores you receive on practice tests predict your actual MCAT VR score reasonably well. AAMC practice tests are excellent predictors of MCAT performance. Keep in mind that the intense pressure can cause you to score a point or two lower on the actual MCAT.

6. Consider investing in computer software that is designed to improve your reading speed, eye movement, and comprehension.

DURING THE TEST:

7. Pacing is king. Pacing makes a tremendous difference regarding your performance on Verbal Reasoning. If you are a fast reader, then slow down to absorb all of the material. If you read slowly, then speed up. Either way, you should complete a passage in eight to nine minutes. As one top performer said, "Timing is everything."

8. You should read each passage only one time. Refer back to it only to verify answers. To answer Inference questions, you should not need to look back at the passage at all.

9. Don't read the questions until *after* you finish reading the passage.

10. Develop your ability to know exactly where something was mentioned in the passage. Many top performers have a keen sense of where details were mentioned in a passage.

11. Speed-reading is not necessary. Top performers read a passage carefully, with speed as a second priority.

12. Be able to identify the main idea of each paragraph. Top performers can document all of the ideas and details of a passage in their minds. Summarize key ideas mentally as you read.

13. Use the strikethrough feature. This tool is very useful for eliminating wrong answer choices. Interestingly, none of the top performers wrote anything on paper, and only a few used the highlight feature.

14. Predict the questions. Being able to predict questions during the MCAT is very important. This skill comes from extensive practice with passages.

15. Verify your answers. Refer back to the passage and make sure your answers are reasonably supported by the material. You will eliminate a good portion of error by verifying your answers.

✓ Doing well on Verbal Reasoning requires many months of reading and passage practice. Be sure to follow the advice and techniques outlined in this book. There are no shortcuts.

PART V

Elevens for the Wise:
Invaluable Information
to Help You Succeed
on the MCAT

Eleven False Assumptions about Verbal Reasoning

CHAPTER
13

IN THIS CHAPTER

False Assumptions:

I. Nothing Can Change Your Verbal Score
II. You Cannot Study for Verbal Reasoning
III. High School SAT Verbal Scores Predict MCAT VR Results
IV. Speed-Reading is the Best Approach
V. You Should Read the Questions First
VI. Finishing on Time is Not Realistic
VII. The Verbal Reasoning Grading Scale is Unfairly Steep
VIII. Science Nerds and Engineers are Doomed
IX. A Word-Search Function Exists on Verbal Reasoning
X. High PS and BS Scores Can Compensate for a Low VR Score
XI. Reading the Daily Paper is Sufficient Practice

On any given college campus, most pre-med students can probably tell you at least one horror story about the MCAT, from students falling asleep during the exam, to computers crashing. Somewhere in all of these stories are fantasies and rumors about Verbal Reasoning, which students love to embellish:

"It's impossible to pull up your Verbal Score..."

"Just speed-read and you'll be fine..."

"The questions on my MCAT didn't match the passage..."

"The computer opened up and ate me alive!"

FALSE ASSUMPTION #1: NOTHING CAN CHANGE YOUR VERBAL SCORE

Why do you think I wrote this book? Because you can indeed change your verbal score. You can improve your score by boosting your reading ability, increasing your strategic thinking skills when tackling answers, anticipating questions, improving your command of the clock, understanding the psychology of the test, and practicing, practicing, practicing. Have you read chapters one through five yet?

Verbal scores will probably NOT improve if you

1. wait and cram, taking practice tests soon before the test;

2. read only occasionally;

3. choose not to follow a long-term reading program.

FALSE ASSUMPTION #2: YOU CANNOT STUDY FOR VERBAL REASONING

If you have read any section of this book, then you must know that this assumption is hogwash. It's hard to believe, but some students actually think that there is no benefit to studying for Verbal Reasoning. Nothing can be further from the truth. Students unwisely think that no one can prepare for Verbal Reasoning, and use this as an excuse to avoid hard work.

This entire book is about how **you can study to improve your Verbal score.** As a matter of personal experience, I used the same techniques in this book to pull up a Verbal score of 6 to 11s and 12s.

Suppose that you are one of those students who prefer to cram for an exam. If this is your tendency, then you are setting yourself up for unnecessary failure on Verbal Reasoning. The self-fulfilling prophecy would become a reality, and you literally "couldn't study for VR." Why?

Simply, cramming cannot improve reading skills, time management, confidence, and test-taking strategies.

The fact is that **you can improve** your VR score by making improvements in each of the Three Pillars of Verbal Reasoning:

I. Reading & Comprehension Skills

II. Exam Psychology

III. Time Management

Your score will improve when you have mastered all three pillars, and each one requires a few months of practice. Obviously, if you can dedicate a year to this then you can expect big gains in your score. For others, **six to eight months** should be enough time to help anyone make great strides in reading and comprehension abilities, exam psychology, and time management.

Do not shortcut yourself. **Shortcuts simply do not work when it comes to preparing for Verbal Reasoning.** Ironically, most books about MCAT preparation put very little focus on how to study properly for Verbal Reasoning.

FALSE ASSUMPTION #3: HIGH SCHOOL SAT VERBAL SCORES PREDICT MCAT VR RESULTS

Did you take the SAT last month? Not likely. Probably years have passed since your days in high school, and since then your mental capacities have grown tremendously (hopefully). If the SAT Verbal section was your weakness, then let it be your past. That described you many years ago. There is no necessary correlation between your SAT verbal result and your MCAT verbal performance. Your vocabulary has certainly grown since your days in high school.

Follow the long-term program as described in this book and you should knock the socks off any MCAT Verbal Reasoning section. Basically, six to eight months of solid reading practice should boost your critical thinking abilities greatly, turning any verbal struggles of your past into mere puffs of smoke.

FALSE ASSUMPTION #4: SPEED-READING IS THE BEST APPROACH

A common misconception of scoring well on Verbal Reasoning is that the faster you read, the better you score.

You may hear some students say that doing well is all about speed-reading your way through Verbal Reasoning. These same students will also tell you that they used every ounce of their energy to barely achieve an 8 or 9 just as time was running out.

What does this suggest? It suggests that these students used the *fast-and-furious* approach where they rushed through the passages, and then rushed through the questions (having had to go back and re-read portions over and over). If these fast-and-furious students had soaked up all the details and information the **first time** through each passage, then they would have finished with minutes to spare. Since they struggled to finish on time, however, we can conclude that **the fast-and-furious approach really wastes time.**

When a student speed-reads and rushes through the material, he or she is in danger of glossing over important details and inferences. There is a difference between reading at a speed that pushes your ability to comprehend and retain information, and reading at a speed that feels like a uncontrollable rollercoaster.

On the day of your test, never read beyond your ability to comprehend material. **It is better to work through six of the seven passages very**

diligently, than to rush through all seven. Of course, you should be so well prepared after you follow the reading program in this book that you will manage all seven passages without difficulty.

> Never read faster than you can comprehend material.

FALSE ASSUMPTION #5: YOU SHOULD READ THE QUESTIONS FIRST

Many students think that reading the questions first is a good approach. Reading the questions of a passage before you actually read the passage can be a great strategy for attacking Physical Sciences and Biological Science passages, but not for Verbal Reasoning. Why? Skimming the questions before reading the passage is counterproductive for three reasons:

1. A single question can require a deep understanding of several portions of the passage. By keeping a question in mind as you read, you tend to search for only the most relevant part of the passage dealing with that question. The question in your mind focuses your attention too much, and you miss other parts of the passage that are necessary to answer the question correctly.

2. By the time you finish reading the passage the first time through, you may forget a few of the questions. After reading the forgotten questions again, you then will have to read the passage a second time to find their answers. This wastes too much time. You should only have to read the passage in its entirety once.

3. For many students, trying to remember something while reading text becomes a big distraction from fully comprehending the passage material.

Overall, you will either focus on remembering the questions instead of remembering what you are reading, and will have to go back and re-read the passage, or you will forget the questions. **Either way, you will waste time that you cannot afford to throw away.**

The better approach is to read the passage carefully yet steadily, remembering details using Neuro-Visualization programming. Then proceed to the questions. There should be no need to preview the questions before you read the passage. In fact, by the time you complete the verbal training program in this book, you will be able to **predict** questions on the MCAT.

FALSE ASSUMPTION #6: FINISHING ON TIME IS NOT REALISTIC

Students who earn top scores on Verbal Reasoning finish the section on time. In many cases, these examinees have a minute or two to spare during which time they check marked answers. However, hearing about other students not finishing one or two entire passages is quite common. Many students run out of time, unfortunately, for a number of reasons. They spend too much time re-reading the passages, answering questions, thinking, or even panicking. The importance of staying obedient to the clock cannot be overstated. Using solid pacing skills is the first step towards finishing all seven passages on time.

You have only one hour for seven passages, which equates to eight-and-a-half minutes per passage. You can deviate from this a bit depending on the difficulty of the passage. For example, if you encounter one or two very challenging passages, then give yourself nine to ten minutes to complete each one. But, be sure to catch up by spending only six to seven minutes on the easier passages. How do you recognize easy from difficult passages? The easier ones discuss a core concept or theory without interjecting competing theories that are potentially confusing. The easier passages are sometimes shorter in length as well. You will recognize easy and difficult passages automatically as you read. Some will feel much easier to manage and comprehend versus others. Do not waste time searching for the easy passages; they will come to you.

The ultimate goal is to finish on time by knowing exactly where you should be at various time points. You should know that when the clock on the screen reads, say, 30:00, you should be on passage four. The following table is your overall guide (from Chapter 6). You will deviate from this schedule slightly when you encounter very easy or difficult passages. Just be sure to get back on track.

Table 13.1 Time points during Verbal Reasoning.

Time on clock (counts down)	Begin this VR Passage
60:00	I
51:00	II
43:00	III
34:00	IV
26:00	V
17:00	VI
9:00	VII

FALSE ASSUMPTION #7: THE VERBAL REASONING GRADING SCALE IS UNFAIRLY STEEP

Yes, it is true that the grading scale for Verbal Reasoning is more steep than that of other MCAT sections when considering scores of 12 and above. The number of students who achieve a 12 or higher decreases more rapidly on the Verbal Reasoning section than on the Biological Sciences or Physical Sciences sections.

Of the 67,828 students who took the MCAT in 2007, **only 4.8% scored a 12 or higher on Verbal Reasoning**. Compare this to 10.9% of examinees achieving a score of 12 or higher on the Physical Sciences section, and 12.3% of test-takers scoring a 12 or higher on the Biological Sciences section.

Interestingly, the picture changes when considering the number of students who scored an 8, 9, or 10 on these sections. For the same pool, 45.9% of test-takers scored in the 8 to 10 range on Verbal Reasoning. This is **above** the number of examinees who scored in the same range on Physical Sciences, which turned out to be 41.8%. On Biological Sciences, 50.4% of test-takers scored in the 8 to 10 range.

The grading scale for Verbal Reasoning is, therefore, not unfair, but only biased away from the upper range. Why might this be so? With only 40 questions to discriminate performance across a 15-tiered scale, the ability to resolve the quality of performance that warrants a 14 versus a 15 becomes quite challenging. However, the question of why someone who scores in the 95% to 97% range on all three sections warrants a 13 on Physical Sciences, 13 on Biological Sciences, and only a 12 on Verbal Reasoning remains a mystery.

FALSE ASSUMPTION #8: SCIENCE NERDS AND ENGINEERS ARE DOOMED

My response to this is: not necessarily! Do you have to be a Humanities major to score a 10 or better on Verbal Reasoning? Of course not.

But many science majors do face a tougher challenge. Testing results for 2005 show that the average score on Verbal Reasoning for Humanities majors was 9.3, versus an average of 7.9 for Biological Sciences majors. Surprisingly, however, those students who majored in Math and Statistics achieved an average score of 8.6, which is above not only their biological counterparts, but also above the national average of 8.1.

What does this suggest? **Clearly, taking classes in the Humanities will help prepare students for the rigorous reading demands of Verbal Reasoning.** For those examinees who did not major in the Humanities (like the author of this book), they must create an independent intense reading schedule to boost their speed and comprehension (which is one way this book becomes extremely useful).

Notice that the examinee data suggests that science and math majors can score very well on Verbal Reasoning, as is evident from the 8.6 average for Math majors. In fact, students who majored in the Physical Sciences achieved an average score of 8.4. So, what sets one major apart from another? I would say **the quality and amount of reading material makes a sizable difference.** Large amounts of critical reading is demanded of the Humanities major. Unfortunately for the science major, he or she must read large volumes of scientific material that, while boosting analytical thinking skills, does not enhance critical reading skills. So the nature of the material is influential. The more scholarly and challenging the material, the more a student can improve essential reading skills (regardless of whether he or she has a Math or Humanities background). In other words, science nerds need not worry if they work hard at it.

FALSE ASSUMPTION #9: A WORD-SEARCH FUNCTION EXISTS ON VERBAL REASONING

Not true! Contrary to rumors, the computerized MCAT exam provides no word-search function on the Verbal Reasoning section to locate words or key phrases (as of 2008). Oddly enough, several computer-based AAMC practice MCAT exams have provided test-takers a search function (a small box to enter text and search for matches) on Verbal Reasoning. These particular practice exams have caused many students to assume with great anticipation and gladness that such a feature will appear on the actual MCAT exam. Such a search function would be most useful. To the surprise of many, however, the real MCAT contains no word-search feature.

✓ Sometimes, a Verbal question will make reference to a specific word without providing the line number where that word can be found. Line references were once provided on the paper MCAT exams of the past. So how should students handle this?

> Without a line reference or a search feature, the recommended tactic is to first attempt the question without looking back at the passage, eliminate wrong answers, and glance at the pertinent paragraph to confirm your answer if needed.

A good reader will remember the context of the word, and not need to re-read the passage. But if you cannot narrow down the answer choices, and you do not recall the location of the word, then you will need to skim the passage as a last resort. In general, searching a passage for a word wastes too much time, so try to avoid doing so at all costs.

FALSE ASSUMPTION #10: HIGH *PS* AND *BS* SCORES CAN COMPENSATE FOR A LOW *VR* SCORE

I once asked an admissions officer at a prominent East-coast medical school whether she thought that a BS score of 13 and a PS score of 13 would compensate for a VR score of 6. Her answer was a flat out "No." To the chagrin of many, a high Physical Sciences score and a high Biological Sciences score will not compensate for a low Verbal Reasoning score. A Verbal score of 8 or less is considered low. **The Verbal score is a very important factor that impacts your candidacy to medical schools, and should not be underestimated.**

Some applicants to medical schools have received offers to interview based largely on a high VR score. For many others, a low VR score knocked them out of the running, **despite having high science scores**. One applicant I know scored a 15 on Physical Sciences, a 14 on Biological Sciences, and a 4 on Verbal Reasoning; she did not received a single acceptance letter from a US medical school. A low VR score has poor implications about a candidate's ability to not only comprehend material, but also communicate ideas (a key requirement of all physicians). **The moral of the story is that high science scores will not compensate for a low Verbal score.**

FALSE ASSUMPTION #11: READING THE DAILY PAPER IS SUFFICIENT PRACTICE

If you believe this, then you are in for a surprise. The material presented on Verbal Reasoning can be quite challenging, dense, and scholarly. Most mainstream newspapers and coffee-table journals are simply not rigorous enough.

The typical Verbal passage discusses two or more theories that share similarities and differences on a number of clear and subtle levels. Often, passages are truncated excerpts from books and journals published by professors and other leaders in their fields. Therefore, anything at your fingertips around the house or apartment is, generally, not sufficient. Even the majority of books in your typical bookstore will not reach the critical rigor demanded of serious readers.

Where do students find good material to read? As was previously explained in Chapter 11, a great place to begin is at a college library. For a reasonable price (or for free), a student can obtain a library card and check out challenging books and journals that measure up to the difficulty of MCAT passages. Begin by looking for authors in the subjects of Anthropology, Sociology, Philosophy, Natural Science, Government or Public Policy, Artistic or Literary Criticism, and Religion (see Chapter 11).

> Professors from leading universities and academic departments generally publish material of excellent quality and complexity.

At the same time, the good student would do well to subscribe to a publication that offers an archive of articles on the Internet. One of my favorite online sources for MCAT preparation was *American Scientist* (the official publication of Sigma Xi, The Scientific Research Society). The online subscription exposed me to hundreds of complex MCAT-caliber articles, and provided great practice with reading on a computer screen. Those who are computer-savvy do have a slight edge over the rest of the pack, so do not get left behind!

CHAPTER

14

Eleven Things You Must Do on Test Day

On the day of your exam, entering the testing center with a solid plan of attack can influence your final MCAT score by as much as a point or two, maybe more. Why is this? Your mental state has a large influence on your performance. Two points can mean the difference between acceptance and rejection at a choice medical school, so controlling your mental state is critical.

The benefits of walking in with a winning mindset and an effective strategy are many-fold: less stress, better concentration, higher confidence, improved pacing, just to name a few. In order to reach your full potential on Verbal Reasoning, you should equip yourself with eleven key strategies on the day of the MCAT.

> If you have the knowledge and skills to achieve a score of, say,
> 30 on the MCAT, but let yourself lose focus and be thrown out of
> your zone resulting in a score of, say, 27, then you have
> done yourself a great disservice.

I. POSSESS THE PRIZE-FIGHTER MENTALITY

GENUINE CONFIDENCE IS CRUCIAL

One of the most entertaining moments of a boxing match happens *before* the fight, when the two opponents appear face-to-face. While the entertainment and marketing value of this act appears to be high, the fighters experience an added benefit. Confronting each other charges them up. Tensions rise, adrenaline pumps, and both walk away determined to be the next champion.

In a slightly similar fashion, you should walk into the MCAT exam determined to be a champion. For months, or years perhaps, the MCAT may have taunted you. You may have struggled with this monster daily, and gone to bed worrying about it night after night. It probably intimidated you with rough passages and tough questions, swinging and throwing punches. Now is the time for you to knock it down with a whopping blow. On the day of your fight - MCAT day - you must emerge as the champion. If you do not have this conviction, then it is best to wait another day.

✓ The key is to walk into the test ready for the challenge, knowing that you will win. The question then arises, "how will you gain the confidence, energy, and mindset of a champion set on winning?" Well, **the first step is to study excessively.** You need to study until you turn blue in the face. You need to dedicate months to studying until you cannot stand it. And just when you feel like stopping, after you have covered all material, you must keep studying until you really feel like quitting. Then, you should take an AAMC practice MCAT to discover the areas that need improvement. Your results will reveal topics that need more review, which means that you will have to go back and study those areas. Take a few more AAMC practice tests. Study the subjects where you are weak. Repeat this cycle. (This may take up to a month.)

For some, studying for the MCAT lasts three to four months. For others, studying can last a year or so. Whichever schedule you follow, study hard enough so that you are ready to kick the pants off the test. For most, this can mean six months to a year, easily.

In addition, realize that you are not competing against the MCAT, but against yourself. Improving your score is a function of your knowledge and effort. Increase your knowledge, boost your effort, take more practice tests, and your score will rise. It's that simple. You may wonder what your target score should be on practice tests. Your goal is to achieve a score that is a few points above the score you wish to achieve on the actual exam. If you goal is to achieve a 35 on the actual MCAT, for example, then you should aim for a 37 on practice tests.

Strategy #1: Maintain the mindset of a champion. If you do not have a high level of confidence, then you are not ready to take the MCAT.

II. STAY FED AND ENERGIZED

REFUEL ON BREAKS
The best instruments in the world become useless when their source of power runs dry. Every tool requires energy in order to function, whether it be a pencil or computer. Without a hand to move the pencil, it cannot write. Without electricity, microprocessors cannot activate. Every machine or instrument needs energy input.

There are two systems that must work on MCAT day: the computer, and your brain (along with your body of course). You can be sure that the computer will receive all the power it needs. But will your brain? Have you thought about how to feed your brain for five and a half hours so it can perform at its highest capacity?

You want to start the day with a complete meal, avoiding foods with a high sugar or glycemic index. But, **a large breakfast will not keep you fed for the duration of the test.**

So, how should you eat on test day? Consider eating natural foods like oatmeal, bananas, whole grain bread, eggs, etc. Stay away from very starchy foods that may make you sleepy, such as pasta and pizza. Avoid processed foods. **Foods rich in sugar can give you an energy spike followed by a sense of lethargy and fatigue.** Avoid eating lots of syrup, jelly, and cereals rich in sugar. Also, if you are not accustomed to drinking caffeinated beverages, then avoid doing so on the day of your test.

During each of the three 10-minute breaks throughout the MCAT, be sure to eat a nutritious snack. Your brain will burn energy faster than usual when dealing with complex passages under stress. Your job is to enable it to think as quickly and efficiently as possible.

Eat and drink on your breaks to give your brain the power it needs.

Suggested foods include the following: oranges, bananas, strawberries, granola bars (not power bars), yogurt, peanut butter and jelly sandwich (on wheat or whole grain bread), vegetables, cheese, salad with tomatoes, and drinks that do not contain high fructose corn syrup or caffeine.

Strategy #2: Eat the right foods for breakfast and during your breaks.

III. DO NOT PANIC

PANIC INHIBITS YOUR ABILITY TO THINK

Staying calm is easier said than done. You cannot overestimate the importance of remaining calm. **Plenty of practice with timed exams will help you handle stress and fear.** Many students who succumb to pressure begin to panic, and panic blocks their ability to think.

Those who succumb to the panic factor will most likely miss a few more questions than usual, which could potentially lower their scores in each section. Panicking could mean the difference between, say, a score of 27, and a score of 30. **Here is why remaining calm is so critical: when you panic, you stop thinking critically.** If you stop thinking on the MCAT, you might as well go home. Therefore, panicking is not an option. You must do what you can to remain calm. But how? Chapter fifteen covers in detail eleven ways to stay calm. In general, altering your breathing is a very effective way to improve your mood. Either on your breaks or during the exam, take five seconds to close your eyes and clear your mind. Take a few long deep breaths. As you inhale, count to four. Hold your breath for three seconds, and then exhale slowly. Relax to the feeling of air escaping from your chest. This will center your mind and calm your nerves.

✔ Feeling nervous or anxious is not the same as falling into a state of panic. When you panic, you become desperate and make impulsive choices instead of thoughtful ones. Feeling a bit nervous, on the other hand, is expected. In fact, feeling somewhat anxious can be to your benefit because it **can heighten your effort and concentration.**

Also realize that this exam is not the end of the world. It may seem that way for many students, but it is not. A strong score does not guarantee admission, just as a low score does not guarantee rejection. Medical schools look at many factors in addition to the MCAT score.

Please note, however, that taking the MCAT more than three times is generally discouraged and could appear problematic to admissions committees.

Strategy #3: Resist any temptation to panic. Use controlled breathing along with other relaxation techniques (covered in Chapter 15) to calm down when things get stressful.

IV. READ A BOOK WHILE WAITING FOR YOUR NAME TO BE CALLED

WARM UP WITH READING

On test day, bring a book to the testing center. The book should be from the reading list that you used during your training - scholarly and challenging. When you arrive at the testing center, you will probably have to wait in the lobby a good 30 minutes or so before starting the MCAT. **Do not talk to any other examinee. Instead, read your book.**

Get your eyes and mind geared for reading because you are about to face the Olympics of reading comprehension tests. Do yourself a favor by warming up your mind, not your mouth.

Strategy #4: Begin reading while waiting to be called into the testing room. By putting your mind into reading mode, you will gain an edge by the time you reach the Verbal Reasoning section.

V. IGNORE SCANNERS, CAMERAS, AND PEOPLE

STAY IN YOUR ZONE

Unfamiliar elements in an environment can be most distracting, especially during the pinnacle test of your pre-medical life. A big help is to know what to expect, which you can realize in three ways. First, visit your testing center a week or two before the MCAT. If you do, then ask for a quick tour of the facility and pay attention to the process of signing in. Second, if possible, talk to people who have taken the computerized MCAT to get first-hand knowledge about the experience. And, third, read this entire book. We recommend you do all three.

I want to bring to your attention a few distractions that will appear on test day, and ask that you do your best to ignore them. First, **do not dwell on the scanning device** that allows people to enter or leave the computer room. Expect to have your thumb scanned every time you wish to enter or leave the room. This means that a ten-minute break is actually seven to eight minutes, because a few minutes are spent scanning in and out. So, plan for this. On your breaks, do not talk to anyone except the staff if you have questions or concerns.

Second, **ignore the camera** in the ceiling above you. Now that I have told you about the overhead camera, you should not be entirely surprised by it. And yes, the staff watches everything you do.

Third, **ignore other examinees.** They will only distract you and break your concentration. Remember, you must stay in your zone. Do not talk to anyone (except for the staff). Chatting with other examinees will take you out of your zone completely. Your best approach is to stay quiet and focused the entire time.

Strategy #5: Do not worry about the scanning device, the cameras, and the students. Disregard distractions in your environment. Stay focused. Stay in your zone.

VI. BECOME ENGROSSED AND NEVER BREAK FOCUS ON EACH SECTION

FOCUS INTENTLY ON THE MATERIAL
During the test you must think of nothing else but the material on the screen. This is easy to do on a single passage (surprisingly, some students struggle even with this). But to maintain focus in blocks of 60 to 70 minutes over the course of more than five hours is much more challenging. To achieve such focus control you need to practice.

Recall the technique called **clutch reading** that we introduced in Chapter 6. You should practice this technique often to build focus. After mastering clutch reading, you will be able to catch yourself and prevent your mind from wandering on a consistent basis, which will greatly improve your reading comprehension. The need for enhanced focus will be evident on all sections of the MCAT, including Verbal Reasoning. By the time you take the MCAT, you should be able to stay focused for more than one hour at a time.

On Verbal Reasoning, you cannot afford to break focus. Take interest in each VR passage. Be curious about the material. Try to learn something from it. Each passage has something very interesting to share. By becoming a curious reader, you will stay fully engaged.

Strategy #6: Do not let your mind wander. Take interest in your passages and stay fully engaged until the end of each section.

VII. MANAGE THE CLOCK CAREFULLY

STAYING ON TIME IS CRITICAL

The computerized MCAT gives you a valuable assistant: the clock. You now have no excuse for running out of time. The clock counts down in seconds and is always visible at the bottom of your screen. Unfortunately, some students will find the clock to be a distraction. So here are a few simple rules to follow on practice tests and on the real MCAT:

1. Do not stare at the clock.
2. Do not look at the clock after *every* question.
3. On Physical Sciences and Biological Sciences, check the clock after **every two or three** passages. Memorize specific time points, and stick to them.

4. On Verbal Reasoning, check the clock after **every passage.**
It is much easier to veer off schedule on Verbal Reasoning,
so be sure you have memorized the time points on a
per-passage basis. Refer to Chapter 8 for pacing details.

Please be aware of the psychological pressure of having a timer count
down right before your eyes. When you near the end of a passage, you
must resist the temptation to panic or feel pressured by the clock. The
timer is meant to act as a guide, not as a drill sergeant. **Lots of practice
with timed exams will enable you to overcome the stress of a clock
always counting down.** The importance of taking practice MCAT exams
cannot be emphasized enough.

Strategy #7: Use the clock to your advantage. Memorize time points to stay on schedule.

VIII. FORGET ABOUT THE PREVIOUS PASSAGE

YOUR GUT FEELING IS OFTEN WRONG

Have you ever felt awful about your performance on a test, and later
discovered that you had earned a great score? Or perhaps you were sure
that you aced an exam, only to discover that you had performed poorly.
This has happened to nearly all of us. The moral of the story is that **your
gut feeling about how you performed on a question is not reliable.**
Therefore, worrying about a previous passage on the MCAT can waste
valuable time and energy. So don't do it.

What happens when you encounter a very difficult passage? You can either
skip it (and return later), or attempt it. When you do decide to tackle a
rather challenging passage, simply do your best, stay on time, and move on.
**When you move to the next passage, do not think about your
performance on the previous passage.** Let it go. Forget about the
previous passage, because you cannot predict your performance. Just
because you struggled on a question does not mean you missed it.

Keeping your mind fresh and clear is extremely important for focus control.

✓ Remember, everyone will face challenging passages. The MCAT contains questions of varying difficulty, so expect to struggle on occasion. Most questions should seem feasible, but a few may seem impossible. This is to be expected. Do not dwell on the few impossible questions. In general, keep moving when you tackle very difficult material. Do not fall into a time trap and get bogged down. Why spend more time on material that you are more likely to get wrong?

Strategy #8: Do not dwell on previous passages or questions. Focus completely on your current passage. Return to challenging questions only as time permits.

IX. DO NOT FEAR THE IMPOSSIBLE QUESTION

EXPECT A FEW VERY DIFFICULT QUESTIONS

There you sit, reading passages and questions, staying focused and on schedule. Suddenly, you come across a very difficult question. You read the question again, and it looks ever harder. What should you do?

Your options are to skip it, take a guess, or figure it out. First, do not fear the impossible question. It is intended to be extremely challenging. If you happen to mark it correctly, then you are one step ahead of the curve. Second, never skip the impossible question. Since there is no penalty for guessing, you should always pick an answer. Leaving a question blank risks forgetting about it later. Third, since the question is very difficult, **do not waste precious time on it.** The chance of figuring out the correct answer is slim.

So, all things considered, your best strategy is to spend about a minute on a very difficult question, place a check in the small box to mark the question, select an educated answer choice, and move on. If you have time left over, then you can locate your marked questions and spend more time on them. Ultimately, you should spend the bulk of your time on questions that you have a decent chance of marking correctly.

✓ Above all, never panic when you see a seemingly impossible question. Every MCAT is designed to contain some very challenging questions. Give your best effort in a short amount of time, and move on. Be efficient.

Strategy #9: On the most difficult questions, take your best guess and quickly move on. If time permits, attempt them with more thought later. Never leave a question blank.

X. TALK TO THE AUTHOR AND ANTICIPATE QUESTIONS

BECOME AN ACTIVE READER

This may sound unusual or even strange, but having an internal dialogue with the author can be very helpful. What does it mean to have an internal dialogue? Imagine that you are sitting in a room with the author; the words of the passage are the words that he or she is speaking to you. You would enter the room and take a seat with some level of curiosity about what the author will tell you. As the author begins to share his or her ideas, you should not only listen, but also **ask questions**. Pretend to be an inquisitive journalist. After every few sentences, prod the author with questions:

> *"Why is that true Miss Author?"*
>
> *"How does that make you feel Miss Author?"*
>
> *"Why do you come to that conclusion Miss Author?"*
>
> *"What else can you tell me Miss Author?"*

You will find that as you read Verbal Reasoning passages in this manner, as if you were having a dialogue, your ability to focus on the material and comprehend it will improve significantly. Couple this with NVP, and you should drastically improve your level of comprehension. NVP acts like a blank slate where you take note of everything the author says. **Reading with an active internal dialogue requires extensive practice.** It takes time for your mind to naturally ask questions as it reads, which is partly why developing your reading comprehension requires several months of reading.

In addition to having a mental dialogue with the author, **anticipating questions is very helpful.** Anticipating questions involves predicting the most likely questions to appear based on passage material. As you saw in Chapter 12, top performers of Verbal Reasoning have the ability to predict questions. Anticipating questions is an extremely useful skill which comes after much reading and passage practice.

> Remember the four common passage constructs (see Chapter 6) typically seen on Verbal Reasoning: Thesis Development, Competing Theories, A Process, and Opinions.

To develop the skill of anticipation, you must read for many months and then take many practice tests (going through a large volume of questions). Again, turn to test preparation courses for an ample source of passages. The goal is for you to develop a feel of what questions seem most probable based on the information itself, and on how the information is presented.

Strategy #10: Engage in a mental dialogue with the author, and anticipate questions as you read. Both should happen naturally by the time you take the MCAT. Only after months of practice with sample passages will you be able to anticipate Verbal Reasoning questions.

XI. ENGAGE YOUR NEURO-VISUAL PROGRAMMING

USE NVP WHEN POSSIBLE

Finally, be sure to take full advantage of Neuro-Visual Programming. We saw in Chapter 9 how NVP is the process of transforming ideas in the passage into visual images and symbols in your mind. NVP is like a muscle - the more your exercise it, the more material it can process. The average learning curve to master NVP is approximately four to six months, since you must train your brain to perform new and demanding tasks.

Throughout your Verbal Reasoning section, you should **use NVP on each passage** in a manner that feels very natural to you. If NVP still feels difficult to use by the time you take the MCAT, then *do not* use it. My hope is that you read this book far enough in advance to you give yourself the necessary time to learn and use NVP quite effectively.

Strategy #11: Do not forget to use NVP as you read the passages. Given that you are well prepared, you can use NVP on all sections of the MCAT.

XII. IN YOUR OWN WORDS -
THE ELEVEN STRATEGIES

Use the space below to describe each of the eleven strategies in your own words. Studies have shown that when we write things down, we have a much better chance of remembering and doing them.

1. _____

2. _____

3. _____

4. _____

5. _____

6. _____

7. _____

8. _____

9. _____

10. _____

11. _____

Eleven Ways to Reduce Anxiety Before and During the MCAT

Feeling nervous about the MCAT is natural. On the day of your test, you will see students attempting to ignore their worries and insecurities while waiting in the lobby before the exam begins. Some will chat with their neighbor, walk around, or stare at the walls, while others will close their eyes, or even talk on their cell phones (none of these are recommended). Performing at your very best means controlling pressure and anxiety leading up to the MCAT exam in an intelligent, calm manner. What follows are eleven techniques to maintain focus and composure.

Anxiety about the MCAT has its roots in factors that relate both directly and indirectly to the exam. Everyone is familiar with the obvious concerns:

handling a challenging science passage, pacing and staying on time, reading difficult Verbal passages, dealing with anxiety, and so on. But many overlook the more subtle sources of anxiety, like the fear of taking a test with strangers, or being in a different environment, or facing traffic in the morning.

I. VISIT THE TESTING CENTER BEFORE TAKING THE MCAT

A clear recommendation for all test-takers is to visit, if at all possible, the testing center two weeks before the day of your exam. Call the center in advance and speak to the staff to arrange for an opportune time to visit. When you visit, take a good look around. Notice the locations of the computers, lockers, and restrooms. Try to feel relaxed. Ask for an informal tour of the testing center and be sure free to ask questions.

While you are not allowed to enter the actual testing room, you can look in through the rather large windows and imagine yourself taking the test with dozens of other students. Find out if your particular testing center provides noise-canceling headphones, or ear plugs. Also find out if they provide pencil and paper, or marker and laminated sheets. Also, take note of the length of time it takes to get to the location.

> Once you become more acquainted with the testing center, your mind can recall the experience periodically. Practice visualizing being at the center.

The more you recall your visit, the more you will feel comfortable with the testing center on the day of your MCAT. When you finally arrive to take the MCAT, you may be surprised at how calmly you handle the experience.

By visiting the center, you will eliminate most anxieties you may have about the testing environment, center staff, and trip to that location.

II. CLOSE YOUR EYES AND REHEARSE THE EXPERIENCE

When we rehearse a task in our minds over and over again, we improve how we perform that task. There once was a famous pianist who was imprisoned for many years. Every day he practiced the same piano concerto in his mind, and after he was released he could perform it with near perfection.

Each afternoon, try to close your eyes and **imagine sitting in front of the computer as you take the MCAT.** Imagine in your mind the computer screen, keyboard, mouse, and paper that sit before you. Visualize wearing headphones and focusing intently on each passage. Do this mental exercise daily. When the time comes for you to take the actual MCAT, you will have a sense of calm and composure as if you had taken the test already - you have, in your mind.

III. FLEX YOUR MUSCLES FROM TOE TO HEAD

Have you ever tensed your muscles while sitting in a chair? If not, you are missing out on a very common technique used by many to help alleviate stress.

If your body is in good working order, then try the following. (This exercise requires you to voluntarily tense certain muscles from your toes to your head.) To begin, take a slow deep breath while seated. Now, with both feet on the floor, curl your toes and flex the muscles in your feet. Concentrate on your feet and keep your toes tensed. Next, activate your leg muscles by making them tense. Focus on each body part as you engage it. While holding those tight, squeeze your stomach and tense your back. Move up into your arms and tighten those muscles. Hold your tightened body in this manner and count to five. Then relax. Try it again. You will begin to feel much more relaxed.

✓ The tension you create while sitting will actually help alleviate any tension you felt prior to the exercise. This is a good relaxation technique for stressful moments when you are confined to a chair.

IV. BREATHE IN AND OUT CALMLY

Breathing is a very effective relaxation technique that is often overlooked by students. You may think that breathing is not helpful because you breathe all the time. Well, the key is in how you breathe. **Inhaling slowly, holding your breath, and exhaling in a timed fashion can produce an important calming effect during your MCAT.**

Here are some basic steps to achieve a relaxed state through breathing. Slowly count to ten and exhale a good portion of air in your chest. Then, take a deep breath slowly as you count to seven in your mind until you cannot breathe in any further. Hold all of that air in your chest for four seconds, and then slowly exhale again for ten seconds. Do this three times in a row and notice how your body responds. Is your mind more clear and calm? Do you feel relaxed all throughout your body? When your mind enters this elevated state of calm, you can think much more effectively. **Deep breathing is very effective for attacking anxiety.**

V. TAKE A FIVE-SECOND BREAK AND KEEP YOUR HANDS WARM

While your mind will be running hot, your hands may become very cold during the MCAT. Your extremities may get cold from the air conditioning and lack of motion over a five-hour period. For many examinees, the hand controlling the computer mouse (usually the right hand) notoriously turns into ice. When this happens, a good technique is to squeeze your fingers, roll your wrists around, rub your hands, and try warming them up with your breath.

✓ Should you ever feel overwhelmed by a question, consider looking away from the screen and take a five-second break. You will be surprised by how a quick break can give your mind a fresh boost. In the heat of the MCAT, a five-second break will feel like a pleasant five-minute break.

> Do not be afraid to take a quick five-second break if you feel overwhelmed or lose concentration.

VI. COUNT DOWN IN YOUR MIND

At any point before or during the MCAT you can always stop and take a pause. With your eyes closed, count down from 5 to 0 **silently and slowly**. Give it a try. Did you notice something change? If not, try it again. You will quickly realize the benefit of this technique, which you can use anywhere at any time.

This is a great calming exercise to use on a break between MCAT sections, or during a section if you experience anxiety. You can also use this technique while waiting in the lobby before the start of your exam. **Counting down in your mind gives you a sense of peace and composure.** Depending on how much time you have available, you can count down from 10 for a greater calming effect.

VII. THINK OF A GREAT MOMENT

When I say the phrase "You loved it when…," what first comes to mind? A friend telling a funny joke? A childhood memory fishing on a lake? A trip to the Grand Canyon last summer? Anything will do. You should **have one positive memory ready to recall on the day of your test.** When you encounter a stressful moment during the exam, think of your great memory to calm yourself down and lift your spirits.

VIII. IMAGINE LIFE FIVE MINUTES AFTER THE EXAM

Imagine yourself getting up out of your chair after the MCAT. You have just finished, arguably, the hardest graduate school entrance exam after sacrificing months of your life in diligent preparation. Imagine that you achieved your target score, or a few points above it. Imagine how good that feels and the relief and joy you have. How did you do it? Were you in command of the clock and totally focused, never letting anxiety or doubt enter your mind?

✓ Students who score in the mid 30s or above most often manage the test without distraction or worry. They achieve control over their mental state. Imagine that you are one of those students. **See yourself having complete control** over your anxiety. Imagine maintaining a healthy level of confidence throughout the test, followed by success.

Side note: on the day of your test, you may feel unsure about your performance on a certain section of the MCAT. Do not assume that you scored poorly. A student often feels badly about a particular section only to discover later that he or she scored well on it. See Chapter 14.

IX. REFUEL DURING BREAKS

Hungry people become fussy, and fussy people do not score well on the MCAT. Without a doubt, this exam is a stressful and glucose-demanding experience. Your brain will have to work on overdrive for five-and-a-half hours. Running out of fuel is the last thing you want to have happen. If you do not snack on your MCAT breaks, then your brain will feel tired which can compromise your performance and final score.

During each ten-minute break, be sure to eat quickly. **Plan to eat in six or seven minutes**, because two to three minutes will be spent getting into and out of the testing room.

> You have only six to seven minutes to eat and use the restroom during a ten-minute break, because scanning into and out of the testing room takes a couple minutes.

What should you eat? As was mentioned in the previous chapter, avoid anything with a high glycemic index or high starch content. Several suggested foods include a banana, granola bar, apple, or peanut-butter sandwich. Avoid foods like pizza, pasta, and caffeinated drinks. **Also, be careful not to drink too much water. You cannot pause the test in the middle of a section to take a trip to the bathroom.**

X. DRESS COMFORTABLY AND WARMLY

Dress in layers. If the room is too hot, then you can always remove a sweatshirt or sweater. But if the room is too cold, and you are wearing just one layer, then you will shiver for five-and-a-half hours. You may wish to wear either a sweatshirt, or sweater on top of two T-shirts. **Be aware that**

most testing centers generally do not allow jackets with many pockets. As with any responsible computer facility, the colder a room, the longer its computer equipment will stay in good functioning order. You simply have to prepare for cold ambient temperatures. Taking a test while shivering will surely compromise your ability to stay comfortable and focused. This anxiety will threaten your chances of scoring your very best.

XI. SLEEP WELL THE PREVIOUS NIGHT AND ARRIVE EARLY

What destroys Verbal scores? No, not a live rock band playing music in the testing center (which would actually help some students wake up). In reality, a lack of sleep will cut down Verbal scores faster than a chainsaw. When students get only three to four hours of sleep, they cannot rapidly comprehend material (or even walk straight). **Be sure to sleep for about seven hours the night before your exam.**

Also, be sure to arrive early. Arriving early is not for impressing the students and the testing staff. It's for starting the test before most other examinees start their tests. All students do not begin the MCAT at the same time. Instead, **the staff purposely staggers the starting times on a first-come, first-serve basis.** If you are one of the unlucky few to sign in late, then you will begin your Verbal Reasoning section later than others. Why is this a disadvantage? If this should happen, then you will hear people typing their essays by the time you reach the Verbal Reasoning section (because they have already begun their Writing Sample). Nothing is more annoying than hearing many little fingers typing away while you are trying to read challenging material. Noise-canceling headphones cancel most sounds, but not the clicking of keys. Therefore, **be one of the first students to arrive. Sign in at the testing center right away.** Arriving a good 45 minutes to an hour before the official start time should be early enough.

READING COMPREHENSION
AND
MEMORY EXERCISES

UNIT 1
BASIC LEVEL A

READING SPEED EXERCISE - BASIC LEVEL A

DIRECTIONS: This exercise is designed to measure your relative reading speed. Read the passage at an accelerated rate while monitoring your time. Be sure to comprehend as much material as possible. At the end of the passage, record the number of minutes and seconds you spent reading. Refer to the Appendix for your calculated reading rate.

Of all the traditional precepts, the one most frequently cited in theoretical treatises on the voice is, "Place the tone forward." For this precept it is generally believed that a satisfactory explanation has been found in the accepted doctrine of tone emission.

The characteristic effect of perfect singing known as the "forward tone" is thoroughly well known to every lover of singing. In some peculiar way the tone, when perfectly produced, seems to issue directly from the singer's mouth. When we listen to a poorly trained and faulty singer the tones seem to be caught somewhere in the singer's throat. We feel instinctively that if the singer could only lift the voice off the throat, and bring it forward in the mouth, the tones would be greatly improved in character. It is commonly believed that the old masters knew some way in which this can be done. Just what means they used for this purpose is not known. But the accepted scientific interpretation of the "forward tone" precept is held by vocal theorists to render the subject perfectly clear.

To the vocal theorists this is no doubt thoroughly convincing and satisfactory. But as a topic of practical instruction in singing this theory of tone emission is utterly valueless. How can the "column of vocalized breath" be voluntarily directed in its passage through the pharynx and mouth? No muscular process has ever been located, by which the singer can influence the course of the expired breath, and direct it to any specific point in the mouth. Even if the expired breath does, in perfect singing, take the course described, knowledge of this fact cannot enable the singer to bring this about. The accepted doctrine of tone emission is of no benefit whatever to the teacher of singing. He knows what the "forward tone" is, that is, what it sounds like, just as well no doubt as did the old Italian master. But if the latter knew how to enable his pupils to obtain the

"forward" character of tone, the modern teacher is to that extent not so well off.

In view of the prevailing ignorance of any means for securing the (supposedly) correct emission of tone, intelligible instruction on this topic is hardly to be expected. But the great majority of teachers lay great stress on the need of acquiring the correct emission. The best they can do is to explain the scientific doctrine to their pupils; the students are generally left to find for themselves some way of applying the explanation. In many cases the master tries to assist the student by describing the singer's sensations, experienced when producing a "forward" tone.

Certain vowels and consonants are usually held to be especially favored by a "forward position," and exercises on these are very widely used for securing a "forward" tone. These exercises are described in a later paragraph. It will be noticed however that this use of vowels is not an application of the theory of "forward emission." The vowel sounds are believed to owe their "forward position" to resonance, while "emission" is purely a matter of direction or focusing of the breath-blast. The whole subject of emission and forward placing is in a very unsatisfactory condition.

All instruction based on the singer's sensations is purely empirical, in the meaning ordinarily attached to this word in treatises on Vocal Science. Theoretical works on the voice seldom touch on the subject of sensations, nor do the vocal teachers generally make this subject prominent when speaking of their methods.

Sensations occupy a rather peculiar position in modern methods. They are a distinctly subsidiary element of instruction and are seldom raised to the dignity accorded to the mechanical doctrines of vocal management. The use of the singer's sensations, as applied in practical instruction, is almost exclusively interpretive. In the mechanical sense the traditional precepts have no meaning whatever; this is also true of several of the accepted doctrines of Vocal Science. For example, the precept "Support the tone," is absolutely meaningless as a principle of mechanical vocal action. But, when interpreted as referring to a set of sensations experienced by the singer, this precept takes on a very definite meaning. Nobody knows what the support of the tone is, but every vocal teacher knows how it feels. In the same way, no means is known for directly throwing the air in the nasal cavities into vibration. But the sensation in the front of the head, which indicates, presumably, the proper action of nasal resonance, is familiar to all teachers. Most of the positive materials of modern methods are thus interpreted in terms of sensations.

True, the accepted theory of Vocal Science does not directly countenance this interpretation. The basic principle of modern Voice Culture is the idea of mechanical vocal management. All instruction is supposed to aim at direct, conscious, and voluntary control of the muscular operations of singing. Teachers always impart to their pupils this idea of the mechanical control of the voice. The vocal action is always considered from the mechanical side. Even those expressions whose mechanical meaning is vague or unscientific are yet used as referring definitely to muscular actions. The conscious thought of the teacher is always turned to the mechanical idea supposedly conveyed by scientific doctrine and empirical precept. The translation of this idea into a description of sensations is almost always the result of a sub-conscious mental process.

It therefore follows that in practical instruction the appeal to sensations is more often indirect than direct. For example, when a student's tones are caught in the throat, the master says explicitly,"Free the tone by opening your throat." The master explains the (supposed) wrong vocal action, and describes how the tone should be produced. Incidentally, the master may also tell how and where the tone should be felt.

There is also a great deal of instruction based frankly and directly on the singer's sensations. Instruction of this type usually takes the form of special exercises on certain vowels and consonants, which are believed to be peculiarly suited for imparting command of particular features of the correct vocal action. The topics generally covered are chest resonance, nasal resonance, open throat, and forward placing of the tone. This form of instruction is held to be referable in some way to scientific principles. The laws of vowel and consonant formation formulated by Helmholtz are often cited in proof of the efficacy of exercises of this type. There is also much discussion of the "location" of the tone. But there is little justification for the statement that instruction based on the singer's sensations is scientific in character. A misconception of acoustic principles is evidenced by most of the statements made concerning the use of special vowels and consonants in securing the correct vocal action. (Taylor)

TOTAL TIME:

....

PARAGRAPH SUMMARY EXERCISE - BASIC LEVEL A

DIRECTIONS: This exercise is designed to improve your ability to summarize main concepts. Read the material at a comfortable rate. After you have read EACH paragraph, write a brief summary of its key points in the right column. Include main ideas, conclusions, and opinions. Do not include details.

The Greeks pretended, that they had the use of the sphere, and were acquainted with the zodiac, and its asterisms very early. But it is plain from their mistakes, that they received the knowledge of these things very late; at a time when the terms were obsolete, and the true purport of them not to be obtained. They borrowed all the schemes under which the stars are comprehended from the Egyptians: who had formed them of old, and named them from circumstances in their own religion and mythology.

1st PARAGRAPH SUMMARY:

They had particularly conferred the titles of their Deities upon those stars, which appeared the brightest in their hemisphere. One of the most remarkable and brilliant they called Cahen Sehor; another they termed Purcahen; a third Cahen Ourah, or Cun Ourah. These were all misconstrued, and changed by the Greeks; Cahen-Sehor to Canis Sirius; P'urcahen to Procyon; and Cahen Ourah to Cunosoura, the dog's tail. In respect to this last name I think, from the application of it in other instances, we may be assured that it could not be in acceptation what the Greeks would persuade us: nor had it any relation to a dog.

2nd PARAGRAPH SUMMARY:

There was the summit of a hill in Arcadia of this name: also a promontory in Attica; and another in Eubœa. How could it possibly in its common acceptation be applicable to these places? And as a constellation if it signified a dog's tail, how came it to be a name given to the tail of a bear? It was a term brought from Sidon, and Egypt: and the purport was to be sought for from the language of the Amonians.

3rd PARAGRAPH SUMMARY:

We find the same mistake occur in the account transmitted to us concerning the first discovery of purple. The ancients very gratefully gave the merit of every useful and salutary invention to the Gods. Ceres was supposed to have discovered to men corn, and

4th PARAGRAPH SUMMARY:

UNIT 1 - BASIC

bread: Osiris showed them the use of the plough; Cinyras of the harp. Vesta taught them to build. Every Deity was looked up to as the cause of some blessing.

There was a tradition concerning Antæus, that he covered the roof of a temple, sacred to Poseidon, with the sculls of foreigners, whom he forced to engage with him. The manner of the engagement was by wrestling. Eryx in Sicily was a proficient in this art, and did much mischief to strangers: till he was in his turn slain. The Deity was the same in these parts, as was alluded to under the name of Taurus, and Minotaurus, in Crete; and the rites were the same. Hence Lycophron speaks of Eryx by the name of Taurus; and calls the place of exercise before the temple, *The Gymnasium of Eryx, who used to murder strangers*.

When the Spaniards got access to the Western world, there were to be observed many rites, and many terms, similar to those, which were so common among the sons of Ham. Among others was this particular custom of making the person, who was designed for a victim, engage in fight with a priest of the temple. In this manner he was slaughtered: and this procedure was esteemed a proper method of sacrifice.

The histories of which I have been speaking were founded in truth, though the personages are not real. Such customs did prevail in the first ages: and in consequence of these customs we find those beggarly attributes of wrestling and boxing conferred upon some of the chief Divinities. Hercules and Pollux were of that number, who were as imaginary beings, as any mentioned above: yet represented upon earth as sturdy fellows, who righted some, and wronged many. They were in short a kind of honorable Banditti, who would suffer nobody to do any mischief, but themselves. From these customs were derived the Isthmian, Nemean, Pythic, and Olympic games, together with those at Delos. Of these last Homer gives a fine description in his Hymn to Apollo. (Bryant)

5th PARAGRAPH SUMMARY:

6th PARAGRAPH SUMMARY:

7th PARAGRAPH SUMMARY:

VISUAL MEMORY EXERCISE - BASIC LEVEL A

DIRECTIONS: This exercise is designed to improve your visual memory. Four grids of four objects are presented. Look at each grid for one minute. Memorize as best you can the design and placement of each symbol. When you have all objects memorized for one grid, turn to the next page and draw the four objects in the corresponding grid FROM MEMORY. If you need to look back at the grid, then document how many times you looked at the objects.

GRID 1

ε	Ω
3	☰

GRID 2

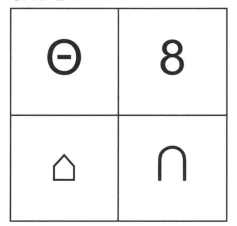

GRID 3

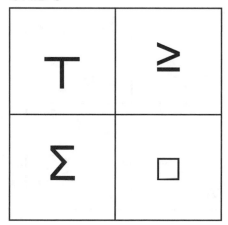

GRID 4

○	Ш
6	¾

VISUAL MEMORY *CONTINUED*

GRID 1   looked back _____ time(s)

GRID 2   looked back _____ time(s)

GRID 3   looked back _____ time(s)

GRID 4   looked back _____ time(s)

SENTENCE RECALL EXERCISE - BASIC LEVEL A

DIRECTIONS: This exercise is designed to improve your memory. Read each sentence carefully, remembering as much as possible. In the space immediately below, write the sentence FROM MEMORY, word for word. Resist the temptation to look back at the sentence after you have read it. Try to read each sentence only once.

Sentence #1:
Manet was certainly one of the most noteworthy painters that France or any other country has produced. (Brownell)

Recall #1:

Sentence #2:
There are, of course, innumerable substances, more or less, capable of talismanic virtue to particular individuals. (Wagner)

Recall #2:

Sentence #3:
Pitt once said that "British policy is British trade." (Baring)

Recall #3:

Sentence #4:
The Hermetic brethren encircled my astral body, which was deeply entranced. (Wagner)

Recall #4:

UNIT 1 - BASIC

Sentence #5:
He wrote a small book setting forth the Six Canons or Requirements of painting. (Petrucci)

Recall #5:

Sentence #6:
The only necessity is for the singer to have a clear mental conception of the effects to be obtained, and to listen attentively to the voice. (Taylor)

Recall #6:

Sentence #7:
All ideas are symbols, and symbols are reservoirs for the conservation of thought. (Wagner)

Recall #7:

Sentence #8:
This last opinion would fit in very well with the views of Mr. Rhys, the Celtic professor at Oxford. (Allen)

Recall #8:

Sentence #9:
Faith in the imitative faculty was gradually undermined by the progress of the mechanical idea. (Taylor)

Recall #9:

SENTENCE RECALL *CONTINUED*

Sentence #10:
The confusion is like that of a kaleidoscope, which though possessing a life of its own, belongs to another sphere. (Kandinsky)

Recall #10:

Sentence #11:
The soul sees the light beyond, and, emerging from the dark chasm of matter, knows the battle that must be fought against wrong. (Wagner)

Recall #11:

Sentence #12:
Our minds, which are even now only just awakening after years of materialism, are infected with the despair of unbelief, of lack of purpose and ideal. (Kandinsky)

Recall #12:

Sentence #13:
It produced splendid compositions in which the golden age of Chinese painting continued to be manifest. (Petrucci)

Recall #13:

Sentence #14:
Now, the struggle for life is fiercest, and the wealth of nature is greatest, one need hardly say, in tropical climates. (Allen)

Recall #14:

UNIT 2
BASIC LEVEL B

READING SPEED EXERCISE - BASIC LEVEL B

DIRECTIONS: This exercise is designed to measure your relative reading speed. Read the passage at an accelerated rate while monitoring your time. Be sure to comprehend as much material as possible. At the end of the passage, record the number of minutes and seconds you spent reading. Refer to the Appendix for your calculated reading rate.

The Blowpipe is a small instrument, made generally out of brass, silver, or German silver, and was principally used in earlier times for the purpose of soldering small pieces of metals together. It is generally made in the form of a tube, bent at a right angle, but without a sharp corner. The largest one is about seven inches long, and the smallest about two inches. The latter one terminates with a small point, with a small orifice. The first use of the blowpipe that we have recorded is that of a Swedish mining officer, who used it in the year 1738 for chemical purposes, but we have the most meager accounts of his operations. In 1758 another Swedish mining officer, by the name of Cronstedt, published his "Use of the Blowpipe in Chemistry and Mineralogy," translated into English, in 1770, by Van Engestroem. Bergman extended its use, and after him Ghan and the venerable Berzelius.

Dr. Black's blowpipe is as good an instrument and cheaper. It consists of two tubes, soldered at a right angle; the larger one, into which the air is blown, is of sufficient capacity to serve as a reservoir. A chemist can, with a blowpipe and a piece of charcoal, determine many substances without any reagents, thus enabling him, even when traveling, to make useful investigations with means which are always at his disposal. There are pocket blowpipes as portable as a pencil case, such as Wollaston's and Mitscherlich's; these are objectionable for continued use as their construction requires the use of a metallic mouthpiece. Mr. Casamajor, of New York, has made one lately which has an ivory mouthpiece, and which, when in use, is like Dr. Black's.

The length of the blowpipe is generally seven or eight inches, but this depends very much upon the visual angle of the operators. A short-sighted person, of course, would require an instrument of less length than would suit a far-sighted person. The purpose required of the blowpipe is to introduce a fine current of air into the flame of a candle or lamp, by which a higher degree of heat is induced, and consequently combustion is more rapidly accomplished.

Any flame of sufficient size can be used for blowpipe operations. It may be either the flame of a candle of tallow or wax, or the flame of a lamp. The flame of a wax candle, or of an oil lamp is most generally used. Sometimes a lamp is used filled with a solution of spirits of turpentine in strong alcohol. If a candle is used, it is well to cut the wick off short, and to bend the wick a little toward the substance experimented upon. But candles are not the best for blowpipe operations, as the radiant heat, reflecting from the substance upon the wax or tallow, will cause it to melt and run down the side of the candle; while again, candles do not give heat enough. The lamp is much the most desirable.

The metal platinum is infusible in the blowpipe flame, and is such a poor conductor of heat that a strip of it may be held close to that portion of it which is red hot without the least inconvenience to the fingers. It is necessary that the student should be cognizant of those substances which would not be appropriate to experiment upon if placed on platinum. Metals should not be treated upon platinum apparatus, nor should the easily reducible oxides, sulfides, nor chlorides, as these substances will combine with the platinum, and thus render it unfit for further use in analysis.

As the color of the flame cannot be well discerned when the substance is supported upon charcoal, in consequence of the latter furnishing false colors, by its own reflection, to the substances under examination, we use platinum wire for that purpose, when we wish to examine those substances which give

UNIT 2 - BASIC

indications by the peculiar color which they impart to fluxes. The wire should be about as thick as No. 16 or 18 wire, or about 0.4 millimeter, and cut into pieces about from two and a half to three inches in length. The end of each piece is crooked. In order that these pieces should remain clear of dirt, and ready for use, they should be kept in a glass of water. To use them, we dip the wetted hooked end into the powdered flux (borax or microcosmic salt) some of which will adhere, when we fuse it in the flame of the blowpipe to a bead. This bead hanging in the hook, must be clear and colorless. Should there not adhere a sufficient quantity of the flux in the first trial to form a bead sufficiently large, the hook must be dipped a second time in the flux and again submitted to the blowpipe flame. To fix the substance to be examined to the bead, it is necessary, while the latter is hot, to dip it in the powdered substance. If the hook is cold, we moisten the powder a little, and then dip the hook into it, and then expose it to the oxidation flame, by keeping it exposed to a regular blast until the substance and the flux are fused together, and no further alteration is produced by the flame.

The glass of which the bulb is made should be entirely free from lead, otherwise fictitious results will ensue. If the bulb be of flint glass, then by heating it, there is a slightly iridescent film caused upon the surface of the glass, which may easily be mistaken for arsenic. Besides, this kind of glass is easily fusible in the oxidizing flame of the blowpipe, while, in the reducing flame, its ready decomposition would preclude its use entirely. The tube should be composed of the potash or hard Bohemian glass, should be perfectly white, and very thin, or the heat will crack it. The tube should be perfectly clean, which can be easily attained by wrapping a clean cotton rag around a small stick, and inserting it in the tube. Before using the tube, see also that it is perfectly dry. The quantity of the substance put into the tube for examination should be small. From one to three grains is quite sufficient, as a general rule, but circumstances vary the quantity. The sides of the tube should not catch any of the substance as it is being placed at the bottom of the tube, or into the bulb. If any of the powder, however, should adhere, it should be pushed down with a roll of clean paper, or the clean cotton rag referred to above. In submitting the

tube to the flame, it should be heated at first very gently, the heat being increased until the glass begins to soften, when the observations of what is ensuing within it may be made.

If the substance contains water, it will condense upon the cold portion of the tube, and may be there examined as to whether it is acid or alkaline. If the former, the matter under examination is, perhaps, vegetable; if the latter, it is of an animal nature.
Of the metallic chlorides there are many which, when heated on charcoal with the blowpipe flame, are volatilized and redeposited as a white incrustation. Among these are the chlorides of potassium, sodium, and lithium, which volatilize and cover the charcoal immediately around the assay with a thin white film, after they have been fused and absorbed into the charcoal, chloride of potassium forms the thickest deposit, and chloride of lithium the thinnest, the latter being moreover of a greyish-white color. The chlorides of ammonium, mercury, and antimony volatilize without fusing. The chlorides of zinc, cadmium, lead, bismuth, and tin first fuse and then cover the charcoal with two different incrustations, one of which is a white volatile chloride, and the other a less volatile oxide of the metal.

Some of the incrustations formed by metallic chlorides disappear with a colored flame when heated with the reducing flame; thus chloride of potassium affords a violet flame, chloride of sodium an orange one, chloride of lithium a crimson flame, and chloride of lead a blue one. The other metals mentioned above volatilize without coloring the flame. (System)

TOTAL TIME:

....

PARAGRAPH SUMMARY EXERCISE - BASIC LEVEL B

DIRECTIONS: This exercise is designed to improve your ability to summarize main concepts. Read the material at a comfortable rate. After you have read EACH paragraph, write a brief summary of its key points in the right column. Include main ideas, conclusions, and opinions. Do not include details.

You will say that I am old and mad, but I answer that there is no better way of keeping sane and free from anxiety than by being mad.

1st PARAGRAPH SUMMARY:

Had Michelangelo been less poetic and more explicit in his language, he might have said there is nothing so conducive to mental and physical wholeness as saturation of body and mind with work. The great artist was so prone to over-anxiety and met (whether needlessly or not) with so many rebuffs and disappointments, that only constant absorption in manual labor prevented spirit from fretting itself free from flesh. He toiled "furiously" in all his mighty undertakings and body and mind remained one and in superior harmony—in abundant health—for nearly four score and ten years.

2nd PARAGRAPH SUMMARY:

This Titan got his start in life in the rugged country three miles outside Florence: a place of quarries, where stone cutters and sculptors lived and worked. His mother's health was failing and it was to the wife of one of these artisans that her baby was given to nurse. Half in jest, half in earnest, Michelangelo said one day to Vasari:

3rd PARAGRAPH SUMMARY:

"If I have anything good in me, that comes from my birth in the pure air of your country of Arezzo, and perhaps also from the feet that with the milk of my nurse, I sucked in the chisels and hammers wherewith I make my figures."

4th PARAGRAPH SUMMARY:

He began his serious study of art (and with it his course in "physical training") at fourteen, when he became apprenticed to a painter. He was not vigorous as a child, but his bodily powers unfolded and were intensified through their active expression of his imagination.

5th PARAGRAPH SUMMARY:

UNIT 2 - BASIC

His life was devoted with passion to art. He had from the start no time for frivolity. Art became his religion—and required of him the sacrifice of all that might keep him below his highest level of power for work. His father early warned him to have a care for his health, "for," said he, "in your profession, if once you were to fall ill you would be a ruined man."

To one so intent on perfection and so keenly alive to imperfection such advice must have been nearly superfluous, for the artist could not but observe the effect upon his work of any depression of his bodily well-being. He was, besides, too thrifty in all respects to think of lapsing into bodily neglect or abuse. He was severely temperate, but not ascetic, save in those times when devotion to work caused him to sleep with his clothes on, that he might not lose time in seizing the chisel when he awoke. He ate to live and to labor, and was pleased with a present of "fifteen marzolino cheeses and fourteen pounds of sausage—the latter very welcome, as was also the cheese."

Over a gift of choice wines he is not so enthusiastic and the bottles found their way mostly to the tables of his friends and patrons. When intent on some work he usually "confined his diet to a piece of bread which he ate in the middle of his labors." Few hours (we have no accurate statement in the matter) were devoted to sleep. He ate comparatively little because he worked better: he slept less than many men because he worked better in consequence. Partly for protection against cold, partly perhaps for economy of time, he sometimes left his high dog-skin boots on for so long that when he removed them the scarf skin came away like the skin of a molting serpent.

The blemish of nearsight he considered a no small defect and sufficient to render a young woman unworthy of entry into the proud family of the Buonarroti. To his own father he wrote: "Look to your life and health, for a man does not come back again to patch up things ill done." (Rogers)

6th PARAGRAPH SUMMARY:

7th PARAGRAPH SUMMARY:

8th PARAGRAPH SUMMARY:

9th PARAGRAPH SUMMARY:

VISUAL MEMORY EXERCISE - BASIC LEVEL B

DIRECTIONS: This exercise is designed to improve your visual memory. Four grids of nine objects are presented. Look at each grid for one minute. Memorize as best you can the design and placement of each symbol. When you have all objects memorized for one grid, turn to the next page and draw the nine objects in the corresponding grid FROM MEMORY. If you need to look back at the grid, then document how many times you looked at the objects.

GRID 1

g	6	d
a	35	0
z	i	w

GRID 2

y	x	6
p	9	h5
c	d	e

GRID 3

to	of	8
t	Yw	Zp
mn	4	7

GRID 4

d	9e	v3
tq	76	K
5V	fw	2k

VISUAL MEMORY *CONTINUED*

GRID 1   looked back _____ time(s)

GRID 2   looked back _____ time(s)

GRID 3   looked back _____ time(s)

GRID 4   looked back _____ time(s)

SENTENCE RECALL EXERCISE - BASIC LEVEL B

DIRECTIONS: This exercise is designed to improve your memory. Read each sentence carefully, remembering as much as possible. In the space immediately below, write the sentence FROM MEMORY, word-for-word. Resist the temptation to look back at the sentence after you have read it. Try to read each sentence only once.

___

Sentence #1:
This powder should then be fused in the oxidation flame until it mixes with, and is thoroughly dissolved by the borax bead. (System)

Recall #1:

___

Sentence #2:
That the analogy contains a grain of truth does not make it the less mischievous. (Kandinsky)

Recall #2:

___

Sentence #3:
Our first difficulty arises from a matter which, viewed in another light, is one of our greatest blessings. (Ackland)
Recall #3:

___

Sentence #4:
It had unwittingly achieved unity for China, despite itself and against its own inclination. (Petrucci)

Recall #4:

UNIT 2 - BASIC

Sentence #5:
The capacity for acquisition is confounded with the opportunity for acquisition. (Ackland)

Recall #5:

_____

Sentence #6:
Maeterlinck is perhaps one of the first prophets, one of the first artistic reformers and seers to herald the end of the decadence just described. (Kandinsky)

Recall #6:

_____

Sentence #7:
Their oxides are, in both flames, reduced to a metallic and infusible powder. (System)

Recall #7:

_____

Sentence #8:
Their skill in music must have been very great: and though they have been changed into birds, they retain that faculty, and, I am told, sing most melodiously. (Bryant)

Recall #8:

_____

Sentence #9:
Manet was certainly one of the most noteworthy painters that France or any other country has produced. (Brownell)

Recall #9:

_____

SENTENCE RECALL *CONTINUED*

Sentence #10:
A "possum up a gum-tree" is accepted by the observant American mind as the very incarnation of animal cleverness, cunning, and duplicity. (Allen)

Recall #10:

Sentence #11:
A great critic of the Sung period said of him that "his soul entered into communion with all things, his spirit penetrated the mysteries and the secrets of nature." (Petrucci)

Recall #11:

Sentence #12:
It is said of Jupiter, that he was the son of Saturn; and that he carried away Europa, before the arrival of Cadmus. (Bryant)

Recall #12:

Sentence #13:
The metallic oxides are allowed to subside, and the above solution decanted off into another porcelain vessel. (System)

Recall #13:

Sentence #14:
The stronghold of the Institute had been mined many times by revolutionary painters before Dalou took the grand medal of the Salon. (Brownell)

Recall #14:

UNIT 3
MEDIUM LEVEL A

READING SPEED EXERCISE - MEDIUM LEVEL A

DIRECTIONS: This exercise is designed to measure your relative reading speed. Read the passage at an accelerated rate while monitoring your time. Be sure to comprehend as much material as possible. At the end of the passage, record the number of minutes and seconds you spent reading. Refer to the Appendix for your calculated reading rate.

Everybody knows mountain flowers are beautiful. As one rises up any minor height in the Alps or the Pyrenees below snow-level, one notices at once the extraordinary brilliancy and richness of the blossoms one meets there. All nature is dressed in its brightest robes. Great belts of blue gentian hang like a zone on the mountain slopes; masses of yellow globe-flower star the upland pastures; nodding heads of soldanella lurk low among the rugged boulders by the glacier's side. No lowland blossoms have such vividness of coloring, or grow in such conspicuous patches. To strike the eye from afar, to attract and allure at a distance, is the great aim and end in life of the Alpine flora.

Now, why are Alpine plants so anxious to be seen of men and angels? Why do they flaunt their golden glories so openly before the world, instead of shrinking in modest reserve beneath their own green leaves, like the Puritan primrose and the retiring violet? The answer is, Because of the extreme rarity of the mountain air. It's the barometer that does it. At first sight, I will readily admit, this explanation seems as fanciful as the traditional connection between Goodwin Sands and Tenterden Steeple. But, like the amateur stories in country papers, it is 'founded on fact,' for all that. (Imagine, by the way, a tale founded entirely on fiction! How charmingly aerial!) By a roundabout road, through varying chains of cause and effect, the rarity of the air does really account in the long run for the beauty and conspicuousness of the mountain flowers.

For bees, the common go-betweens of the loves of the plants, cease to range about a thousand or fifteen hundred feet below snow-level. And why? Because it's too cold for them? Oh, dear, no: on sunny days in early English spring, when the thermometer doesn't rise above freezing in the shade, you will see both the honey-bees and the great black bumble as busy as their conventional character demands of them among the golden cups of the first timid crocuses. Give the bee sunshine, indeed, with a temperature just about freezing-point, and he'll flit about joyously on his communistic errand. But bees, one must remember, have heavy bodies and relatively small wings: in the rarefied air of mountain heights they can't manage to support themselves in the most literal sense. Hence their place in these high stations of the world is taken by the gay and airy butterflies, which have lighter bodies and a much bigger expanse of wing-area to buoy them up. In the valleys and plains the bee competes at an advantage with the butterflies for all the sweets of life: but in this broad sub-glacial belt on the mountain-sides the butterflies in turn have things all their own way. They flit about like monarchs of all they survey, without a rival in the world to dispute their supremacy.

And how does the preponderance of butterflies in the upper regions of the air affect the colour and brilliancy of the flowers? Simply thus. Bees, as we are all aware on the authority of the great Dr. Watts, are industrious creatures which employ each shining hour (well-chosen epithet, 'shining') for the good of the community, and to the best purpose. The bee, in fact, is the bon bourgeois of the insect world: he attends strictly to business, loses no time in wild or reckless excursions, and flies by the straightest path from flower to flower of the same species with mathematical precision. Moreover, he is careful, cautious, observant, and steady-going—a model business man, in fact, of sound middle-class morals and sober middle-class intelligence. No flitting for him, no coquetting, no fickleness. Therefore, the flowers that have adapted themselves to his needs, and that depend upon him mainly or solely for fertilization, waste no unnecessary material on those big flaunting colored posters which we human observers know as petals. They have, for the most part, simple blue or purple flowers, tubular in shape and, individually, inconspicuous in hue; and they are oftenest arranged in long spikes of blossom to avoid wasting the time of their winged Mr. Bultitudes. So long as they are just bright enough to catch the bee's eye a few yards away, they are certain to receive a visit in due season from that industrious and persistent commercial traveler. Having a circle of good customers upon whom they can depend with certainty for fertilization, they have no need to waste any large proportion of their substance upon expensive advertisements or gaudy petals.

It is just the opposite with butterflies. Those gay and irrepressible creatures, the fashionable and frivolous element in the insect world, gad about from flower to flower over great distances at once, and think much more of sunning themselves and of attracting their fellows than of attention to business. And the reason is obvious, if one considers for a moment the difference in the political and domestic economy of the two opposed groups. For the honey-bees are neuters, sexless purveyors of the hive, with no interest on earth save the storing of honey for the common benefit of the phalanstery to which they belong. But the butterflies are full-fledged males and females, on the hunt through the world for suitable partners: they think far less of feeding than of displaying their charms: a little honey to support them during their flight is all they need:— 'For the bee, a long round of ceaseless toil; for me,' says the gay butterfly, 'a short life and a merry one.' Mr. Harold Skimpole needed only 'music, sunshine, a few grapes.' The butterflies are of his kind. The high mountain zone is for them a true ball-room: the flowers are light refreshments laid out in the vestibule. Their real business in life is not to gorge and lay by, but to coquette and display themselves and find fitting partners.

So while the bees with their honey-bags, like the financier with his money-bags, are storing up profit for the composite community, the butterfly, on the contrary, lays himself out for an agreeable flutter, and sips nectar where he will, over large areas of country. He flies rather high, flaunting his wings in the sun, because he wants to show himself off in all his airy beauty: and when he spies a bed of bright flowers afar off on the sun-smitten slopes, he sails off towards them lazily, like a grand signior who amuses himself. No regular plodding through a monotonous spike of plain little bells for him: what he wants is brilliant color, bold advertisement, good honey, and plenty of it. He doesn't care to search. Who wants his favors must make himself conspicuous.

Now, plants are good shopkeepers; they lay themselves out strictly to attract their customers. Hence the character of the flowers on this bee-less belt of mountain side is entirely determined by the character of the butterfly fertilizers. Only those plants which laid themselves out from time immemorial to suit the butterflies, in other words, have succeeded in the long run in the struggle for existence. So the butterfly-plants of the butterfly-zone are all strictly adapted to butterfly tastes and butterfly fancies. They are, for the most part, individually large and brilliantly colored: they have lots of honey, often stored at the base of a deep and open bell which the long proboscis of the insect can easily penetrate: and they habitually grow close together in broad belts or patches, so that the color of each reinforces and aids the color of the others. It is this cumulative habit that accounts for the marked flowerbed or jam-tart character which everybody must have noticed in the high Alpine flora.

Aristocracies usually pride themselves on their antiquity: and the high life of the mountains is undeniably ancient. The plants and animals of the butterfly-zone belong to a special group which appears everywhere in Europe and America about the limit of snow, whether northward or upward. For example, I was pleased to note near the summit of Mount Washington (the highest peak in New Hampshire) that a large number of the flowers belonged to species well known on the open plains of Lapland and Finland. The plants of the High Alps are found also, as a rule, not only on the High Pyrenees, the Carpathians, the Scotch Grampians, and the Norwegian fields, but also round the Arctic Circle in Europe and America. They reappear at long distances where suitable conditions recur: they follow the snow-line as the snow-line recedes ever in summer higher north toward the pole

READING SPEED *CONTINUED*

or higher vertically toward the mountain summits. And this bespeaks in one way to the reasoning mind a very ancient ancestry. It shows they date back to a very old and cold epoch.

A couple of hundred thousand years ago or thereabouts—don't let us haggle, I beg of you, over a few casual centuries—the whole of northern Europe and America was covered from end to end, as everybody knows, by a sheet of solid ice, like the one which Frithiof Nansen crossed from sea to sea on his own account in Greenland. For many thousand years, with occasional warmer spells, that vast ice-sheet brooded, silent and grim, over the face of the two continents. Life was extinct as far south as the latitude of New York and London. No plant or animal survived the general freezing. Not a creature broke the monotony of that endless glacial desert. At last, as the celestial cycle came round in due season, fresh conditions supervened. Warmer weather set in, and the ice began to melt. Then the plants and animals of the sub-glacial district were pushed slowly northward by the warmth after the retreating ice-cap. As time went on, the climate of the plains got too hot to hold them. The summer was too much for the glacial types to endure. They remained only on the highest mountain peaks or close to the southern limit of eternal snow. In this way, every isolated range in either continent has its own little colony of arctic or glacial plants and animals, which still survive by themselves, unaffected by intercourse with their unknown and unsuspected fellow-creatures elsewhere.

Not only has the Glacial epoch left these organic traces of its existence, however; in some parts of New Hampshire, where the glaciers were unusually thick and deep, fragments of the primeval ice itself still remain on the spots where they were originally stranded. Among the shady glens of the white mountains there occur here and there great masses of ancient ice, the unmelted remnant of primeval glaciers; and one of these is so large that an artificial cave has been cleverly excavated in it, as an attraction for tourists, by the canny Yankee proprietor. Elsewhere the old ice-blocks are buried under the débris of moraine-stuff and alluvium, and are only accidentally

discovered by the sinking of what are locally known as ice-wells. No existing conditions can account for the formation of such solid rocks of ice at such a depth in the soil. They are essentially glacier-like in origin and character: they result from the pressure of snow into a crystalline mass in a mountain valley: and they must have remained there unmelted ever since the close of the Glacial epoch, which, by Dr. Croll's calculations, must most probably have ceased to plague our earth some eighty thousand years ago. Modern America, however, has no respect for antiquity: and it is at present engaged in using up this paleocrystic deposit—this belated storehouse of prehistoric ice—in the manufacture of gin slings and brandy cocktails.

As one scales a mountain of moderate height— say seven or eight thousand feet—in a temperate climate, one is sure to be struck by the gradual diminution as one goes in the size of the trees, till at last they tail off into mere shrubs and bushes. This diminution—an old commonplace of tourists—is a marked characteristic of mountain plants, and it depends, of course, in the main upon the effect of cold, and of the wind in winter. Cold, however, is by far the more potent factor of the two, though it is the least often insisted upon: and this can be seen in a moment by anyone who remembers that trees shade off in just the self-same manner near the southern limit of permanent snow in the Arctic regions. And the way the cold acts is simply this: it nips off the young buds in spring in exposed situations, as the chilly sea-breeze does with coast plants, which, as we commonly but incorrectly say, are "blown sideways" from seaward.

Of course, the lower down one gets, and the nearer to the soil, the warmer the layer of air becomes, both because there is greater radiation, and because one can secure a little more shelter. So, very far north, and very near the snow-line on mountains, you always find the vegetation runs low and stunted. It takes advantage of every crack, every cranny in the rocks, every sunny little nook, every jutting point or wee promontory of shelter. And as the mountain plants have been accustomed for ages to the strenuous conditions of such cold and wind-swept situations, they have ended, of course, by adapting themselves to that station in life

UNIT 3 - MEDIUM

to which it has pleased the powers that be to call them. They grow quite naturally low and stumpy and rosette-shaped: they are compact of form and very hard of fiber: they present no surface of resistance to the wind in any way; rounded and boss-like, they seldom rise above the level of the rooks and stones, whose interstices they occupy. It is this combination of characters that makes mountain plants such favorites with florists: for they possess of themselves that close-grown habit and that rich profusion of clustered flowers which it is the grand object of the gardener by artificial selection to produce and encourage.

When one talks of the 'the limit of trees' on a mountain side, however, it must be remembered that the phrase is used in a strictly human or Pickwickian sense, and that it is only the size, not the type, of the vegetation that is really in question. For trees exist even on the highest hill-tops: only they have accommodated themselves to the exigencies of the situation. Smaller and ever smaller species have been developed by natural selection to suit the peculiarities of these inclement spots. Take, for example, the willow and poplar group. Nobody would deny that a weeping willow by an English river, or a Lombardy poplar in an Italian avenue, was as much of a true tree as an oak or a chestnut. But as one mounts towards the bare and wind-swept mountain heights one finds that the willows begin to grow downward gradually. The 'netted willow' of the Alps and Pyrenees, which shelters itself under the lee of little jutting rocks, attains the height of only a few inches; while the 'herbaceous willow,' common on all very high mountains in Western Europe, is a tiny creeping weed, which nobody would ever take for a forest tree by origin at all, unless he happened to see it in the catkin-bearing stage, when its true nature and history would become at once apparent to him.

Yet this little herb-like willow, one of the most northerly and hardy of European plants, is a true tree at heart none the less for all that. Soft and succulent as it looks in branch and leaf, you may yet count on it sometimes as many rings of annual growth as on a lordly Scotch fir-tree. But where? Why, underground. For see how cunning it is, this little stunted descendant of proud forest lords: hard-pressed by nature, it has learnt to make the best of its difficult and precarious position. It has a woody trunk at core, like all other trees; but this trunk never appears above the level of the soil: it creeps and roots underground in tortuous zigzags between the crags and boulders that lie strewn through its thin sheet of upland leaf-mould. By this simple plan the willow manages to get protection in winter, on the same principle as when we human gardeners lay down the stems of vines: only the willow remains laid down all the year and always. But in summer it sends up its short-lived herbaceous branches, covered with tiny green leaves, and ending at last in a single silky catkin. Yet between the great weeping willow and this last degraded mountain representative of the same primitive type, you can trace in Europe alone at least a dozen distinct intermediate forms, all well marked in their differences, and all progressively dwarfed by long stress of unfavorable conditions. (Allen)

TOTAL TIME:

....

PARAGRAPH SUMMARY EXERCISE - MEDIUM LEVEL A

DIRECTIONS: This exercise is designed to improve your ability to summarize main concepts. Read the material at a comfortable rate. After you have read EACH paragraph, write a brief summary of its key points in the right column. Include main ideas, conclusions, and opinions. Do not include details.

Where our painters have chosen wood or canvas as a ground, the Chinese have employed silk or paper. While our art recognizes that drawing itself, quite apart from painting, is a sufficient objective, drawing and painting have always been closely intermingled in the Far East. While the mediums used in Europe for painting in color, distemper, tempera and oil, led to an exact study of form, the colors employed by the Orientals—at times brilliant, at times subdued with an almost studied restraint—preserved a singular fluidity and lent themselves to undefined evanescence which gave them a surprising charm.

The early paintings were generally done on cotton, coarse silk or paper. In the eighth century, under the T'ang dynasty, the use of finer silk began. The dressing was removed with boiling water, the silk was then sized and smoothed with a paddle. The use of silken fabric of the finest weave, prepared with a thick sizing, became general during the Sung dynasty. Papers were made of vegetable fibers, principally of bamboo. Being prepared, as was the silk, with a sizing of alum, they became practically indestructible. Upon these silks and papers the painter worked with brush and Chinese ink, color being introduced with more or less freedom or restraint.

The brushes are of different types. Each position of the brush conforms to a specific quality of the line, either sharp and precise or broad and quivering, the ink spreading in strong touches or thinning to delicate shades.

The colors are simple, of mineral or vegetable origin. Chinese painters have always avoided mixing colors so far as possible. From malachite they obtained several shades of green, from cinnabar or sulfide of mercury, a number of reds. They knew also how to

1st PARAGRAPH SUMMARY:

2nd PARAGRAPH SUMMARY:

3rd PARAGRAPH SUMMARY:

4th PARAGRAPH SUMMARY:

284

UNIT 3 - MEDIUM

combine mercury, sulfur and potash to produce vermilion. From peroxide of mercury they drew coloring powders which furnished shades ranging from brick red to orange yellow. During the T'ang dynasty coral was ground to secure a special red, while white was extracted from burnt oyster shells. White lead was later substituted for this lime white. Carmine lake they obtained from madder, yellows from the sap of the rattan, blues from indigo. To these must be added the different shades of Chinese ink and lastly, gold in leaf and in powder.

The brush-stroke in the painting of the Far East is of supreme importance. We know that this could not be otherwise if we recall that the characters in Chinese writing are ideographs, not actually written, but rather drawn. The stroke is not a mere formal, lifeless sign. It is an expression in which is reflected the beauty of the thought that inspired it as well as the quality of the soul of him who gives it form. In writing, as in painting, it reveals to us the character and the conception of its author. Placed at the service of certain philosophical ideas, which will be set forth later on, this technique was bound to lead to a special code of Aesthetics. The painter seeks to suggest with an unbroken line the fundamental character of a form. His endeavor, in this respect, is to simplify the objective images of the world to the extreme, replacing them with ideal images, which prolonged meditation shall have freed from every non-essential. It may therefore be readily understood how the brush-stroke becomes so personal a thing, that in itself it serves to reveal the hand of the master. There is no Chinese book treating of painting which does not discuss and lay stress upon the value of its aesthetic code.

It has often been said that in Chinese painting, as in Japanese painting, perspective is ignored. Nothing is further from the truth. This error arises from the fact that we have confused one system of perspective with perspective as a whole. There are as many systems of perspective as there are conventional laws for the representation of space.

The practice of drawing and painting offers the student the following problem in descriptive geometry: to represent the three dimensions of space by means of

5th PARAGRAPH SUMMARY:

6th PARAGRAPH SUMMARY:

7th PARAGRAPH SUMMARY:

8th PARAGRAPH SUMMARY:

a plane surface of two dimensions. The Egyptians and Assyrians solved this problem by throwing down vertical objects upon one plane, which demands a great effort of abstraction on the part of the observer. European perspective, built up in the fifteenth century upon the remains of the geometric knowledge of the Greeks, is based on the monocular theory used by the latter. In this system, it is assumed that the picture is viewed with the eye fixed on a single point. Therefore the conditions of foreshortening—or distorting the actual dimensions according to the angle from which they are seen—are governed by placing in harmony the distance of the eye from the scheme of the picture, the height of the eye in relation to the objects to be depicted, and the relative position of these objects with reference to the surface employed.

But, in assuming that the picture is viewed with the eye fixed on a single point, we put ourselves in conditions which are not those of nature. The European painter must therefore compromise with the exigencies of binocular vision, modify the too abrupt fading of forms and, in fine, evade over-exact principles. Thus he arrives at a *perspective de sentiment*, which is the one used by our masters.

Chinese perspective was formulated long before that of the Europeans and its origins are therefore different. It was evolved in an age when the method of superimposing different registers to indicate different planes was still being practiced in bas-reliefs. The succession of planes, one above the other, when codified, led to a system that was totally different from our monocular perspective. It resulted in a perspective as seen from a height. No account is taken of the habitual height of the eye in relation to the picture. The line of the horizon is placed very high, parallel lines, instead of joining at the horizon, remain parallel, and the different planes range one above the other in such a way that the glance embraces a vast space. Under these conditions, the picture becomes either high and narrow—a hanging picture—to show the successive planes, or broad in the form of a scroll, unrolling to reveal an endless panorama. These are the two forms best known under their Japanese names of kakemono and makimono.

9th PARAGRAPH SUMMARY:

10th PARAGRAPH SUMMARY:

11th PARAGRAPH SUMMARY:

UNIT 3 - MEDIUM

But the Chinese painter must attenuate the forms where they are parallel, give a natural appearance to their position on different levels and consider the degree of their reduction demanded by the various planes. Even he must compromise with binocular vision and arrive at a perspective de sentiment which, like our own, while scientifically false, is artistically true. To this linear perspective is added moreover an atmospheric perspective.

Having elected from a very early time to paint in monochrome, Chinese painters were led by the nature of this medium to seek to express atmospheric perspective by means of tone values and harmony of shading instead of by color. Thus they were familiar with chiaroscuro before the European painters. Wang Wei established the principles of atmospheric perspective in the eighth century. He explains how tints are graded, how the increasing thickness of layers of air deprives distant objects of their true coloring, substituting a bluish tinge, and how forms become indistinct in proportion as their distance from the observer increases. His testimony in this respect is similar to that of Leonardo da Vinci in his "Treatise on Painting."

The Chinese divide the subjects of painting into four principal classes, as follows: Landscape, Man and Objects, Flowers and Birds, Plants and Insects. Nowhere do we see a predominant place assigned to the drawing or painting of the human figure. This alone is sufficient to mark the wide difference between Chinese and European painting.

The exact name for Landscape is translated by the words mountain and water picture. They recall the ancient conception of Creation on which the Oriental system of the world is founded. The mountain exemplifies the teeming life of the earth. It is threaded by veins wherein waters continuously flow. Cascades, brooks and torrents are the outward evidence of this inner travail. By its own superabundance of life, it brings forth clouds and arrays itself in mists, thus being a manifestation of the two principles which rule the life of the universe. (Petrucci)

12th PARAGRAPH SUMMARY:

13th PARAGRAPH SUMMARY:

14th PARAGRAPH SUMMARY:

15th PARAGRAPH SUMMARY:

VISUAL MEMORY EXERCISE - MEDIUM LEVEL A

DIRECTIONS: This exercise is designed to improve your visual memory. Four grids of nine objects are presented. Look at each grid for one minute. Memorize as best you can the design and placement of each symbol. When you have all objects memorized for one grid, turn to the next page and draw the nine objects in the corresponding grid FROM MEMORY. If you need to look back at the grid, then document how many times you looked at the objects.

GRID 1

€	≥	‡
Ω	O	∏
∫	5	›

GRID 2

⅞	≈	∂
≤	◇	√
3	Þ	$

GRID 3

¢	μ	¼
⌂	<	⊣
π	Γ	C

GRID 4

ē	›	•
4	+	≡
/	°	ε

VISUAL MEMORY *CONTINUED*

GRID 1   looked back _____ time(s)

GRID 2   looked back _____ time(s)

GRID 3   looked back _____ time(s)

GRID 4   looked back _____ time(s)

SENTENCE RECALL EXERCISE - MEDIUM LEVEL A

DIRECTIONS: This exercise is designed to improve your memory. Read each sentence carefully, remembering as much as possible. In the space immediately below, write the sentence FROM MEMORY, word-for-word. Resist the temptation to look back at the sentence after you have read it. Try to read each sentence only once.

Sentence #1:
Form, in the narrow sense, is nothing but the separating line between surfaces of colour. (Kandinsky)

Recall #1:

Sentence #2:
Solidity and power, rather than beauty and grace, are what they aim at; and in this, Michael Angelo was a true Tuscan. (Allen)

Recall #2:

Sentence #3:
It is certainly not too much to say that in the sculpture of the present day the sense of individual character is conveyed mainly by convention. (Brownell)

Recall #3:

Sentence #4:
They so interblend that, the dividing line cannot be detected by the untrained eye of the exact scientist. (Wagner)

Recall #4:

UNIT 3 - MEDIUM

Sentence #5:
Business enterprise and politics, the all-absorbing interests of the majority of mankind, work in an endless circle. (Robertson)

Recall #5:

Sentence #6:
This is the first step of the upward journey, or evolution, from the inert mineralstate. (Wagner)

Recall #6:

Sentence #7:
Reds and purples became dominant notes amidst rich greens which set them off and enhanced their brilliancy. (Petrucci)

Recall #7:

Sentence #8:
In addition to this, the idea of eternity precludes from its very nature the idea of possible change. (Ackland)

Recall #8:

Sentence #9:
A great silence, like an impenetrable wall, shrouds its life from our understanding. (Kandinsky)

Recall #9:

SENTENCE RECALL *CONTINUED*

Sentence #10:
But in the neighborhood of the Thames, the high road to the great commercial port of London, the mementoes of their presence are particularly frequent. (Allen)

Recall #10:

_____

Sentence #11:
Detail that is neglected really acquires a greater prominence than detail that is carried too far, because it is sensuously disagreeable. (Brownell)

Recall #11:

_____

Sentence #12:
Investigations made on school children by the Binet test indicate Ward's estimate is conservative. (Gillette)

Recall #12:

_____

Sentence #13:
These compounds are taken into the body as food, and after undergoing certain modifications and arrangements are finally decomposed. (Ackland)

Recall #13:

_____

Sentence #14:
Literature, music and art are the first and most sensitive spheres in which this spiritual revolution makes itself felt. (Kandinsky)

Recall #14:

UNIT 4
MEDIUM LEVEL B

READING SPEED EXERCISE - MEDIUM LEVEL B

DIRECTIONS: This exercise is designed to measure your relative reading speed. Read the passage at an accelerated rate while monitoring your time. Be sure to comprehend as much material as possible. At the end of the passage, record the number of minutes and seconds you spent reading. Refer to the Appendix for your calculated reading rate.

So thoroughly have modern men fastened their attention upon the problems of the immediate present, that one feels driven to justify oneself in taking up an historical investigation of any subject presented in a popular manner. And yet it takes little argument to show that what we shall be depends in large measure on what we are; and that what we are rests back on what we have been. In anything we try to think or feel or do, we quickly reach a limit; and this limit is determined by the original quality of our nervous system plus the training it has received. For here is the curious fact about this instrument of thought and feeling which at once takes it away from comparison with mechanical instruments. Whatever it does, becomes a part of itself, and then helps to determine what it will do the next time and how it will do it. With the making easy of mental operations through repetition, and with the formation of associations based on our choices, it may be truly said that we become whatever we habitually think and feel and do.

Every choice we make is thus literally built into our character and becomes a part of ourselves. After that, the old choice will help determine the new, and we shall find ourselves being directed by all of our past choices, and even by the choices of our ancestors. Since, then, all our earlier selves are continued in us and make us what we are, we are simply studying ourselves when we study the history of our ancestors. If we would go forward, we must first look backward; for we must rise on stepping-stones of our dead selves.

But history is not merely the story of the past. To relate that, would take as long as it took to live it, and the result would be but weariness of spirit. History, to be significant, must select the events with which it will deal; it must arrange these in series that are in accord with the constitution of things; and then it must use the generalizations it reaches to interpret the present, and even to forecast the future. It is obvious that this interprctation will depend on the point of view held by the interpreter.

Hence we must ask in what fundamental beliefs this presentation rests. These are, first, that life tends to move along certain lines that constitute the law of human nature. Just as the infant tends first to wriggle, then creep, then walk, then run and dance, so human nature tends to move upward from savagery through primitive settled life to the complex forms of larger settled units. In this progress, material or economic forces play a large part; but ideas, originally born out of circumstances, but sometimes borrowed from other people, sometimes degenerate remnants of past utilities, also play a large part. The progress we finally make is thus directed by this human tendency, by material circumstances, and by ideas. Sometimes it keeps pretty closely to what seems to us to be upward human growth; sometimes it stagnates; sometimes it gives us perverted products; and sometimes it destroys itself.

Thus it becomes necessary to trace the past experiences of woman that we may see with what heritage she faces the future. She is all that she has felt and thought and done. She started with at least half of the destiny of the race in her keeping. Handicapped in size and agility, and periodically weighted down by the burdens of maternity, she still possessed charms and was mistress of pleasures which made her, for savage man, the dearest possession next to food; and for civilized man, the companion, joy and inspiration of his days.

Of woman's position in early savage times we know only what we can learn from fragmentary

UNIT 4 - MEDIUM

prehistoric remains, from the structure of early languages, from records of travelers and students among savages of more recent times; or what can be inferred from human nature in general. Most of this data is difficult to interpret, but it is probable that woman's position was not much worse than man's. It is a bad beast that fouls its own food or its own nest; and the female had always the protection of the male's desire. If she could not entirely control her body, she could still control her own expressions of affection and desire; and, without these, mere possession lost much of its charm.

As keeper of the cave, cultivator of the soil, and guardian of the child, woman, rather than her more foot-loose mate, probably became the center of the earliest civilization. The jealousy of men formed tribal rules for her protection; and to these, religion early gave its powerful sanctions. Thus there came a day when the woman took her mate home to her tribe and gave her children her own name. Even if the matriarchal period was not so important as has sometimes been assumed, woman certainly had large influence over tribal affairs in early savage life.

With the increase in population, and the consequent disappearance of game, man was forced to turn his attention to the crude agriculture which woman had begun to develop. The superior qualities which he had acquired in war and the chase, enabled him slowly to improve on these beginnings and to shape a body of custom which made settled society possible. With man's leadership in the family the patriarchal form of government developed, and man's power over woman was sanctioned by custom and law. The woman was stolen, or bought; and while sexual attraction did not play the continuous part which it plays in developed society, it must have done much to protect women from abuse and neglect, at least during the years of girlhood and child-bearing. It is at this point that our historical records begin.

In the pages of Homer, or of the Old Testament, in Tacitus's "Germania," or in the writings of Livy, we find woman's position well defined. True, she stands second to the man, but she is his assistant, not his slave. She must be courted, and while marriage presents are exchanged, she is not bought. In times of emergency, she steps to the front and legislates, judges, or fights. It is possible in the pages of the Old Testament to find women doing everything which men can do. Even where the power is not nominally in her own hands, she often, as in the cases of Penelope or Esther, rules by indirection. Her body and her offspring are protected; and the Hebrew woman of the Proverbs shows us a singularly free and secure industrial position. Such was the condition in primitive Judea, in early Greece, in republican Rome, or among the Germans who invaded southern Europe in the third and fourth centuries of our era.

Man's jealousy of his woman as a source of pleasure and honor to himself, and to his family, must have always acted to limit woman's freedom, even while it gave her protection and a secure position in society. With the development of settled government in city states, like Athens or early Rome, the necessity for defining citizenship made the family increasingly a political institution. A man's offspring through slave women, concubines, or "strangers" lived outside the citizen group, and so were negligible; but the citizen woman's children were citizens, and so she became a jealously guarded political institution. The established family became the test of civic, military, and property rights. The regulations limiting the freedom of girls and women were jealously enforced, since mismatches might open the treasures of citizenship to any low born or foreign adventurer.

In the ancient Orient, in Greece, Rome, and in later Europe, these stages have been repeated again and again. Woman is first a slave, stolen or bought, protected by sexual interest to which is later added social custom and religious sanction. Early civilization centers around the woman, so that she becomes in some degree the center of the home-staying group. In primitive civilization man takes over woman's most important activities; but she gains a fixed position, protected, though still further enslaved, by political necessities.

But with the increase of wealth, whether in terms of money, slaves, or trade, woman found herself subject to a fourth form of enslavement more subtly dangerous than brute force, lust, or political and religious institutionalism. This was the desire of man to protect her and make her happy because he loved her. He put golden chains about her neck and bracelets on her arms, clothed her in silks and satins, fed her with dainty fare, gave her a retinue of attendants to spare her fatigue, and put her in the safest rear rooms of the habitation. But it is foolish to talk of conscious enslavement in this connection. Rich men and luxurious civilizations have always enslaved women in the same way that rich, fond, and foolish mothers have enslaved their children, by robbing them of opportunity, by taking away that needful work and that vital experience of real life which alone can develop the powers of the soul.

Thus in the Periclean age in Greece, in the Eastern Kingdoms established by Alexander, in Imperial Rome, in the later Italian Renaissance, in France under Louis XIV and Louis XV, in England under the Stuart kings, and in many centers of our own contemporary world, women have given up their legitimate heritage of work and independent thought for trinkets, silks, and servants, and have quickly degenerated, like the children of rich and foolish mothers, into luxury-loving parasites and playthings.

To maintain this luxurious setting for their mistresses, whether wives or irregular concubines, men of the Occident have generally been driven to ever fiercer struggle with their fellows. Thus a Pericles, at the zenith of his powers, facing difficulties which strained and developed all his forces, had for his legitimate wife a woman, bound hand and foot by conventions and immured in her house in Athens. But a man is only half a complete human being, and the other half cannot be furnished by a weak and ignorant kept-woman, no matter how legal the bond. Hence the forces always driving men to completeness and unity drove Pericles away from his house and his legitimate children and his mere wife to find the completion of his life.

In these cases, as elsewhere, demand creates supply, and there were to be found everywhere in Athens able and cultivated foreign women, many of

whom had come over from the mainland of Asia Minor; and one of these, Aspasia, became the mistress of Pericles and bore him children. She was no adventuress of the street, but an educated and brilliant woman, in whose home you might have met not only Pericles, but also Socrates, Phidias, Anaxagoras, Sophocles and Euripides.

This is the stage that always follows the period of the luxury-loving wife. It was so in Imperial Rome, in later Carthage, in Venice, and in eighteenth-century France. But the normal human unit is the man and woman who love each other, not these combinations of illegality, law, lust, love and dishonor. Such a triangle of two women and a man rests its base in shame, and its lines are lies, and its value is destruction. So virile republican Rome swept over decadent Greece and made it into the Roman province of Achaia; later the chaste Germans swarmed over the decadent Roman Empire and then slowly rebuilt modern Europe; the ascetic Puritans destroyed the Stuarts; while the French Revolution was the deluge that swept away Louis XVI and put the virtuous, if commonplace, bourgeoisie in power.

So far we have dealt with the position of women as though it depended alone on human hungers, passions and environment; but while these are the driving forces of life, they are very subject to the repressing and diverting power of ideas, working in an environment of economic conditions. These ideas may themselves date back to earlier passions and economic conditions, but they often survive the time which created them, and then they enter into life and conduct as seemingly independent forces. These ideas played a large part, even in the ancient world.

The Protestant Revolution went far to restore the special functions of women to respect. Belief in her individual soul, and in its need of salvation through individual choice, was supplemented by the belief that this choice must be guided by her individual judgment. Celibacy ceased to be a sign of righteousness; and the best men and women married. But beliefs cannot be directly destroyed by revolution; they can only be disturbed and modified. The

UNIT 4 - MEDIUM

teachings of Paul, Augustine, Tertullian and St. Jerome were still authoritative, and Calvin and Knox reaffirmed many of them. The family was still subordinate to the Church; and marriage still remained a sacrament, with theological significances, rather than the simple union of a man and woman who loved each other. The choice of a mate once made was final, because theological, and it could be broken only with infinite pain and disgrace.

The great political upheaval, which we call the French Revolution, carried in its fundamental teachings freedom and opportunity for men and for women; but like the corresponding revolution in religion, it required time to make adjustments, and so we have been content to live for more than a hundred years in the midst of verbal affirmations which we denied in all our institutional life.

In America, conditions have always been favorable for women to work out their freedom. Among the immigrants who came to our shores before 1840 there were, of course, a few traders, adventurers and servants who hoped to improve their financial conditions; but the leaders, and most of the rank and file, came that they might be free to think their own thoughts and live their own lives. If this selection of colonists, through religious and political persecution, sometimes gave us bigots with one idea, it also gave us people who knew that ideas can change. Along with Cotton Mather it gave us Anne Hutchinson, Roger Williams and William Penn.

Most of these who came in the early days belonged to extreme dissenting sects believing in salvation through individual choice, based on personal judgments. Preaching was exalted at the expense of ritual; and by substituting new thinking for old habits in religion, the American settlers made it less difficult for other adjustments to be made, even in such a conservative matter as woman's position. It is through no accident that Methodists, Friends, Unitarians and the Salvation Army have been much more sympathetic to woman's progress than have the older ritualistic faiths. And these theological ideas had to be worked out under the material conditions of the New World, which were also favorable to the emancipation of women. Facing primitive conditions in the forest, it became a habit to do new things in new ways. Woman's work and judgment were indispensable; and these picked women showed themselves capable in every direction. They did every kind of work; and when it came to enduring privation or even to starving, they set an example for men.

But while every new movement in ideas always carries with it other radical ideas, the practical difficulties of mental, social and legal adjustment always prevent the full and harmonious development of all that is involved in any new point of view. In the American colonies the need for new adjustments in religion, government and practical living made it inevitable that any very important change in woman's position should linger. In fact, the student of colonial records finds many traces of ultra conservatism in the treatment of women, though the forces had been liberated which must inevitably open the way for her through the New World of America into a new world of the spirit.

And before the quickening influence of the new life had time to become commonplace, the struggle with England began. The Revolutionary period was a time of intense political education for every one. War and sacrifice glorified the new ideas; and even the children and women could not escape their influence. Why then did not the American Revolution pass on to full freedom and opportunity for women? For the same reason that it did not forever abolish slavery in America. The vested interests involved were so many, and the changes so momentous and difficult, that only the most imperative needs could receive attention. (Barnes)

TOTAL TIME:

....

PARAGRAPH SUMMARY EXERCISE - MEDIUM LEVEL B

DIRECTIONS: This exercise is designed to improve your ability to summarize main concepts. Read the material at a comfortable rate. After you have read EACH paragraph, write a brief summary of its key points in the right column. Include main ideas, conclusions, and opinions. Do not include details.

The first name of which the history of anatomy keeps record is that of Alcmaeon, a contemporary of Pythagoras (6th century B.C.). His interests appear to have been rather physiological than anatomical. He traced the chief nerves of sense to the brain, which he considered to be the seat of the soul, and he made some good guesses at the mechanism of the organs of special sense. He showed that, contrary to the received opinion, the seminal fluid did not originate in the spinal cord. Two comparisons are recorded of his, one that puberty is the equivalent of the flowering time in plants, the other that milk is the equivalent of white of egg. Both show his bias towards looking at the functional side of living things. The latter comparison reappears in Aristotle.

A century later Diogenes of Apollonia gave a description of the venous system. He too placed the seat of sensation in the brain. He assumed a vital air in all living things, being in this influenced by Anaximenes whose primitive matter was infinite air. In following out this thought he tried to prove that both fishes and oysters have the power of breathing.

A more strictly morphological note is struck by a curious saying of Empedocles (4th century B.C.), that "hair and foliage and the thick plumage of birds are one." In the collected writings of Hippocrates and his school, the Corpus Hippocraticum, of which no part is later than the end of the 5th century, there are recorded many anatomical facts. The author of the treatise "On the Muscles" knew, for instance, that the spinal marrow is different from ordinary marrow and has membranes continuous with those of the brain. Embryos of seven days have all the parts of the body plainly visible. Work on comparative embryology is contained in the treatise "On the Development of the Child."

1st PARAGRAPH SUMMARY:

2nd PARAGRAPH SUMMARY:

3rd PARAGRAPH SUMMARY:

UNIT 4 - MEDIUM

The author of the treatise "On the Joints," which Littré calls "the great surgical monument of antiquity," is to be credited with the first systematic attempt at comparative anatomy, for he compared the human skeleton with that of other Vertebrates.

Aristotle (384-322 B.C.) may fairly be said to be the founder of comparative anatomy, not because he was specially interested in problems of "pure morphology," but because he described the structure of many animals and classified them in a scientific way. We shall discuss here the morphological ideas which occur in his writings upon animals—in the Historia Animalium, the De Partibus Animalium, and the De Generatione Animalium.

The Historia Animalium is a most comprehensive work, in some ways the finest text-book of Zoology ever written. Certainly few modern text-books take such a broad and sane view of living creatures. Aristotle never forgets that form and structure are but one of the many properties of living things; he takes quite as much interest in their behaviour, their ecology, distribution, comparative physiology. He takes a special interest in the comparative physiology of reproduction. The Historia Animalium contains a description of the form and structure of man and of as many animals as Aristotle was acquainted with—and he was acquainted with an astonishingly large number. The later De Partibus Animalium is a treatise on the causes of the form and structure of animals. Owing to the importance which Aristotle ascribed to the final cause this work became really a treatise on the functions of the parts, a discussion of the problems of the relation of form to function, and the adaptation of structure.

Aristotle was quite well aware that each of the big groups of animals was built upon one plan of structure, which showed endless variations "in excess and defect" in the different members of the group. But he did not realize that this fact of community of plan constituted a problem in itself. His interest was turned towards the functional side of living things, form was for him a secondary result of function.

4th PARAGRAPH SUMMARY:

5th PARAGRAPH SUMMARY:

6th PARAGRAPH SUMMARY:

7th PARAGRAPH SUMMARY:

Yet he was not unaware of facts of form for which he could not quite find a place in his theory of organic form, facts of form which were not, at first sight at least, facts of function. Thus he was aware of certain facts of "correlation," which could not be explained off-hand as due to correlation of the functions of the parts. He knew, for instance, that all animals without front teeth in the upper jaw have cotyledons, while most that have front teeth on both jaws and no horns have no cotyledons.

Speaking generally, however, we find in Aristotle no purely morphological concepts. What then does morphology owe to Aristotle? It owes to him, first, a great mass of facts about the structure of animals; second, the first scientific classification of animals; third, a clear enunciation of the fact of community of plan within each of the big groups; fourth, an attempt to explain certain instances of the correlation of parts; fifth, a pregnant distinction between homogeneous and heterogeneous parts; sixth, a generalization on the succession of forms in development; and seventh, the first enunciation of the idea of the Échelle des êtres.

What surprises the modern reader of the Historia Animalium perhaps more than anything else is the extent and variety of Aristotle's knowledge of animals. He describes more than 500 kinds. Not only does he know the ordinary beasts, birds, and fishes with which everyone is acquainted, but he knows a great deal about cuttlefish, snails and oysters, about crabs, crawfish (Palinurus), lobsters, shrimps, and hermit crabs, about sea-urchins and starfish, sea-anemones and sponges, about ascidians (which seem to have puzzled him not a little!). He has noticed even fish-lice and intestinal worms, both flat and round. Of the smaller land animals, he knows a great many insects and their larva.

The extent of his anatomical knowledge is equally surprising, and much of it is clearly the result of personal observation. No one can read his account of the internal anatomy of the chameleon, or his description of the structure of cuttlefish, or that touch in the description of the hermit crab—"Two large eyes ... not ... turned on one side like those of crabs, but straight forward"—without being convinced that Aristotle is

8th PARAGRAPH SUMMARY:

9th PARAGRAPH SUMMARY:

10th PARAGRAPH SUMMARY:

11th PARAGRAPH SUMMARY:

UNIT 4 - MEDIUM

speaking of what he has seen. Naturally he could not make much of the anatomy of small insects and snails, and, to tell the truth, he does not seem to have cared greatly about the minutia of structure. He was too much of a Greek and an aristocrat to care about laborious detail.

Not only did he lay a foundation for comparative anatomy, but he made a real start with comparative embryology. Medical men before him had known many facts about human development; Aristotle seems to have been the first to study in any detail the development of the chick. He describes this as it appears to the naked eye, the position of the embryo on the yolk, the palpitating spot at the third day, the formation of the body and of the large sightless eyes, the veins on the yolk, the embryonic membranes, of which he distinguished two. Aristotle had various systems of classifying animals. They could be classified, he thought, according to their structure, their manner of reproduction, their manner of life, their mode of locomotion, their food, and so on. Thus you might, in addition to structural classifications, divide animals into gregarious, solitary and social, or land animals into troglodytes, surface-dwellers, and burrowers.

He knew that dichotomous classifications were of little use for animals and he explicitly and in so many words accepted the principle of all "natural" classification, that affinities must be judged by comparing not one but the sum total of characters. As everyone knows, he was the first to distinguish the big groups of animals, many of which were already distinguished roughly by the common usages of speech. Among his Sanguinea he did little more than define with greater exactitude the limits of the groups established by the popular classification. Among the "exsanguinous" animals, however, corresponding to our Invertebrates, he established a much more definite classification than the popular, which is apt to call them indiscriminately "shellfish," "insects," or "creeping things." (Russell)

12th PARAGRAPH SUMMARY:

13th PARAGRAPH SUMMARY:

VISUAL MEMORY EXERCISE - MEDIUM LEVEL B

DIRECTIONS: This exercise is designed to improve your visual memory. Four grids of nine objects are presented. Look at each grid for one minute. Memorize as best you can the design and placement of each symbol. When you have all objects memorized for one grid, turn to the next page and draw the nine objects in the corresponding grid FROM MEMORY. If you need to look back at the grid, then document how many times you looked at the objects.

GRID 1

Φ	∫	+
)(	θ	Ø
«	≈	☼

GRID 2

Ю	¢	!!
5	Ψ	☺
•	≤	¼

GRID 3

↑	∏	×
⊩	□	ε
≥	○	▪

GRID 4

%	√	μ
∧	∩	⌂
»	4	Γ

VISUAL MEMORY *CONTINUED*

GRID 1   looked back _____ time(s)

GRID 2   looked back _____ time(s)

GRID 3   looked back _____ time(s)

GRID 4   looked back _____ time(s)

SENTENCE RECALL EXERCISE - MEDIUM LEVEL B

DIRECTIONS: This exercise is designed to improve your memory. Read each sentence carefully, remembering as much as possible. In the space immediately below, write the sentence FROM MEMORY, word-for-word. Resist the temptation to look back at the sentence after you have read it. Try to read each sentence only once.

Sentence #1:

The harbour at Gades was a very fine one; and had several Tor, or Towers to direct shipping. (Bryant)

Recall #1:

Sentence #2:

Müller was, of course, very ready to accept Rathke's opinions on this subject, for he considered that they supported his own theory of the vertebral nature of the skull. (Russell)

Recall #2:

Sentence #3:

But the accepted scientific interpretation of the "forward tone" precept is held by vocal theorists to render the subject perfectly clear. (Taylor)

Recall #3:

Sentence #4:

The carbonate of soda is pulverized and then kneaded to a paste with water; the substance to be examined, in fine powder, is also mixed with it. (System)

Recall #4:

UNIT 4 - MEDIUM

Sentence #5:
Ships now went past the North Foreland to London, and knew it only as a dangerous point, not without a sinister reputation for wrecking. (Allen)

Recall #5:

Sentence #6:
It had, in fact, acquired an independent existence; but it was still in a chaotic state. (Ackland)

Recall #6:

Sentence #7:
The same is true of the elephant near by, in which it seems as if he had designedly attacked the difficult problem of rendering embodied awkwardness decorative. (Brownell)

Recall #7:

Sentence #8:
When we consider that von Baer worked chiefly with a simple microscope and dissecting needles, the minuteness and accuracy of his observations are astonishing. (Russell)

Recall #8:

Sentence #9:
During the hundred years of the Mercian Supremacy, coincident, roughly speaking, with the eighth century, we hear little of Sussex. (Allen)

Recall #9:

SENTENCE RECALL *CONTINUED*

Sentence #10:
Expose this bead to the oxidation flame until it ceases to change, then allow it to cool, when it should be exposed to the reduction flame. (System)

Recall #10:

Sentence #11:
In respect to the legends about dragons, I am persuaded that the antients sometimes did wilfully misrepresent things, in order to increase the wonder. (Bryant)

Recall #11:

Sentence #12:
It is the still, small voice of the awakened soul, that purges the conscience from suffering, and the spiritual body from earthy dross. (Wagner)

Recall #12:

Sentence #13:
To perform this test the singer is instructed to practise the exercises for breath-control while holding a lighted candle with the flame an inch or two in front of the lips. (Taylor)

Recall #13:

Sentence #14:
Old age is simply the petrifaction of the body through lime, and the incorporating of erroneous thoughts into the organism. (Wagner)

Recall #14:

UNIT 5
MEDIUM LEVEL C

READING SPEED EXERCISE - MEDIUM LEVEL C

DIRECTIONS: This exercise is designed to measure your relative reading speed. Read the passage at an accelerated rate while monitoring your time. Be sure to comprehend as much material as possible. At the end of the passage, record the number of minutes and seconds you spent reading. Refer to the Appendix for your calculated reading rate.

Unfortunately, we entirely lack the means of carrying back the history of human speech to its first beginnings. In the latter half of the last century, whilst the ferment of Darwinism was freshly seething, all sorts of speculations were rife concerning the origin of language. One school sought the source of the earliest words in imitative sounds of the type of bow-wow; another in interjectional expressions of the type of tut-tut. Or, again, as was natural in Europe, where, with the exception of Basque in a corner of the west, and of certain Asiatic languages, Turkish, Hungarian and Finnish, on the eastern border, all spoken tongues present certain obvious affinities, the comparative philologist undertook to construct sundry great families of speech; and it was hoped that sooner or later, by working back to some linguistic parting of the ways, the central problem would be solved of the dispersal of the world's races.

These painted bubbles have burst. The further examination of the forms of speech current amongst peoples of rude culture has not revealed a conspicuous wealth either of imitative or of interjectional sounds. On the other hand, the comparative study of the European, or, as they must be termed in virtue of the branch stretching through Persia into India, the Indo-European stock of languages, carries us back three or four thousand years at most—a mere nothing in terms of anthropological time. Moreover, a more extended search through the world, which in many of its less cultured parts furnishes no literary remains that may serve to illustrate linguistic evolution, shows endless diversity of tongues in place of the hoped-for system of a few families; so that half a hundred apparently independent types must be distinguished in North America alone. For the rest, it has become increasingly clear that race and language need not go together at all. What philologist, for instance, could ever discover, if

he had no history to help him, but must rely wholly on the examination of modern French, that the bulk of the population of France is connected by way of blood with ancient Gauls who spoke Celtic, until the Roman conquest caused them to adopt a vulgar form of Latin in its place. The Celtic tongue, in its turn, had, doubtless not so very long before, ousted some earlier type of language, perhaps one allied to the still surviving Basque; though it is not in the least necessary, therefore, to suppose that the Celtic-speaking invaders wiped out the previous inhabitants of the land to a corresponding extent. Races, in short, mix readily; languages, except in very special circumstances, hardly at all.

Disappointed in its hope of presiding over the reconstruction of the distant past of man, the study of language has in recent years tended somewhat to renounce the historical—that is to say, anthropological—method altogether. The alternative is a purely formal treatment of the subject. Thus, whereas vocabularies seem hopelessly divergent in their special contents, the general apparatus of vocal expression is broadly the same everywhere. That all men alike communicate by talking, other symbols and codes into which thoughts can be translated, such as gestures, the various kinds of writing, drum-taps, smoke signals, and so on, being in the main but secondary and derivative, is a fact of which the very universality may easily blind us to its profound significance. Meanwhile, the science of phonetics—having lost that "guild conceit of itself" which once led it to discuss at large whether the art of talking evolved at a single geographical centre, or at many centers owing to similar capacities of body and mind—contents itself now-a-days for the most part with conducting an analytic survey of the modes of vocal expression as correlated with the observed tendencies of the human speech-organs. And what is true of phonetics in particular is hardly less true of comparative philology as a whole. Its present procedure is in the main analytic or formal. Thus its fundamental distinction between isolating, agglutinative and inflectional languages is arrived at simply by contrasting the different ways in which words are affected by being put together into a sentence. No attempt is made to show that one type of arrangement normally precedes another in time, or that it is in any way more rudimentary—that is to say, less adapted to the needs of human intercourse. It is not even pretended that a given language is bound to exemplify one, and one alone, of these three types; though the process known as analogy—that is, the regularizing of exceptions by treating the unlike as if it were like—will always be apt to establish one system at the expense of the rest.

If, then, the study of language is to recover its old pre-eminence amongst anthropological studies, it looks as if a new direction must be given to its inquiries. And there is much to be said for any change that would bring about this result. Without constant help from the philologist, anthropology is bound to languish. To thoroughly understand the speech of the people under investigation is the field-worker's master-key; so much so, that the critic's first question in determining the value of an ethnographical work must always be, Could the author talk freely with the natives in their own tongue? But how is the study of particular languages to be pursued successfully, if it lack the stimulus and inspiration which only the search for general principles can impart to any branch of science?

To relieve the hack-work of compiling vocabularies and grammars, there must be present a sense of wider issues involved, and such issues as may directly interest a student devoted to language for its own sake. The formal method of investigating language, in the meantime, can hardly supply the needed spur. Analysis is all very well so long as its ultimate purpose is to subserve genesis—that is to say, evolutionary history. If, however, it tries to set up on its own account, it is in danger of degenerating into sheer futility. Out of time and history is, in the long run, out of meaning and use. The philologist, then, if he is

to help anthropology, must himself be an anthropologist, with a full appreciation of the importance of the historical method. He must be able to set each language or group of languages that he studies in its historical setting. He must seek to show how it has evolved in relation to the needs of a given time. In short, he must correlate words with thoughts; must treat language as a function of the social life.

For instance, I-cut-bear's-leg-at-the-joint-with-a-flint-now corresponds fairly well with the total impression produced by the particular act; though, even so, I have doubtless selectively reduced the notion to something I can comfortably take in, by leaving out a lot of unnecessary detail—for instance, that I was hungry, in a hurry, doing it for the benefit of others as well as myself, and so on. Well, American languages of the ruder sort, by running a great number of sounds or syllables together, manage to utter a portmanteau word—"holophrase" is the technical name for it—into which is packed away enough suggestions to reproduce the situation in all its detail, the cutting, the fact that I did it, the object, the instrument, the time of the cutting, and who knows what besides. Amusing examples of such portmanteau words meet one in all the text-books.

To go back to the Fuegians, their expression mamihlapinatapai is said to mean "to look at each other hoping that either will offer to do something which both parties desire but are unwilling to do." Now, since exactly the same situation never recurs, but is partly the same and partly different, it is clear that, if the holophrase really tried to hit off in each case the whole outstanding impression that a given situation provoked, then the same combination of sounds would never recur either; one could never open one's mouth without coining a new word. Ridiculous as this notion sounds, it may serve to mark a downward limit from which the rudest types of human speech are not so very far removed. Their well-known tendency to alter their whole character in twenty years or less is due largely to the fluid nature of primitive utterance; it being found hard to detach portions, capable of repeated use in an unchanged form, from the composite vocals wherein they register their highly concrete experiences.

READING SPEED *CONTINUED*

The evolution of language, then, on this view, may be regarded as a movement out of, and away from, the holophrastic in the direction of the analytic. When every piece in your play-box of verbal bricks can be dealt with separately, because it is not joined on in all sorts of ways to the other pieces, then only can you compose new constructions to your liking. Order and emphasis, as is shown by English, and still more conspicuously by Chinese, suffice for sentence-building. Ideally, words should be individual and atomic. Every modification they suffer by internal change of sound, or by having prefixes or suffixes tacked on to them, involves a curtailment of their free use and a sacrifice of distinctness. It is quite easy, of course, to think confusedly, even whilst employing the clearest type of language; though in such a case it is very hard to do so without being quickly brought to book.

On the other hand, it is not feasible to attain to a high degree of clear thinking, when the only method of speech available is one that tends towards wordlessness—that is to say, is relatively deficient in verbal forms that preserve their identity in all contexts. Wordless thinking is not in the strictest sense impossible; but its somewhat restricted opportunities lie almost wholly on the farther side, as it were, of a clean-cut vocabulary. For the very fact that the words are crystallized into permanent shape invests them with a suggestion of interrupted continuity, an overtone of un-utilized significance, that of itself invites the mind to play with the corresponding fringe of meaning attaching to the concepts that the words embody.

It would prove an endless task if I were to try here to illustrate at all extensively the stickiness, as one might almost call it, of primitive modes of speech. Person, number, case, tense, mood and gender—all these, even in the relatively analytical phraseology of the most cultured peoples, are apt to impress themselves on the very body of the words of which they qualify the sense. But the meager list of determinations thus produced in an evolved type of language can yield one no idea of the vast medley of complicated forms that serve the same ends at the lower levels of human experience. Moreover, there are many other shades of secondary and circumstantial meaning which in advanced languages are invariably represented by distinct words, so that when not wanted they can be left out, but in a more primitive tongue are apt to run right through the very grammar of the sentence, thus mixing themselves up inextricably with the really substantial elements in the thought to be conveyed.

For instance, in some American languages, things are either animate or inanimate, and must be distinguished accordingly by accompanying particles. Or, again, they are classed by similar means as rational or irrational; women, by the bye, being designated amongst the Chiquitos by the irrational sign. Reverential particles, again, are used to distinguish what is high or low in the tribal estimation; and we get in this connection such oddities as the Tamil practice of restricting the privilege of having a plural to high-caste names, such as those applied to gods and human beings, as distinguished from the beasts, which are mere casteless "things." Or, once more, my transferable belongings, "my-spear," or "my-canoe," undergo verbal modifications which are denied to non-transferable possessions such as "my-hand"; "my-child," be it observed, falling within the latter class.

Most interesting of all are distinctions of person. These cannot but bite into the forms of speech, since the native mind is taken up mostly with the personal aspect of things, attaining to the conception of a bloodless system of "its" with the greatest difficulty, if at all. Even the third person, which is naturally the most colorless, because excluded from a direct part of the conversational game, undergoes multitudinous leavening in the light of conditions which the primitive mind regards as highly important, whereas we should banish them from our thoughts as so much irrelevant "accident." Thus the Abipones in the first place distinguished "he-present," eneha, and "she-present," anaha, from "he-absent" and "she-absent." But presence by itself gave too little of the speaker's impression. So, if "he" or "she" were sitting, it was necessary to say hiniha and haneha; if they were walking and in sight ehaha and ahaha, but, if walking

UNIT 5 - MEDIUM

and out of sight, ekaha and akaha; if they were lying down, hiriha and haraha, and so on. Moreover, these were all "collective" forms, implying that there were others involved as well. If "he" or "she" were alone in the matter, an entirely different set of words was needed, "he-sitting (alone)" becoming ynitara, and so forth. The modest requirements of Fuegian intercourse have called more than twenty such separate pronouns into being.

Without attempting to go thoroughly into the efforts of primitive speech to curtail its interest in the personnel of its world by gradually acquiring a stock of de-individualized words, let us glance at another aspect of the subject, because it helps to bring out the fundamental fact that language is a social product, a means of intersubjective intercourse developed within a society that hands on to a new generation the verbal experiments that are found to succeed best. Payne shows reason for believing that the collective "we" precedes "I" in the order of linguistic evolution. To begin with, in America and elsewhere, "we" may be inclusive and mean "all-of-us," or selective, meaning "some-of-us-only." Hence, we are told, a missionary must be very careful, and, if he is preaching, must use the inclusive "we" in saying "we have sinned," lest the congregation assume that only the clergy have sinned; whereas, in praying, he must use the selective "we," or God would be included in the list of sinners. Similarly, "I" has a collective form amongst some American languages, and this is ordinarily employed, whereas the corresponding selective form is used only in special cases. Thus if the question be "Who will help?" the Apache will reply "I-amongst-others," "I-for-one"; but, if he were recounting his own personal exploits, he says sheedah, "I-by-myself," to show that they were wholly his own. Here we seem to have group-consciousness holding its own against individual self-consciousness, as being for primitive folk on the whole the more normal attitude of mind.

Another illustration of the sociality engrained in primitive speech is to be found in the terms employed to denote relationship. "My-mother," to the child of nature, is something more than an ordinary mother like yours. Thus, as we have already seen, there may be a special particle applying to blood-relations as non-transferable possessions. Or, again, one Australian language has special duals, "we-two," one to be used between relations generally, another between father and child only. Or an American language supplies one kind of plural suffix for blood-relations, another for the rest of human beings. These linguistic concretions are enough to show how hard it is for primitive thought to disjoin what is joined fast in the world of everyday experience.

No wonder that it is usually found impracticable by the European traveller who lacks an anthropological training to extract from natives any coherent account of their system of relationships; for his questions are apt to take the form of "Can a man marry his deceased wife's sister?" or what not. Such generalities do not enter at all into the highly concrete scheme of viewing the customs of his tribe imposed on the savage alike by his manner of life and by the very forms of his speech. The so-called "genealogical method" initiated by Dr. Rivers, which the scientific explorer now invariably employs, rests mainly on the use of a concrete type of procedure corresponding to the mental habits of the simple folk under investigation. John, whom you address here, can tell you exactly whether he may, or may not, marry Mary Anne over there; also he can point out his mother, and tell you her name, and the names of his brothers and sisters. You work round the whole group—it very possibly contains no more than a few hundred members at most—and interrogate them one and all about their relationships to this and that individual whom you name. In course of time you have a scheme which you can treat in your own analytic way to your heart's content; whilst against your system of reckoning affinity you can set up by way of contrast the native system; which can always be obtained by asking each informant what relationship-terms he would apply to the different members of his pedigree, and, reciprocally, what terms they would each apply to him. (Marett)

TOTAL TIME:
....

PARAGRAPH SUMMARY EXERCISE - MEDIUM LEVEL C

DIRECTIONS: This exercise is designed to improve your ability to summarize main concepts. Read the material at a comfortable rate. After you have read EACH paragraph, write a brief summary of its key points in the right column. Include main ideas, conclusions, and opinions. Do not include details.

I do not know how fully people appreciate the importance of the eye as an agent, or factor, of human cultivation. Judging from the amount of work it is being made to do in our schools and in nearly all our processes of education, we might perhaps be led to feel that its importance is fully appreciated, indeed, that it is being looked upon as the sole factor, or agent. But, on the other hand, this very excessive use, especially in the early school years, leading, as it does in such a large percentage of cases, to serious impairment of vision, almost tells us that its great value is not appreciated. If it were, should we be likely to abuse it as we do in these early years and thus render it incapable of performing its larger, fuller use later on? The attitude seems rather to be that its conservation is not thought to be necessary. That, however, springs from ignorance rather than from studied disregard.

But let us look for a moment at the processes of education and note where the eye comes in. If there is anything upon which leading educators are now practically agreed, or upon which they tend to agree, it is that education as a process is a matter of development rather than the learning of knowledge facts. Now, that development is analogous to the growth and development of the plant, that is, it is brought about through nourishment. In the plant this nourishment is taken in through the roots, becomes absorbed and assimilated and thus ministers to growth and development. In the child, looking at it from the physical point of view and having in mind psychical, not physical, nourishment, the sense organs serve this purpose.

Did you ever stop to think that the sense organs form the only connecting link between the great outside world, which serves as raw material for the nourishment, and the inner life of the child, the

1st PARAGRAPH SUMMARY:

2nd PARAGRAPH SUMMARY:

3rd PARAGRAPH SUMMARY:

UNIT 5 - MEDIUM

development of which we are seeking? Did you ever stop to think that these sense organs, the eye, the ear, the nose, the tongue, and the surface of the body as the organ of touch, form the only possible avenue of approach to that inner life? Cut off, or close up, these avenues and no development of this inner life would be possible in the slightest degree. Thus considered, these same sense organs, simple as they seem to be, leap into importance that almost staggers one's thought. The most priceless possession of any child, I often say to my classes in education, is made up of their eyes, their ears, their noses, their tongues, and their finger tips—simply because through them is poured the nourishment that sustains psychic life and ministers to the development of the same.

Of these five sense organs, the eye is, par excellence, the one of value. More psychic nourishment is poured into the laboratory of psychic life through this one channel alone than through all others combined. Indeed, one of our most eminent scientific psychologists after making most careful investigation of the matter, estimates that the eye's contribution is about 74% as against the other 26% that comes through all the other sources. If this relative value of the eye be even approximately correct, how eminently important it is that it be studied with close scientific accuracy, that it be guarded with the utmost and intelligent jealousy, and that it be cared for with the most scrupulous fidelity!

But what is the situation? The Optician and the Oculist have made the most careful, scientific study of the eye. They know it thoroughly, both its possibilities of service and its limitations. And they have told the rest of us all about it. But let us see how intelligent we are in the use of the knowledge they have given us. They tell us that the eye of the child is undeveloped and that in the undeveloped state it should not be much used on small or close work. In other words, the child's eye is far-sighted.

But at the age of six years we place the child in the school room, put a book in its hands, and compel its use, eyes or no eyes, as long as the child remains in any institution of learning. Why, gentlemen, we have gone mad on this book proposition. We act as though we

4th PARAGRAPH SUMMARY:

5th PARAGRAPH SUMMARY:

6th PARAGRAPH SUMMARY:

think that it is only in the book that knowledge can be found. We act as though we think that it is only through the printed page that psychic nourishment can reach the inner life of the child, whereas, as a matter of fact, both the knowledge and the nourishment that are appropriate to the child in all its early years are better obtained through direct contact with the great outside world itself and by direct communication from the lips of the teacher. If this fact were fully appreciated and acted upon, we should, in two very definite ways, conserve this very important organ; for we should use the eyes upon objects at a greater distance thus preventing unnecessary strain, and allow other organs of sense to share with the eye in the work of gathering information and of appropriating mental nourishment.

Please do not misunderstand me. I am not underestimating the place and value of books, nor decrying their use. They are the storehouse of knowledge and the source of inspiration, but not for children. Our young children in school and out of school read too much—are too much tied to the book. Through this prolonged and close use of the eye upon small and nearby objects for which, in its undeveloped condition, it is not fitted, the organ is permanently weakened and rendered incapable of its legitimate use later in life when the book is a necessity. And again, this excessive use of the eye causes an atrophy of the other organs that is really serious.

Nor is this all. The Optician and the Oculist have studied the matter so carefully and know the eye so thoroughly in its various stages of development that they know exactly the size of type that children of various ages should use. And they know, too, the kind of paper that should be used in books for children. And they have told us all about it. But we systematically disregard all this information gained with such painstaking care, and instead of using the large clear type and the unglazed, soft tinted paper recommended, we persist in tolerating the unsatisfactory merely because it is a little cheaper. Penny wise and pound foolish we surely are. What we save now we shall have to pay later on with compound interest besides compelling our children to undergo physical pain and mental handicap.

7th PARAGRAPH SUMMARY:

8th PARAGRAPH SUMMARY:

UNIT 5 - MEDIUM

And yet again. We are told by our scientific friends the relative amounts of window and floor space that the schoolroom should have in order to be adequately lighted! Not one in ten has as much window space as it should have, and a good portion of what has been provided is frequently covered up by shades through the teacher's perverted notion of relative values—seeming to have greater appreciation for certain so-called artistic effects than for eye comfort and safety in work. And then again, these scientific friends of ours have told us that there should be in the schoolroom no cross lights; that the light should not shine upon the blackboards nor into the faces of the children, but that it should come only from the rear and the left and from above.

They have found out, too, and told us, the proper shades of color for the walls—scientific knowledge, all of it, and therefore thoroly reliable. But how systematically do we disregard all this valuable information! In the construction of a new school building there is nothing that should receive more careful and scientific consideration than the matter of lighting, but too often the architect is either entirely ignorant of the entire matter, or else is selfishly interested in so-called architectural effects.

I do not mean that we all disregard all these things, that we have no school houses properly constructed, no school books properly printed, and no teachers intelligent and sensible in their handling of boys and girls. Not at all. During the last twenty years we have made long strides in advance along many of these lines in many places. But the bright spots are still the exception and not the rule. The friends of children and of the race need to keep vigilantly at work. (Ladd)

9th PARAGRAPH SUMMARY:

10th PARAGRAPH SUMMARY:

11th PARAGRAPH SUMMARY:

VISUAL MEMORY EXERCISE - MEDIUM LEVEL C

DIRECTIONS: This exercise is designed to improve your visual memory. Four grids of nine objects are presented. Look at each grid for one minute. Memorize as best you can the design and placement of each symbol. When you have all objects memorized for one grid, turn to the next page and draw the nine objects in the corresponding grid FROM MEMORY. If you need to look back at the grid, then document how many times you looked at the objects.

GRID 1

□	Ŧ	3
Ξ	u3	M
X	Ψ	kt

GRID 2

⅝	one	∟
∫	Œ	Ø
O	51	&

GRID 3

π	Ш	Δ
λ	Ι	1
px	∪	u

GRID 4

σ	8r	Θ
↔	∩	θ
32	☻	K

VISUAL MEMORY *CONTINUED*

GRID 1   looked back _____ time(s)

GRID 2   looked back _____ time(s)

GRID 3   looked back _____ time(s)

GRID 4   looked back _____ time(s)

SENTENCE RECALL EXERCISE - MEDIUM LEVEL C

DIRECTIONS: This exercise is designed to improve your memory. Read each sentence carefully, remembering as much as possible. In the space immediately below, write the sentence FROM MEMORY, word-for-word. Resist the temptation to look back at the sentence after you have read it. Try to read each sentence only once.

Sentence #1:
Education has become a science, and its activities, its processes, are being based upon definite scientific principles. (Ladd)

Recall #1:

Sentence #2:
The Greeks pretended that they had the use of the sphere, and were acquainted with the zodiac and its asterisms very early. (Bryant)

Recall #2:

Sentence #3:
They were accordingly very liberal of their favours, and by these means enticed seafaring persons, who paid dearly for their entertainment. (Bryant)

Recall #3:

Sentence #4:
Let us not forget that he pointed out the essentially psychological moment implied in all processes of individual adaptation. (Russell)

Recall #4:

UNIT 5 - MEDIUM

Sentence #5:
They can make a grain of wheat chemically perfect, but they cannot make the invisible germ by which it will grow, become fruitful, and reproduce itself. (Wagner)

Recall #5:

Sentence #6:
One must generalize easily to make skies effective, and perhaps it is not fanciful to note the frequency of high horizons in his work. (Brownell)

Recall #6:

Sentence #7:
This last was a sacred fountain, denominated from the God of light, who was the patron of verse and science. (Bryant)

Recall #7:

Sentence #8:
The rate of speed of the life of the modern American business and professional man, the rate of speed of the life of the modern American society woman, is something terrific. (Ladd)

Recall #8:

Sentence #9:
The Cockatoo-girls and the Crow-girls abide each on their own side of the river, where they are visited by partners from across the water. (Marett)

Recall #9:

SENTENCE RECALL *CONTINUED*

Sentence #10:
This opening led into the mouth-cavity, and according to Huschke it became the external ear-passage. (Russell)

Recall #10:

_____

Sentence #11:
Hence it is but a step to the formal duel, as found, for instance, amongst the Apaches of North America. (Marett)

Recall #11:

_____

Sentence #12:
At night my eight-legged friends slept always in their own homes or nests under shelter of the rose-leaves. (Allen)

Recall #12:

_____

Sentence #13:
No matter where we turn nor where we look, there is spread out to our view a vast panorama of symbolic forms for us to read. (Wagner)

Recall #13:

_____

Sentence #14:
Only one implied its presence by showing, above a dense cluster of bamboos, the little banner which in China denotes the presence of a "winehouse." (Petrucci)

Recall #14:

UNIT 6
MEDIUM LEVEL D

READING SPEED EXERCISE - MEDIUM LEVEL D

DIRECTIONS: This exercise is designed to measure your relative reading speed. Read the passage at an accelerated rate while monitoring your time. Be sure to comprehend as much material as possible. At the end of the passage, record the number of minutes and seconds you spent reading. Refer to the Appendix for your calculated reading rate.

In the very interesting account which Mrs. Devereux Roy has given of the present condition of Algeria, she says that France "is now about to embark upon a radical change of policy in regard to her African colonies." If it be thought presumptuous for a foreigner who has no local knowledge of Algerian affairs to make certain suggestions as to the direction which those changes might profitably assume, an apology must be found in Mrs. Roy's very true remark that England "can no more afford to be indifferent to the relations of France with her Moslem subjects than she can disregard the trend of our policy in Egypt and India." It is, indeed, manifest that somewhat drastic reforms of a liberal character will have to be undertaken in Algeria.

The French Government have adopted the only policy which is worthy of a civilized nation. They have educated the Algerians, albeit Mrs. Roy tells us that grants for educational purposes have been doled out "with a very sparing hand." They must bear the consequences of the generous policy which they have pursued. They must recognize, as Macaulay said years ago, that it is impossible to impart knowledge without stimulating ambition. Reforms are, therefore, imposed by the necessities of the situation.

These reforms may be classified under three heads, namely, fiscal, judicial, and political. The order in which changes under each head should be undertaken would appear to be a matter of vital importance. If responsible French statesmen make a mistake in this matter—if, to use the language of proverbial philosophy, they put the cart before the horse—they may not improbably lay the seeds of very great trouble for their countrymen in the future. Prince Bismarck once said: "Mistakes committed in statesmanship are not always punished at once, but they always do harm in the end. The logic of history is a more exact and a more exacting accountant than is the strictest national auditing department."

It should never be forgotten that, however much local circumstances may differ, there are certain broad features which always exist wherever the European—be he French, English, German, or of any other nationality—is brought in contact with the Oriental—be he Algerian, Indian, or Egyptian. When the former once steps outside the influence acquired by the power of the sword, and seeks for any common ground of understanding with the subject race, he finds that he is, by the elementary facts of the case, debarred from using all those moral influences which, in more homogeneous countries, bind society together.

These are a common religion, a common language, common traditions, and—save in very rare instances—intermarriage and really intimate social relations. What therefore remains? Practically nothing but the bond of material interest, tempered by as much sympathy as it is possible in the difficult circumstances of the case to bring into play. But on this poor material—for it must be admitted that it is poor material—experience has shown that a wise statesmanship can build a political edifice, not indeed on such assured foundations as prevail in more homogeneous societies, but nevertheless of a character which will give some solid guarantees of stability, and which will, in any case, minimize the risk that the sword, which the European would fain leave in the scabbard, shall be constantly flaunted before the eyes both of the subject and the governing races, the latter of whom, on grounds alike of policy and humanity, deprecate its use save in cases of extreme necessity.

In the long course of our history many mistakes have been made in dealing with subject races, and the

UNIT 6 - MEDIUM

line of conduct pursued at various times has often been very erratic. Nevertheless, it would be true to say that, broadly speaking, British policy has been persistently directed towards an endeavor to strengthen political bonds through the medium of attention to material interests. The recent history of Egypt is a case in point.

No one who was well acquainted with the facts could at any time have thought that it would be possible to create in the minds of the Egyptians a feeling of devotion towards England which might in some degree take the place of patriotism. Neither, in spite of the relatively higher degree of social elasticity possessed by the French, is it at all probable that any such feeling towards France will be created in Algeria. But it was thought that by careful attention to the material interests of the people it might eventually be possible to bring into existence a conservative class who, albeit animated by no great love for their foreign rulers, would be sufficiently contented to prevent their becoming easily the prey either of the Nationalist demagogue, who was sure sooner or later to spring into existence, or that of some barbarous religious fanatic, such as the Mahdi, or, finally, that of some wily politician, such as the Sultan Abdul Hamid who would, for his own purposes, fan the flame of religious and racial hatred.

For many years after the British occupation of Egypt began, the efforts of the British administrators in that country were unceasingly directed towards the attainment of that object. The methods adopted, which it should be observed were in the main carried out before any large sums were spent on education, were the relief of taxation, the abolition of fiscal inequality and of the corvée, the improvement of irrigation, and last, but not least, a variety of measures having for their object the maintenance of a peasant proprietary class. The results which have been attained fully justify the adoption of this policy, which has probably never been fully understood on the Continent of Europe, even if—which is very doubtful—it has been understood in England.

What, in fact, has happened in Egypt? Nationalists have enjoyed an excess of license in a free press. The Sultan has preached pan-Islamism. The usual Oriental intrigue has been rife. British politicians and a section of the British press, being very imperfectly informed as to the situation, have occasionally dealt with Egyptian affairs in a manner which, to say the least, was indiscreet. But all has been of no avail. In spite of some outward appearances to the contrary, the whole Nationalist movement in Egypt has been a mere splutter on the surface. It never extended deep down in the social ranks. More than this. When a very well-intentioned but rather rash attempt was made to advance too rapidly in a liberal direction, the inevitable reaction, which was to have been foreseen, took place. Not merely Europeans but also Egyptians cried out loudly for a halt, and, with the appointment of Lord Kitchener, they got what they wanted.

The case would have been very different if the Nationalist, the religious fanatic, or the scheming politician, in dealing with some controversial point or incident of ephemeral interest, had been able to appeal to a mass of deep-seated discontent due to general causes and to the existence of substantial grievances. In that case the Nationalist movement would have been less artificial. It would have extended not merely to the surface but to the core of society. It would have possessed a real rather than, as has been shown to be the case, a spurious vitality. The recent history of Egypt, therefore, is merely an illustration of the general lesson taught by universal history. That lesson is that the best, and indeed the only, way to combat successfully the proceedings of the demagogue or the agitator is to limit his field of action by the removal of any real grievances which, if still existent, he would be able to use as a lever to awaken the blind wrath of Demos.

How far can principles somewhat analogous to these be applied in Algeria?

In the first place, it is abundantly clear that, from many points of view, the French Government have successfully carried out the policy of ministering to the material wants of the native population. Public works of great utility have been constructed. Means of locomotion have been improved. Modern agricultural methods have been introduced. Famine has been rendered impossible. Mutual benefit societies have been established. The creation of economic

READING SPEED *CONTINUED*

habits has been encouraged. In all these matters the French have certainly nothing to learn from us. Possibly, indeed, we may have something to learn from them.

Nevertheless, when it is asked whether the French Government is likely to reap the political fruits which it might have been hoped would be the result of their efforts, whether they are in a fair way towards creating a conservative spirit which would be adverse to any radical change, and whether, in reliance on that spirit, they are in a position to move boldly forward in the direction of that liberal reform, the demand for which has naturally sprung into existence from their educational policy, it is at once clear that they are heavily weighted by the policy originated some seventy years ago by Marshal Bugeaud, under which the interests of the native population were made subservient to those of the colonists, numbering about three-quarters of a million, of whom, Mrs. Roy tells us, less than one-half are of French origin. It may have been wise and necessary to initiate that policy. It may be wise and necessary to continue it with certain modifications.

But it is obvious that the adoption of Marshal Bugeaud's plan has necessarily led to the creation of substantial grievances, which are important alike from the point of view of sentiment and from that of material interests. It appears now that there is some probability that this policy will be modified in at least one very important respect, namely, by the removal of the fiscal inequality which at present exists between the natives and the colonists. The former are at present heavily taxed; the latter pay relatively very little. It may be suggested that it would be worth the while of the French Government to consider whether this change should not occupy the first place in the program of reform. The present system is obviously indefensible on general grounds, whilst its continuance, until its abolition results from the strong native pressure which will certainly ensue after the adoption of any drastic measure of political reform, would appear to be undesirable. It would probably be wise and statesmanlike not to await this pressure, but to let the concession be the spontaneous act of the French Government and nation rather than give the appearance of its having been wrung reluctantly from France by the insistence of the native population and its representatives.

Next, there is the question of judicial reform. Mrs. Roy tells us that, under what is called the Code de l'Indigénat, "a native can be arrested and imprisoned practically without trial at the will of the administrateur for his district." It would require full local knowledge to treat this question adequately, but it would obviously be desirable that the French Government should go as far as possible in the direction of providing that all judicial matters should be settled by judicial officers who would be independent of the executive and, for the most part, irremovable. Some local friction between the executive and the judicial authorities is probably to be expected. That cannot be helped. It might perhaps be mitigated by a very careful choice of the officials in each case.

In the third place, there is the question of political reform. M. Philippe Millet, who has published an interesting article on this subject in the April number of The Nineteenth Century, is of course quite right in saying that political reform is the "key to every other change." Once give the natives of Algeria effective political strength, and the reforms will be forced upon the Government. But, as has been already stated, it would perhaps be wiser and more statesmanlike that these changes should be conceded spontaneously by the French Government, and that then, after a reasonable interval, the bulk of the political reforms should follow.

A distinction, however, has to be made between the various representative institutions which already exist. The Conseil Supérieur and the Délégations Financières have very extensive powers, including that of rejecting or modifying the Budget. At present these bodies may be said, for all practical purposes, to be merely representative of the colonists. It would certainly appear wise eventually to allow the natives both a larger numerical strength on the Conseil and on the Délégations, and also, by rearranging the franchise, to endeavor to secure a more real representation of native interests. It must, however, be borne in mind that the difficulties of securing any real representation of the best interests in the country will almost certainly be very great, if not altogether insuperable. In all probability the loquacious, semi-educated native, who has in him the makings of an agitator, will, under any system, naturally float to the top, whilst the really representative man will sink to the bottom. It would perhaps, therefore, be as well not to move in too great a hurry in this matter, and, when any move is made, that the advance should be of a very cautious and tentative nature.

The Conseils Généraux, which are provincial and municipal bodies, stand on a very different footing. Here it may be safe to move forward in the path of reform with greater boldness and with less delay. But whatever is done it will probably be found that real progress in the direction of self-government will depend more on the attitude of the French officials who are associated with the Councils than on any system which can be devised on paper. It may be assumed that the French officials in Algeria present the usual characteristics of their class, that is to say, that they are courageous, intelligent, zealous, and thoroughly honest. Also it may probably be assumed that they are somewhat inelastic, somewhat unduly wedded to bureaucratic ideas, and more especially that they are possessed with the very natural idea that the main end and object of their lives is to secure the efficiency of the administration. Now if self-government is to be a success, they will have to modify to some extent their ideas as to the supreme necessity of efficiency. That is to say, they will have to recognize that it is politically wiser to put up with an imperfect reform carried with native consent, rather than to insist on some more perfect measure executed in the teeth of strong—albeit often unreasonable—native opposition.

English experience has shown that this is a very hard lesson for officials to learn. Nevertheless, the task of inculcating general principles of this nature is not altogether impossible. It depends mainly on the impulse which is given from above. To entrust the execution of a policy of reform in Algeria to a man of ultra-bureaucratic tendencies, who is hostile to reform of any kind, would, of course, be to court failure. On the other hand, to select an extreme radical visionary, who will probably not recognize the difference between East and West, would be scarcely less disastrous. What, in fact, is required is a man of somewhat exceptional qualities. He must be strong—that is to say, he must impress the natives with the conviction that, albeit an advocate of liberal ideas, he is firmly resolved to consent to nothing which is likely to be detrimental to the true interests of France.

He must also be sufficiently strong to keep his own officials in hand and to make them conform to his policy, whilst at the same time he must be sufficiently tactful to win their confidence and to prevent their being banded together against him. The latter is a point of very special importance, for in a country like Algeria no government, however powerful, will be able to carry out a really beneficial program of reform if the organized strength of the bureaucracy—backed up, as would probably be the case, by the whole of the European unofficial community—is thrown into bitter and irreconcilable opposition. The task, it may be repeated, is a difficult one. Nevertheless, amongst the many men of very high ability in the French service there must assuredly be some who would be able to undertake it with a fair chance of success. (Baring)

TOTAL TIME:

....

PARAGRAPH SUMMARY EXERCISE - MEDIUM LEVEL D

DIRECTIONS: This exercise is designed to improve your ability to summarize main concepts. Read the material at a comfortable rate. After you have read EACH paragraph, write a brief summary of its key points in the right column. Include main ideas, conclusions, and opinions. Do not include details.

The roving tribes call no general council with other nations; indeed, they are suspicious even of those with whom they have been at peace for many years, so that they seldom act together in a large body. With the exception of the Hidatsa, Mandau, and Arikara, who are stationary and live in a manner together, the neighboring tribes are quite ignorant of one another's government, rarely knowing even the names of the principal chiefs and warriors.

1st PARAGRAPH SUMMARY:

In all these tribes there is no such thing as hereditary rank. If a son of a chief is wanting in bravery, generosity, or other desirable qualities, he is regarded merely as an ordinary individual; at the same time it is true that one qualification for the position of chief consists in having a large number of kindred in the tribe. Should there be two or more candidates, equally capable and socially well connected, the question would be decided on the day of the first removal of the camp, or else in council by the principal men. In the former case, each man would follow the leader whom he liked best, and the smaller body of Indians would soon adhere to the majority.

2nd PARAGRAPH SUMMARY:

Women are never acknowledged as chiefs, nor have they anything to say in the council. A chief would be deposed for any conduct causing general disgust or dissatisfaction, such as incest (marrying within his group) or lack of generosity. Though crime in the abstract would not tend to create dissatisfaction with a chief, yet if he murdered, without sufficient cause, one whose kindred were numerous, a fight between the two bodies of kindred would result and an immediate separation of his former adherents would ensue; but should the murdered person be without friends, there would be no attempt to avenge the crime, and the people would fear the chief only the more. To preserve his popularity a chief must give away all his property,

3rd PARAGRAPH SUMMARY:

UNIT 6 - MEDIUM

and he is consequently always the poorest man in the band; but he takes care to distribute his possessions to his own kindred or to the rich, from whom he might draw in times of need.

The duties of a leading chief are to study the welfare of his people, by whom he is regarded as a father, and whom he addresses as his children. He must determine where the camp should be placed and when it should be moved; when war parties are advisable and of whom they should be composed—a custom radically different from that of the Omaha and Ponka,—and all other matters of like character. Power is tacitly committed to the leading chief, to be held so long as he governs to general satisfaction, subject, however, to the advice of the soldiers. Age, debility, or any other natural defect, or incapacity to act, advise, or command, would lead a chief to resign in favor of a younger man.

When war is deemed necessary, any chief, soldier, or brave warrior has the privilege of raising and leading a war party, provided he can get followers. The powers of a warrior and civil chief may be united in one person, thus differing from the Omaha and Ponka custom. The leading chief may and often does lead the whole band to war; in fact, it devolves on him to lead any general expedition.

The Akitcita, soldiers or guards (policemen), form an important body among the Asiniboin as they do among the other Siouan tribes. These soldiers, who are chosen from the band on account of their bravery, are from 25 to 45 years of age, steady, resolute, and respected; and in them is vested the power of executing the decisions of the council. In a camp of 200 lodges these soldiers would number from 50 to 60 men; their lodge is pitched in the center of the camp and is occupied by some of them all the time, though the whole body is called together only when the chief wishes a public meeting or when their hunting regulations are to be decided. In their lodge all tribal and intertribal business is transacted, and all strangers, both white men and Indians, are domiciled. The young men, women, and children are not allowed to enter the soldiers' lodge during the time that tribal matters are being considered, and, indeed, they are seldom, if ever, seen there. All the choicest parts of meat and the

4th PARAGRAPH SUMMARY:

5th PARAGRAPH SUMMARY:

6th PARAGRAPH SUMMARY:

tongues of animals killed in hunting are reserved for the soldiers' lodge, and are furnished by the young men from time to time. A tax is levied on the camp for the tobacco smoked there, which is no small quantity, and the women are obliged to furnish wood and water daily. This lodge corresponds in some degree to the two sacred lodges of the Hañga.

Judging from the meager information which we possess concerning the Asiniboin kinship system, the latter closely resembles that of the Dakota tribes, descent being in the male line. After the smallpox epidemic of 1838, only 400 thinly populated lodges out of 1,000 remained, relationship was nearly annihilated, property lost, and but few, the very young and very old, were left to mourn the loss. Remnants of bands had to be collected and property acquired, and several years elapsed ere the young people were old enough to marry. The names of the wife's parents are never pronounced by the husband; to do so would excite the ridicule of the whole camp. The husband and the father-in-law never look on each other if they can avoid it, nor do they enter the same lodge. In like manner the wife never addresses her father-in-law.

A plurality of wives is required by a good hunter, since in the labors of the chase women are of great service to their husbands. An Indian with one wife can not amass property, as she is constantly occupied in household labors, and has no time for preparing skins for trading. The first wife and the last are generally the favorites, all others being regarded as servants. The right of divorce lies altogether with the husband; if he has children by his wife, he seldom puts her away. Should they separate, all the larger children—those who require no further care—remain with the father, the smaller ones departing with the mother. When the women have no children they are divorced without scruple.

After one gets acquainted with Indians the very opposite of taciturnity exists. The evenings are devoted to jests and amusing stories and the days to gambling. The soldiers' lodge, when the soldiers are not in session, is a very theater of amusement; all sorts of jokes are made and obscene stories are told, scarcely a

7th PARAGRAPH SUMMARY:

8th PARAGRAPH SUMMARY:

9th PARAGRAPH SUMMARY:

UNIT 6 - MEDIUM

woman in the camp escaping the ribaldry; but when business is in order decorum must prevail.

The personal property of these tribes consists chiefly of horses. Possession of an article of small value is a right seldom disputed, if the article has been honestly obtained; but the possession of horses being almost the principal object in life of an Indian of the plains, the retention of them is a matter of great uncertainty, if he has not the large force necessary to defend them. Rights to property are based on the method of acquirement, as (1) articles found; (2) those made by themselves (the sole and undisputed property of the makers); (3) those stolen from enemies, and (4) those given or bought. Nothing is given except with a view to a gift in return. Property obtained by gambling is held by a very indefinite tenure.

Murder is generally avenged by the kindred of the deceased, as among the Omaha and Ponka. Goods, horses, etc, may be offered to expiate the crime, when the murderer's friends are rich in these things, and sometimes they are accepted; but sooner or later the kindred of the murdered man will try to avenge him. Everything except loss of life or personal chastisement can be compensated among these Indians. Rape is nearly unknown, not that the crime is considered morally wrong, but the punishment would be death, as the price of the woman would be depreciated and the chances of marriage lessened. Besides, it would be an insult to her kindred, as implying contempt of their feelings and their power of protection.

Marriage within the group is regarded as incest and is a serious offense. Marriage among the Hidatsa is usually made formal by the distribution of gifts on the part of the man to the woman's kindred. Afterward presents of equal value are commonly returned by the wife's relations, if they have the means of so doing and are satisfied with the conduct of the husband. (Dorsey)

10th PARAGRAPH SUMMARY:

11th PARAGRAPH SUMMARY:

12th PARAGRAPH SUMMARY:

VISUAL MEMORY EXERCISE - MEDIUM LEVEL D

DIRECTIONS: This exercise is designed to improve your visual memory. Four grids of nine objects are presented. Look at each grid for one minute. Memorize as best you can the design and placement of each symbol. When you have all objects memorized for one grid, turn to the next page and draw the nine objects in the corresponding grid FROM MEMORY. If you need to look back at the grid, then document how many times you looked at the objects.

GRID 1

T	Π	k%
37	O	•
√	◊	Δ

GRID 2

Ш	♀	6
þ	Ξ	2g
Σ	Ø	1

GRID 3

∞	∂	‡
Γ	e9	kr
≥	⊥	□

GRID 4

☼	◊	≠m
⊤	⊤⊤	≈
u5	2.6	!!

VISUAL MEMORY *CONTINUED*

GRID 1   looked back _____ time(s)

GRID 2   looked back _____ time(s)

GRID 3   looked back _____ time(s)

GRID 4   looked back _____ time(s)

SENTENCE RECALL EXERCISE - MEDIUM LEVEL D

DIRECTIONS: This exercise is designed to improve your memory. Read each sentence carefully, remembering as much as possible. In the space immediately below, write the sentence FROM MEMORY, word-for-word. Resist the temptation to look back at the sentence after you have read it. Try to read each sentence only once.

Sentence #1:
Yet if life be happy in proportion as the summation of its moments be contented, the Fijians are far happier than we. (Mayer)

Recall #1:

Sentence #2:
Then they go away, neither richer nor poorer than when they came, and are absorbed at once in their business, which has nothing to do with art. (Kandinsky)

Recall #2:

Sentence #3:
The iconoclast both of the revolutionary and of the Napoleonic legends chills alike the heart of the worshippers at either shrine. (Baring)

Recall #3:

Sentence #4:
Among the Omaha both officers and warriors must be taken from the class of "young men," as the chiefs are afraid to act as leaders in war. (Dorsey)

Recall #4:

UNIT 6 - MEDIUM

Sentence #5:
The gods were more monstrous in every way than man, but in all attributes only the exaggerated counterparts of Fijian chiefs. (Mayer)

Recall #5:

Sentence #6:
The blessed in heaven are represented in the Apocalypse by St. John, as standing before the throne in white robes, with branches of Palm in their hands. (Bryant)

Recall #6:

Sentence #7:
Broken scales, "five finger exercises," and mechanical drills of every kind, are altogether objectionable. (Taylor)

Recall #7:

Sentence #8:
The last two hundred years have revolutionized nearly all of our deepest conceptions concerning the relations of human beings to religion, government, property, and to each other. (Barnes)

Recall #8:

Sentence #9:
The Northern temperament, reflective, strong and positive, now began to assume mastery over the bewildered reveries of the Southern nature. (Petrucci)

Recall #9:

SENTENCE RECALL *CONTINUED*

Sentence #10:
The artist and the spectator drift apart, till finally the latter turns his back on the former or regards him as a juggler whose skill and dexterity are worthy of applause. (Kandinsky)

Recall #10:

Sentence #11:
The popular mind, quickened by universal education, and freed from a burden of fixed beliefs, is turning restlessly to inquire about everything that affects human life. (Barnes)

Recall #11:

Sentence #12:
It was evolved in an age when the method of superimposing different registers to indicate different planes was still being practiced in bas-reliefs. (Petrucci)

Recall #12:

Sentence #13:
Like most other great changes in civilization, this industrial transformation was neither preceded nor accompanied by any general consciousness of what was happening. (Dorsey)

Recall #13:

Sentence #14:
Several famous writers on musical subjects would have us believe that the love of vocal melody is outgrown by one who reaches the heights of musical development. (Taylor)

Recall #14:

UNIT 7
MEDIUM LEVEL E

READING SPEED EXERCISE - MEDIUM LEVEL E

DIRECTIONS: This exercise is designed to measure your relative reading speed. Read the passage at an accelerated rate while monitoring your time. Be sure to comprehend as much material as possible. At the end of the passage, record the number of minutes and seconds you spent reading. Refer to the Appendix for your calculated reading rate.

The misfortune rather than the fault of our individual critic is that he is the heir of the false theory and bad manners of the English school. The theory of that school has apparently been that almost any person of glib and lively expression is competent to write of almost any branch of polite literature; its manners are what we know. The American, whom it has largely formed, is by nature very glib and very lively, and commonly his criticism, viewed as imaginative work, is more agreeable than that of the Englishman; but it is, like the art of both countries, apt to be amateurish. In some degree our authors have freed themselves from English models; they have gained some notion of the more serious work of the Continent: but it is still the ambition of the American critic to write like the English critic, to show his wit if not his learning, to strive to eclipse the author under review rather than illustrate him. He has not yet caught on to the fact that it is really no part of his business to display himself, but that it is altogether his duty to place a book in such a light that the reader shall know its class, its function, its character. The vast good-nature of our people preserves us from the worst effects of this criticism without principles. Our critic, at his lowest, is rarely malignant; and when he is rude or untruthful, it is mostly without truculence; I suspect that he is often offensive without knowing that he is so. Now and then he acts simply under instruction from higher authority, and denounces because it is the tradition of his publication to do so. In other cases the critic is obliged to support his journal's repute for severity, or for wit, or for morality, though he may himself be entirely amiable, dull, and wicked; this necessity more or less warps his verdicts.

The worst is that he is personal, perhaps because it is so easy and so natural to be personal, and so instantly attractive. In this respect our criticism has not improved from the accession of numbers of ladies to its ranks, though we still hope so much from women in our politics when they shall come to vote. They have come to write, and with the effect to increase the amount of little-digging, which rather super abounded in our literary criticism before. They "know what they like"—that pernicious maxim of those who do not know what they ought to like and they pass readily from censuring an author's performance to censuring him. They bring a stock of lively misapprehensions and prejudices to their work; they would rather have heard about than known about a book; and they take kindly to the public wish to be amused rather than edified. But neither have they so much harm in them: they, too, are more ignorant than malevolent.

Our criticism is disabled by the unwillingness of the critic to learn from an author, and his readiness to mistrust him. A writer passes his whole life in fitting himself for a certain kind of performance; the critic does not ask why, or whether the performance is good or bad, but if he does not like the kind, he instructs the writer to go off and do some other sort of thing— usually the sort that has been done already, and done sufficiently. If he could once understand that a man who has written the book he dislikes, probably knows infinitely more about its kind and his own fitness for doing it than any one else, the critic might learn something, and might help the reader to learn; but by putting himself in a false position, a position of superiority, he is of no use. He is not to suppose that an author has committed an offence against him by writing the kind of book he does not like; he will be far more profitably employed on behalf of the reader in finding out whether they had better not both like it. Let him conceive of an author as not in any wise on trial before him, but as a reflection of this or that aspect of life, and he will not be tempted to browbeat him or bully him.

UNIT 7 - MEDIUM

The critic need not be impolite even to the youngest and weakest author. A little courtesy, or a good deal, a constant perception of the fact that a book is not a misdemeanor, a decent self-respect that must forbid the civilized man the savage pleasure of wounding, are what I would ask for our criticism, as something which will add sensibly to its present luster.

I would have my fellow-critics consider what they are really in the world for. The critic must perceive, if he will question himself more carefully, that his office is mainly to ascertain facts and traits of literature, not to invent or denounce them; to discover principles, not to establish them; to report, not to create.

It is so much easier to say that you like this or dislike that, than to tell why one thing is, or where another thing comes from, that many flourishing critics will have to go out of business altogether if the scientific method comes in, for then the critic will have to know something besides his own mind. He will have to know something of the laws of that mind, and of its generic history.

The history of all literature shows that even with the youngest and weakest author criticism is quite powerless against his will to do his own work in his own way; and if this is the case in the green wood, how much more in the dry! It has been thought by the sentimentalist that criticism, if it cannot cure, can at least kill, and Keats was long alleged in proof of its efficacy in this sort. But criticism neither cured nor killed Keats, as we all now very well know. It wounded, it cruelly hurt him, no doubt; and it is always in the power of the critic to give pain to the author—the meanest critic to the greatest author —for no one can help feeling a rudeness. But every literary movement has been violently opposed at the start, and yet never stayed in the least, or arrested, by criticism; every author has been condemned for his virtues, but in no wise changed by it. In the beginning he reads the critics; but presently perceiving that he alone makes or mars himself, and that they have no instruction for him, he mostly leaves off reading them, though he is always glad of their kindness or grieved by their harshness when he chances upon it. This, I believe, is the general experience, modified, of course, by exceptions.

Then, are we critics of no use in the world? I should not like to think that, though I am not quite ready to define our use. More than one sober thinker is inclining at present to suspect that aesthetically or specifically we are of no use, and that we are only useful historically; that we may register laws, but not enact them. I am not quite prepared to admit that aesthetic criticism is useless, though in view of its futility in any given instance it is hard to deny that it is so. It certainly seems as useless against a book that strikes the popular fancy, and prospers on in spite of condemnation by the best critics, as it is against a book which does not generally please, and which no critical favor can make acceptable. This is so common a phenomenon that I wonder it has never hitherto suggested to criticism that its point of view was altogether mistaken, and that it was really necessary to judge books not as dead things, but as living things—things which have an influence and a power irrespective of beauty and wisdom, and merely as expressions of actuality in thought and feeling. Perhaps criticism has a cumulative and final effect; perhaps it does some good we do not know of. It apparently does not affect the author directly, but it may reach him through the reader. It may in some cases enlarge or diminish his audience for a while, until he has thoroughly measured and tested his own powers. If criticism is to affect literature at all, it must be through the writers who have newly left the starting-point, and are reasonably uncertain of the race, not with those who have won it again and again in their own way.

Sometimes it has seemed to me that the crudest expression of any creative art is better than the finest comment upon it. I have sometimes suspected that more thinking, more feeling certainly, goes to the creation of a poor novel than to the production of a brilliant criticism; and if any novel of our time fails to live a hundred years, will any censure of it live? Who can endure to read old reviews? One can hardly read them if they are in praise of one's own books.

The author neglected or overlooked need not despair for that reason, if he will reflect that criticism can neither make nor unmake authors; that there have not been greater books since criticism became an art

READING SPEED *CONTINUED*

than there were before; that in fact the greatest books seem to have come much earlier.

That which criticism seems most certainly to have done is to have put a literary consciousness into books unfelt in the early masterpieces, but unfelt now only in the books of men whose lives have been passed in activities, who have been used to employing language as they would have employed any implement, to effect an object, who have regarded a thing to be said as in no wise different from a thing to be done. In this sort I have seen no modern book so unconscious as General Grant's 'Personal Memoirs.' The author's one end and aim is to get the facts out in words. He does not cast about for phrases, but takes the word, whatever it is, that will best give his meaning, as if it were a man or a force of men for the accomplishment of a feat of arms. There is not a moment wasted in preening and prettifying, after the fashion of literary men; there is no thought of style, and so the style is good as it is in the 'Book of Chronicles,' as it is in the 'Pilgrim's Progress,' with a peculiar, almost plebeian, plainness at times. There is no more attempt at dramatic effect than there is at ceremonious pose; things happen in that tale of a mighty war as they happened in the mighty war itself, without setting, without artificial relief one after another, as if they were all of one quality and degree. Judgments are delivered with the same unimposing quiet; no awe surrounds the tribunal except that which comes from the weight and justice of the opinions; it is always an unaffected, unpretentious man who is talking; and throughout he prefers to wear the uniform of a private, with nothing of the general about him but the shoulder-straps, which he sometimes forgets.

Canon Fairfax,'s opinions of literary criticism are very much to my liking, perhaps because when I read them I found them so like my own, already delivered in print. He tells the critics that "they are in no sense the legislators of literature, barely even its judges and police"; and he reminds them of Mr. Ruskin's saying that "a bad critic is probably the most mischievous person in the world," though a sense of their relative proportion to the whole of life would perhaps acquit the worst among them of this extreme of culpability. A bad critic is as bad a thing as can be, but, after all, his mischief does not carry very far. Otherwise it would be mainly the conventional books and not the original books which would survive; for the censor who imagines himself a law-giver can give law only to the imitative and never to the creative mind. Criticism has condemned whatever was, from time to time, fresh and vital in literature; it has always fought the new good thing in behalf of the old good thing; it has invariably fostered and encouraged the tame, the trite, the negative. Yet upon the whole it is the native, the novel, the positive that has survived in literature. Whereas, if bad criticism were the most mischievous thing in the world, in the full implication of the words, it must have been the tame, the trite, the negative, that survived.

Bad criticism is mischievous enough, however; and I think that much if not most current criticism as practiced among the English and Americans is bad, is falsely principled, and is conditioned in evil. It is falsely principled because it is unprincipled, or without principles; and it is conditioned in evil because it is almost wholly anonymous. At the best its opinions are not conclusions from certain easily verifiable principles, but are effects from the worship of certain models. They are in so far quite worthless, for it is the very nature of things that the original mind cannot conform to models; it has its norm within itself; it can work only in its own way, and by its self-given laws.

Criticism does not inquire whether a work is true to life, but tacitly or explicitly compares it with models, and tests it by them. If literary art traveled by any such road as criticism would have it go, it would travel in a vicious circle, and would arrive only at the point of departure. Yet this is the course that criticism must always prescribe when it attempts to give laws. Being itself artificial, it cannot conceive of the original except as the abnormal. It must altogether preconceive its office before it can be of use to literature. It must reduce this to the business of observing, recording, and comparing; to analyzing the material before it, and then synthesizing its impressions. Even then, it is not too much to say that literature as an art could get on perfectly well without it. Just as many good novels,

UNIT 7 - MEDIUM

poems, plays, essays, sketches, would be written if there were no such thing as criticism in the literary world, and no more bad ones.

But it will be long before criticism ceases to imagine itself a controlling force, to give itself airs of sovereignty, and to issue decrees. As it exists it is mostly a mischief, though not the greatest mischief; but it may be greatly ameliorated in character and softened in manner by the total abolition of anonymity.

I think it would be safe to say that in no other relation of life is so much brutality permitted by civilized society as in the criticism of literature and the arts. Canon Farrar is quite right in reproaching literary criticism with the bitterness of judging an author without reference to his aims; with pursuing certain writers from spite and prejudice, and mere habit; with misrepresenting a book by quoting a phrase or passage apart from the context; with magnifying misprints and careless expressions into important faults; with abusing an author for his opinions; with base and personal motives.

Every writer of experience knows that certain critical journals will condemn his work without regard to its quality, even if it has never been his fortune to learn, as one author did from a repentant reviewer, that in a journal pretending to literary taste his books were given out for review with the caution, "Remember that the Clarion is opposed to Mr. Blank's books."

The final conclusion appears to be that the man, or even the young lady, who is given a gun, and told to shoot at some passer from behind a hedge, is placed in circumstances of temptation almost too strong for human nature.

As I have already intimated, I doubt the more lasting effects of unjust criticism. It is no part of my belief that Keats's fame was long delayed by it, or Wordsworth's, or Browning's. Something unwanted, unexpected, in the quality of each delayed his recognition; each was not only a poet, he was a revolution, a new order of things, to which the critical perceptions and habitudes had painfully to adjust themselves: But I have no question of the gross and stupid injustice with which

these great men were used, and of the barbarization of the public mind by the sight of the wrong inflicted on them with impunity. This savage condition still persists in the toleration of anonymous criticism, an abuse that ought to be as extinct as the torture of witnesses. It is hard enough to treat a fellow-author with respect even when one has to address him, name to name, upon the same level, in plain day; swooping down upon him in the dark, covered in the authority of a great journal, it is impossible.

Every now and then some idealist comes forward and declares that you should say nothing in criticism of a man's book which you would not say of it to his face. But I am afraid this is asking too much. I am afraid it would put an end to all criticism; and that if it were practiced literature would be left to purify itself. I have no doubt literature would do this; but in such a state of things there would be no provision for the critics. We ought not to destroy critics, we ought to reform them, or rather transform them, or turn them from the assumption of authority to a realization of their true function in the civilized state. They are no worse at heart, probably, than many others, and there are probably good husbands and tender fathers, loving daughters and careful mothers, among them. (Howells)

TOTAL TIME:

....

PARAGRAPH SUMMARY EXERCISE - MEDIUM LEVEL E

DIRECTIONS: This exercise is designed to improve your ability to summarize main concepts. Read the material at a comfortable rate. After you have read EACH paragraph, write a brief summary of its key points in the right column. Include main ideas, conclusions, and opinions. Do not include details.

Comparatively little is known as yet, even in this age of publicity, about the domestic arrangements and private life of fishes. Not that the creatures themselves shun the wiles of the interviewer, or are at all shy and retiring, as a matter of delicacy, about their family affairs; on the contrary, they display a striking lack of reticence in their native element, and are so far from pushing parental affection to a quixotic extreme that many of them, like the common rabbit immortalized by Mr. Squeers, 'frequently devour their own offspring.'

1st PARAGRAPH SUMMARY:

But nature herself opposes certain obvious obstacles to the pursuit of knowledge in the great deep, which render it difficult for the ardent naturalist, however much he may be so disposed, to carry on his observations with the same facility as in the case of birds and quadrupeds. You can't drop in upon most fish, casually, in their own homes; and when you confine them in aquariums, where your opportunities of watching them through a sheet of plate-glass are considerably greater, most of the captives get huffy under the narrow restrictions of their prison life, and obstinately refuse to rear a brood of hereditary helots for the mere gratification of your scientific curiosity.

2nd PARAGRAPH SUMMARY:

Still, by hook and by crook (especially the former), by observation here and experiment there, naturalists in the end have managed to piece together a considerable mass of curious and interesting information of an out-of-the-way sort about the domestic habits and manners of sundry piscine races. And, indeed, the morals of fish are far more varied and divergent than the uniform nature of the world they inhabit might lead an à priori philosopher to imagine. To the eye of the mere casual observer every fish would seem at first sight to be a mere fish, and to differ but little in sentiments and ethical culture from all the rest of his remote cousins.

3rd PARAGRAPH SUMMARY:

UNIT 7 - MEDIUM

But when one comes to look closer at their character and antecedents, it becomes evident at once that there is a deal of unsuspected originality and caprice about sharks and flat-fish. Instead of conforming throughout to a single plan, as the young, the gay, the giddy, and the thoughtless are too prone to conclude, fish are in reality as various and variable in their mode of life as any other great group in the animal kingdom. Monogamy and polygamy, socialism and individualism, the patriarchal and matriarchal types of government, the oviparous and viviparous methods of reproduction, perhaps even the dissidence of dissent and esoteric Buddhism, all alike are well represented in one family or another of this extremely eclectic and philosophically unprejudiced class of animals.

If you want a perfect model of domestic virtue, for example, where can you find it in higher perfection than in that exemplary and devoted father, the common great pipe-fish of the North Atlantic and the British Seas? This high-principled lophobranch is so careful of its callow and helpless young that it carries about the unhatched eggs with him under his own tail, in what scientific ichthyologists pleasantly describe as a sub caudal pouch or cutaneous receptacle. There they hatch out in perfect security, free from the dangers that beset the spawn and fry of so many other less tender-hearted kinds; and as soon as the little pipe-fish are big enough to look after themselves the sac divides spontaneously down the middle, and allows them to escape, to shift for themselves in the broad Atlantic.

Even so, however, the juniors take care always to keep tolerably near that friendly shelter, and creep back into it again on any threat of danger, exactly as baby-kangaroos do into their mother's pouch. The father-fish, in fact, has gone to the trouble and expense of developing out of his own tissues a membranous bag, on purpose to hold the eggs and young during the first stages of their embryonic evolution. This bag is formed by two folds of the skin, one of which grows out from each side of the body, the free margins being firmly glued together in the middle by a natural exudation, while the eggs are undergoing incubation, but opening once more in the middle to let the little fish out as soon as the process of hatching is fairly finished.

4th PARAGRAPH SUMMARY:

5th PARAGRAPH SUMMARY:

6th PARAGRAPH SUMMARY:

So curious a provision for the safety of the young in the pipe-fish may be compared to some extent, as I hinted above, with the pouch in which kangaroos and other marsupial animals carry their cubs after birth, till they have attained an age of complete independence. But the strangest part of it all is the fact that while in the kangaroo it is the mother who owns the pouch and takes care of the young, in the pipe-fish it is the father, on the contrary, who thus specially provides for the safety of his defenseless offspring. And what is odder still, this topsy-turvy arrangement (as it seems to us) is the common rule throughout the class of fishes. For the most part it must be candidly admitted by their warmest admirer, fish make very bad parents indeed.

They lay their eggs anywhere on a suitable spot, and as soon as they have once deposited them, like the ostrich in Job, they go on their way rejoicing, and never bestow another passing thought upon their deserted progeny. But if ever a fish does take any pains in the education and social upbringing of its young, you're pretty sure to find on enquiry it's the father—not as one would naturally expect, the mother—who devotes his time and attention to the congenial task of hatching or feeding them. It is he who builds the nest, and sits upon the eggs, and nurses the young, and imparts moral instruction (with a snap of his jaw or a swish of his tail) to the bold, the truant, the cheeky, or the imprudent; while his unnatural spouse, well satisfied with her own part in having merely brought the helpless eggs into this world of sorrow, goes off on her own account in the giddy whirl of society, forgetful of the sacred claims of her wriggling offspring upon a mother's heart.

In the pipe-fish family, too, the ardent evolutionist can trace a whole series of instructive and illustrative gradations in the development of this instinct and the corresponding pouch-like structure among the male fish. With the least highly-evolved types, like the long-nosed pipe-fish of the English Channel, and many allied forms from European seas, there is no pouch at all, but the father of the family carries the eggs about with him, glued firmly on to the service of his abdomen by a natural mucus. In a somewhat more advanced tropical kind, the ridges of the abdomen are slightly

7th PARAGRAPH SUMMARY:

8th PARAGRAPH SUMMARY:

9th PARAGRAPH SUMMARY:

UNIT 7 - MEDIUM

dilated, so as to form an open groove, which loosely holds the eggs, though its edges do not meet in the middle as in the great pipe-fish. Then come yet other more progressive forms, like the great pipe-fish himself, where the folds meet so as to produce a complete sac, which opens at maturity, to let out its little inmates.

And finally, in the common Mediterranean sea-horses, which you can pick up by dozens on the Lido at Venice, and a specimen of which exists in the dried form in every domestic museum, the pouch is permanently closed by coalescence of the edges, leaving a narrow opening in front, through which the small hippocampi creep out one by one as soon as they consider themselves capable of buffeting the waves of the Adriatic.

Fish that take much care of their offspring naturally don't need to produce eggs in the same reckless abundance as those dissipated kinds that leave their spawn exposed on the bare sandy bottom, at the mercy of every comer who chooses to take a bite at it. They can afford to lay a smaller number, and to make each individual egg much larger and richer in proportion than their rivals.

This plan, of course, enables the young to begin life far better provided with muscles and fins than the tiny little fry which come out of the eggs of the improvident species. For example, the cod-fish lays nine million odd eggs; but anybody who has ever eaten fried cod's-roe must have noticed that each individual ovum was so very small as to be almost indistinguishable to the naked eye. Thousands of these infinitesimal specks are devoured before they hatch out by predaceous fish; thousands more of the young fry are swallowed alive during their helpless infancy by the enemies of their species. Imagine the very fractional amount of parental affection which each of the nine million must need to put up with! (Allen)

10th PARAGRAPH SUMMARY:

11th PARAGRAPH SUMMARY:

12th PARAGRAPH SUMMARY:

VISUAL MEMORY EXERCISE - MEDIUM LEVEL E

DIRECTIONS: This exercise is designed to improve your visual memory. Four grids of nine objects are presented. Look at each grid for one minute. Memorize as best you can the design and placement of each symbol. When you have all objects memorized for one grid, turn to the next page and draw the nine objects in the corresponding grid FROM MEMORY. If you need to look back at the grid, then document how many times you looked at the objects.

GRID 1

v3	Φ	Θ
≡	∩	⊃
25	tan	□

GRID 2

7⌂	Σ	ā
oe	Ø	Є
Λ	⅝	c8

GRID 3

ε	3	bh
6m	≥	π
⌐	⊬	—

GRID 4

＋	Ψ	Ξ
θ	o	t2
JY	ω	Π

VISUAL MEMORY *CONTINUED*

GRID 1   looked back _____ time(s)

GRID 2   looked back _____ time(s)

GRID 3   looked back _____ time(s)

GRID 4   looked back _____ time(s)

SENTENCE RECALL EXERCISE - MEDIUM LEVEL E

DIRECTIONS: This exercise is designed to improve your memory. Read each sentence carefully, remembering as much as possible. In the space immediately below, write the sentence FROM MEMORY, word-for-word. Resist the temptation to look back at the sentence after you have read it. Try to read each sentence only once.

Sentence #1:
The theory of Evolution then suggests that the same processes which are employed by the cattle-breeder have been in operation through untold ages. (Ackland)

Recall #1:

Sentence #2:
At that point the spelling of the western town has stopped short, but the tongues of the natives have run on till nothing now remains but Cisseter. (Allen)

Recall #2:

Sentence #3:
A man convicted of deliberate falsehood cannot expect to be believed when he pleads that his public conduct is wholly dictated by public motives. (Baring)

Recall #3:

Sentence #4:
The operator now fills his mouth with air, which is to be passed through the pipe by compressing the muscles of the cheeks, while he breathes through the nostrils, and uses the palate as a valve. (System)

Recall #4:

UNIT 7 - MEDIUM

Sentence #5:
For full growth of mind and spirit one must participate; just as in athletics one must leave the spectator's bench and play the game if one would develop one's own powers. (Barnes)

Recall #5:

Sentence #6:
If a son of a chief is wanting in bravery, generosity, or other desirable qualities, he is regarded merely as an ordinary individual. (Dorsey)

Recall #6:

Sentence #7:
If a product which some individual creates can not be utilized by society, its creator is not regarded as having made a contribution to human progress. (Gillette)

Recall #7:

Sentence #8:
She was great and they were beautiful, because she and they were honest, and dealt with nature nearly a hundred years ago as realism deals with it to-day. (Howells)

Recall #8:

Sentence #9:
And the very names of our towns, our rivers, and our hills, go back in many cases, not merely to the Roman corruptions, but to the aboriginal Celtic, and the still more aboriginal Euskarian tongue. (Allen)

Recall #9:

SENTENCE RECALL *CONTINUED*

Sentence #10:
This tradition undoubtedly related to the shepherds, those sons of Chus, who were so long in possession of the country; and whose history was of the highest antiquity. (Bryant)

Recall #10:

Sentence #11:
We poor fellows who work in the language of an old civilization, we may sit and chisel our little verbal felicities, only to find in the end that it is a borrowed jewel we are polishing. (Howells)

Recall #11:

Sentence #12:
Several remains of reptiles have been found, as well as footprints left on the soft mud or sand of a riverbank or sea-beach. (Ackland)

Recall #12:

Sentence #13:
It enables us to gauge the national aspirations of the day, and to estimate the character of the nation whose yearnings found expression in song. (Baring)

Recall #13:

Sentence #14:
A high jump is not so fine a sight as a running race when the horses have got half a mile away and look like a covey of swift birds, but it is still a fine sight. (Howells)

Recall #14:

UNIT 8
ADVANCED LEVEL A

READING SPEED EXERCISE - ADVANCED LEVEL A

DIRECTIONS: This exercise is designed to measure your relative reading speed. Read the passage at an accelerated rate while monitoring your time. Be sure to comprehend as much material as possible. At the end of the passage, record the number of minutes and seconds you spent reading. Refer to the Appendix for your calculated reading rate.

It is well to remind ourselves, from time to time, that "Ethics" is but another word for "righteousness," that for which many men and women of every generation have hungered and thirsted, and without which life becomes meaningless.

Certain forms of personal righteousness have become to a majority of the community almost automatic. It is as easy for most of us to keep from stealing our dinners as it is to digest them, and there is quite as much voluntary morality involved in one process as in the other. To steal would be for us to fall sadly below the standard of habit and expectation which makes virtue easy. In the same way we have been carefully reared to a sense of family obligation, to be kindly and considerate to the members of our own households, and to feel responsible for their well-being. As the rules of conduct have become established in regard to our self-development and our families, so they have been in regard to limited circles of friends. If the fulfillment of these claims were all that a righteous life required, the hunger and thirst would be stilled for many good men and women, and the clew of right living would lie easily in their hands.

But we all know that each generation has its own test, the contemporaneous and current standard by which alone it can adequately judge of its own moral achievements, and that it may not legitimately use a previous and less vigorous test. The advanced test must indeed include that which has already been attained; but if it includes no more, we shall fail to go forward, thinking complacently that we have "arrived" when in reality we have not yet started.

To attain individual morality in an age demanding social morality, to pride one's self on the results of personal effort when the time demands social adjustment, is utterly to fail to apprehend the situation. It is perhaps significant that a German critic has of late reminded us that the one test which the most authoritative and dramatic portrayal of the Day of Judgment offers, is the social test. The stern questions are not in regard to personal and family relations, but did ye visit the poor, the criminal, the sick, and did ye feed the hungry?

All about us are men and women who have become unhappy in regard to their attitude toward the social order itself; toward the dreary round of uninteresting work, the pleasures narrowed down to those of appetite, the declining consciousness of brain power, and the lack of mental food which characterizes the lot of the large proportion of their fellow-citizens. These men and women have caught a moral challenge raised by the exigencies of contemporaneous life; some are bewildered, others who are denied the relief which sturdy action brings are even seeking an escape, but all are increasingly anxious concerning their actual relations to the basic organization of society.

The test which they would apply to their conduct is a social test. They fail to be content with the fulfillment of their family and personal obligations, and find themselves striving to respond to a new demand involving a social obligation; they have become conscious of another requirement, and the contribution they would make is toward a code of social ethics. The conception of life which they hold has not yet expressed itself in social changes or legal enactment, but rather in a mental attitude of maladjustment, and in a sense of divergence between their consciences and their conduct. They desire both a clearer definition of the code of morality adapted to present day demands and a part in its fulfillment, both

---

a creed and a practice of social morality. In the perplexity of this intricate situation at least one thing is becoming clear: if the latter day moral ideal is in reality that of a social morality, it is inevitable that those who desire it must be brought in contact with the moral experiences of the many in order to procure an adequate social motive.

These men and women have realized this and have disclosed the fact in their eagerness for a wider acquaintance with and participation in the life about them. They believe that experience gives the easy and trustworthy impulse toward right action in the broad as well as in the narrow relations. We may indeed imagine many of them saying: "Cast our experiences in a larger mould if our lives are to be animated by the larger social aims. We have met the obligations of our family life, not because we had made resolutions to that end, but spontaneously, because of a common fund of memories and affections, from which the obligation naturally develops, and we see no other way in which to prepare ourselves for the larger social duties." Such a demand is reasonable, for by our daily experience we have discovered that we cannot mechanically hold up a moral standard, then jump at it in rare moments of exhilaration when we have the strength for it, but that even as the ideal itself must be a rational development of life, so the strength to attain it must be secured from interest in life itself. We slowly learn that life consists of processes as well as results, and that failure may come quite as easily from ignoring the adequacy of one's method as from selfish or ignoble aims. We are thus brought to a conception of Democracy not merely as a sentiment which desires the well-being of all men, nor yet as a creed which believes in the essential dignity and equality of all men, but as that which affords a rule of living as well as a test of faith.

We are learning that a standard of social ethics is not attained by traveling a sequestered byway, but by mixing on the thronged and common road where all must turn out for one another, and at least see the size of one another's burdens. To follow the path of social morality results perforce in the temper if not the practice of the democratic spirit, for it implies that diversified human experience and resultant sympathy which are the foundation and guarantee of Democracy.

There are many indications that this conception of Democracy is growing among us. We have come to have an enormous interest in human life as such, accompanied by confidence in its essential soundness. We do not believe that genuine experience can lead us astray any more than scientific data can.

We realize, too, that social perspective and sanity of judgment come only from contact with social experience; that such contact is the surest corrective of opinions concerning the social order, and concerning efforts, however humble, for its improvement. Indeed, it is a consciousness of the illuminating and dynamic value of this wider and more thorough human experience which explains in no small degree that new curiosity regarding human life which has more of a moral basis than an intellectual one.

The newspapers, in a frank reflection of popular demand, exhibit an omnivorous curiosity equally insistent upon the trivial and the important. They are perhaps the most obvious manifestations of that desire to know, that "What is this?" and "Why do you do that?" of the child. The first dawn of the social consciousness takes this form, as the dawning intelligence of the child takes the form of constant question and insatiate curiosity.

Literature, too, portrays an equally absorbing though better adjusted desire to know all kinds of life. The popular books are the novels, dealing with life under all possible conditions, and they are widely read not only because they are entertaining, but also because they in a measure satisfy an unformulated belief that to see farther, to know all sorts of men, in an indefinite way, is a preparation for better social adjustment—for the remedying of social ills.

Doubtless one under the conviction of sin in regard to social ills finds a vague consolation in reading about the lives of the poor, and derives a sense of complicity in doing good. He likes to feel that he knows about social wrongs even if he does not remedy them, and in a very genuine sense there is a foundation for this belief.

READING SPEED *CONTINUED*

Partly through this wide reading of human life, we find in ourselves a new affinity for all men, which probably never existed in the world before. Evil itself does not shock us as it once did, and we count only that man merciful in whom we recognize an understanding of the criminal. We have learned as common knowledge that much of the insensibility and hardness of the world is due to the lack of imagination which prevents a realization of the experiences of other people. Already there is a conviction that we are under a moral obligation in choosing our experiences, since the result of those experiences must ultimately determine our understanding of life. We know instinctively that if we grow contemptuous of our fellows, and consciously limit our intercourse to certain kinds of people whom we have previously decided to respect, we not only tremendously circumscribe our range of life, but limit the scope of our ethics.

We can recall among the selfish people of our acquaintance at least one common characteristic,—the conviction that they are different from other men and women, that they need peculiar consideration because they are more sensitive or more refined. Such people "refuse to be bound by any relation save the personally luxurious ones of love and admiration, or the identity of political opinion, or religious creed." We have learned to recognize them as selfish, although we blame them not for the will which chooses to be selfish, but for a narrowness of interest which deliberately selects its experience within a limited sphere, and we say that they illustrate the danger of concentrating the mind on narrow and unprogressive issues.

We know, at last, that we can only discover truth by a rational and democratic interest in life, and to give truth complete social expression is the endeavor upon which we are entering. Thus the identification with the common lot which is the essential idea of Democracy becomes the source and expression of social ethics. It is as though we thirsted to drink at the great wells of human experience, because we knew that a daintier or less potent draught would not carry us to the end of the journey, going forward as we must in the heat and jostle of the crowd.

The six following chapters are studies of various types and groups who are being impelled by the newer conception of Democracy to an acceptance of social obligations involving in each instance a new line of conduct. No attempt is made to reach a conclusion, nor to offer advice beyond the assumption that the cure for the ills of Democracy is more Democracy, but the quite unlooked-for result of the studies would seem to indicate that while the strain and perplexity of the situation is felt most keenly by the educated and self-conscious members of the community, the tentative and actual attempts at adjustment are largely coming through those who are simpler and less analytical.

There are many people in every community who have not felt the "social compunction," who do not share the effort toward a higher social morality, who are even unable to sympathetically interpret it. Some of these have been shielded from the inevitable and salutary failures which the trial of new powers involve, because they are content to attain standards of virtue demanded by an easy public opinion, and others of them have exhausted their moral energy in attaining to the current standard of individual and family righteousness.

Such people, who form the bulk of contented society, demand that the radical, the reformer, shall be without stain or question in his personal and family relations, and judge most harshly any deviation from the established standards. There is a certain justice in this: it expresses the inherent conservatism of the mass of men, that none of the established virtues which have been so slowly and hardly acquired shall be sacrificed for the sake of making problematic advance; that the individual, in his attempt to develop and use the new and exalted virtue, shall not fall into the easy temptation of letting the ordinary ones slip through his fingers.

This instinct to conserve the old standards, combined with a distrust of the new standard, is a constant difficulty in the way of those experiments and advances depending upon the initiative of women, both because women are the more sensitive to the individual and family claims, and because their

UNIT 8 - ADVANCED

training has tended to make them content with the response to these claims alone.

There is no doubt that, in the effort to sustain the moral energy necessary to work out a more satisfactory social relation, the individual often sacrifices the energy which should legitimately go into the fulfillment of personal and family claims, to what he considers the higher claim.

In considering the changes which our increasing democracy is constantly making upon various relationships, it is impossible to ignore the filial relation. This chapter deals with the relation between parents and their grown-up daughters, as affording an explicit illustration of the perplexity and mal-adjustment brought about by the various attempts of young women to secure a more active share in the community life. We constantly see parents very much disconcerted and perplexed in regard to their daughters when these daughters undertake work lying quite outside of traditional and family interests. These parents insist that the girl is carried away by a foolish enthusiasm, that she is in search of a career, that she is restless and does not know what she wants. They will give any reason, almost, rather than the recognition of a genuine and dignified claim. Possibly all this is due to the fact that for so many hundreds of years women have had no larger interests, no participation in the affairs lying quite outside personal and family claims. Any attempt that the individual woman formerly made to subordinate or renounce the family claim was inevitably construed to mean that she was setting up her own will against that of her family's for selfish ends. It was concluded that she could have no motive larger than a desire to serve her family, and her attempt to break away must therefore be willful and self-indulgent.

The family logically consented to give her up at her marriage, when she was enlarging the family tie by founding another family. It was easy to understand that they permitted and even promoted her going to college, traveling in Europe, or any other means of self-improvement, because these merely meant the development and cultivation of one of its own members. When, however, she responded to her

impulse to fulfill the social or democratic claim, she violated every tradition.

The mind of each one of us reaches back to our first struggles as we emerged from self-willed childhood into a recognition of family obligations. We have all gradually learned to respond to them, and yet most of us have had at least fleeting glimpses of what it might be to disregard them and the elemental claim they make upon us. We have yielded at times to the temptation of ignoring them for selfish aims, of considering the individual and not the family convenience, and we remember with shame the self-pity which inevitably followed. But just as we have learned to adjust the personal and family claims, and to find an orderly development impossible without recognition of both, so perhaps we are called upon now to make a second adjustment between the family and the social claim, in which neither shall lose and both be ennobled.

The attempt to bring about a healing compromise in which the two shall be adjusted in proper relation is not an easy one. It is difficult to distinguish between the outward act of him who in following one legitimate claim has been led into the temporary violation of another, and the outward act of him who deliberately renounces a just claim and throws aside all obligation for the sake of his own selfish and individual development. The man, for instance, who deserts his family that he may cultivate an artistic sensibility, or acquire what he considers more fullness of life for himself, must always arouse our contempt. Breaking the marriage tie as Ibsen's "Nora" did, to obtain a larger self-development, or holding to it as George Eliot's "Romola" did, because of the larger claim of the state and society, must always remain two distinct paths.

The collision of interests, each of which has a real moral basis and a right to its own place in life, is bound to be more or less tragic. It is the struggle between two claims, the destruction of either of which would bring ruin to the ethical life. Curiously enough, it is almost exactly this contradiction which is the tragedy set forth by the Greek dramatist, who asserted that the gods who watch over the sanctity of the family

READING SPEED *CONTINUED*

bond must yield to the higher claims of the gods of the state. The failure to recognize the social claim as legitimate causes the trouble; the suspicion constantly remains that woman's public efforts are merely selfish and captious, and are not directed to the general good. This suspicion will never be dissipated until parents, as well as daughters, feel the democratic impulse and recognize the social claim.

Our democracy is making inroads upon the family, the oldest of human institutions, and a claim is being advanced which in a certain sense is larger than the family claim. The claim of the state in time of war has long been recognized, so that in its name the family has given up sons and husbands and even the fathers of little children. If we can once see the claims of society in any such light, if its misery and need can be made clear and urged as an explicit claim, as the state urges its claims in the time of danger, then for the first time the daughter who desires to minister to that need will be recognized as acting conscientiously. This recognition may easily come first through the emotions, and may be admitted as a response to pity and mercy long before it is formulated and perceived by the intellect.

The family as well as the state we are all called upon to maintain as the highest institutions which the race has evolved for its safeguard and protection. But merely to preserve these institutions is not enough. There come periods of reconstruction, during which the task is laid upon a passing generation, to enlarge the function and carry forward the ideal of a long-established institution. There is no doubt that many women, consciously and unconsciously, are struggling with this task. The family, like every other element of human life, is susceptible of progress, and from epoch to epoch its tendencies and aspirations are enlarged, although its duties can never be abrogated and its obligations can never be cancelled. It is impossible to bring about the higher development by any self-assertion or breaking away of the individual will. The new growth in the plant swelling against the sheath, which at the same time imprisons and protects it, must still be the truest type of progress. The family in its entirety must be carried out into the larger life. Its various members together must recognize and acknowledge the validity of the social obligation. When this does not occur we have a most flagrant example of the ill-adjustment and misery arising when an ethical code is applied too rigorously and too conscientiously to conditions which are no longer the same as when the code was instituted, and for which it was never designed. We have all seen parental control and the family claim assert their authority in fields of effort which belong to the adult judgment of the child and pertain to activity quite outside the family life. Probably the distinctively family tragedy of which we all catch glimpses now and then, is the assertion of this authority through all the entanglements of wounded affection and misunderstanding. We see parents and children acting from conscientious motives and with the most tender affection, yet bringing about a misery which can scarcely be hidden.

Such glimpses remind us of that tragedy enacted centuries ago in Assisi, when the eager young noble cast his very clothing at his father's feet, dramatically renouncing his filial allegiance, and formally subjecting the narrow family claim to the wider and more universal duty. All the conflict of tragedy ensued which might have been averted, had the father recognized the higher claim, and had he been willing to subordinate and adjust his own claim to it. The father considered his son disrespectful and hard-hearted, yet we know St. Francis to have been the most tender and loving of men, responsive to all possible ties, even to those of inanimate nature. We know that by his affections he freed the frozen life of his time. The elements of tragedy lay in the narrowness of the father's mind; in his lack of comprehension and his lack of sympathy with the power which was moving his son, and which was but part of the religious revival which swept Europe from end to end in the early part of the thirteenth century; the same power which built the cathedrals of the North, and produced the saints and sages of the South.

But the father's situation was nevertheless genuine; he felt his heart sore and angry, and his dignity covered with disrespect. He could not, indeed, have felt otherwise, unless he had been touched by the

UNIT 8 - ADVANCED

fire of the same revival, and lifted out of and away from the contemplation of himself and his narrower claim. It is another proof that the notion of a larger obligation can only come through the response to an enlarged interest in life and in the social movements around us. The grown-up son has so long been considered a citizen with well-defined duties and a need of "making his way in the world," that the family claim is urged much less strenuously in his case, and as a matter of authority, it ceases gradually to be made at all. In the case of the grown-up daughter, however, who is under no necessity of earning a living, and who has no strong artistic bent, taking her to Paris to study painting or to Germany to study music, the years immediately following her graduation from college are too often filled with a restlessness and unhappiness which might be avoided by a little clear thinking, and by an adaptation of our code of family ethics to modern conditions.

It is always difficult for the family to regard the daughter otherwise than as a family possession. From her babyhood she has been the charm and grace of the household, and it is hard to think of her as an integral part of the social order, hard to believe that she has duties outside of the family, to the state and to society in the larger sense. This assumption that the daughter is solely an inspiration and refinement to the family itself and its own immediate circle, that her delicacy and polish are but outward symbols of her father's protection and prosperity, worked very smoothly for the most part so long as her education was in line with it. When there was absolutely no recognition of the entity of woman's life beyond the family, when the outside claims upon her were still wholly unrecognized, the situation was simple, and the finishing school harmoniously and elegantly answered all requirements.

She was fitted to grace the fireside and to add luster to that social circle which her parents selected for her. But this family assumption has been notably broken into, and educational ideas no longer fit it. Modern education recognizes woman quite apart from family or society claims, and gives her the training which for many years has been deemed successful for highly developing a man's individuality and freeing his powers for independent action. Perplexities often occur when the daughter returns from college and finds that this recognition has been but partially accomplished. When she attempts to act upon the assumption of its accomplishment, she finds herself jarring upon ideals which are so entwined with filial piety, so rooted in the most tender affections of which the human heart is capable, that both daughter and parents are shocked and startled when they discover what is happening, and they scarcely venture to analyze the situation. The ideal for the education of woman has changed under the pressure of a new claim. The family has responded to the extent of granting the education, but they are jealous of the new claim and assert the family claim as over against it.

The modern woman finds herself educated to recognize a stress of social obligation which her family did not in the least anticipate when they sent her to college. She finds herself, in addition, under an impulse to act her part as a citizen of the world. She accepts her family inheritance with loyalty and affection, but she has entered into a wider inheritance as well, which, for lack of a better phrase, we call the social claim. This claim has been recognized for four years in her training, but after her return from college the family claim is again exclusively and strenuously asserted. The situation has all the discomfort of transition and compromise. The daughter finds a constant and totally unnecessary conflict between the social and the family claims. In most cases the former is repressed and gives way to the family claim, because the latter is concrete and definitely asserted, while the social demand is vague and unformulated. In such instances the girl quietly submits, but she feels wronged whenever she allows her mind to dwell upon the situation. She either hides her hurt, and splendid reserves of enthusiasm and capacity go to waste, or her zeal and emotions are turned inward, and the result is an unhappy woman, whose heart is consumed by vain regrets and desires. (Addams)

TOTAL TIME:

....

PARAGRAPH SUMMARY EXERCISE - ADVANCED LEVEL A

DIRECTIONS: This exercise is designed to improve your ability to summarize main concepts. Read the material at a comfortable rate. After you have read EACH paragraph, write a brief summary of its key points in the right column. Include main ideas, conclusions, and opinions. Do not include details.

In order to examine a substance in borax, the loop of the platinum wire should, after being thoroughly cleaned, and heated to redness, be quickly dipped into the powdered borax, and then quickly transferred to the flame of oxidation, and there fused. If the bead is not large enough to fill the loop of the wire, it must be subjected again to the same process. By examining the bead, both when hot and cold, by holding it up against the light, it can be soon ascertained whether it is free from dirt by the transparency, or the want of it, of the bead.

1st PARAGRAPH SUMMARY:

In order to make the examination of a substance, the bead should be melted and pressed against it, when enough will adhere to answer the purpose. This powder should then be fused in the oxidation flame until it mixes with, and is thoroughly dissolved by the borax bead.

2nd PARAGRAPH SUMMARY:

The principal objects to be determined now are: the color of the borax bead, both when heated and when cooled; also the rapidity with which the substance dissolves in the bead, and if any gas is eliminated. If the color of the bead is the object desired, the quantity of the substance employed must be very small, else the bead will be so deeply colored, as in some cases to appear almost opaque, as, for instance, in that of cobalt. Should this be the case, then, while the bead is still red hot, it should be pressed flat with the forceps; or it may, while soft, be pulled out to a thin thread, whereby the color can be distinctly discovered.

3rd PARAGRAPH SUMMARY:

Some bodies, when heated in the borax bead, present a clear bead both while hot and cold; but if the bead be heated with the intermittent flame, or in the flame of reduction, it becomes opalescent, opaque or milk-white. The alkaline earths are instances of this kind of reaction, also glucina oxide of cerium, tantalic

4th PARAGRAPH SUMMARY:

UNIT 8 - ADVANCED

and titanic acids, yttria and zirconia. But if a small portion of silica should be present, then the bead becomes clear. This is likewise the case with some silicates, provided there be not too large a quantity present, that is: over the quantity necessary to saturate the borax, for, in that case, the bead will be opaque when cool.

If the bead be heated on charcoal, a small tube or cavity must be scooped out of the charcoal, the bead placed in it, and the flame of reduction played upon it. When the bead is perfectly fused, it is taken up between the platinum forceps and pressed flat, so that the color may be the more readily discerned. This quick cooling also prevents the protoxides, if there be any present, from passing into a higher degree of oxidation.

The bead should first be submitted to the oxidation flame, and any reaction carefully observed. Then the bead should be submitted to the flame of reduction. It must be observed that the platinum forceps should not be used when there is danger of a metallic oxide being reduced, as in this case the metal would alloy with the platinum and spoil the forceps. In this case charcoal should be used for the support. If, however, there be oxides present which are not reduced by the borax, then the platinum loop may be used. Tin is frequently used for the purpose of enabling the bead to acquire a color for an oxide in the reducing flame, by its affinity for oxygen. The oxide, thus being reduced to a lower degree of oxidation, imparts its peculiar tinge to the bead as it cools.

The arsenides and sulphides, before being examined, should be roasted, and then heated with the borax bead. The arsenic of the former, it should be observed, will act on the glass tube in which the sublimation is proceeding, if the glass should contain lead.

It should be recollected that earths, metallic oxides, and metallic acids are soluble in borax, except those of the easily reducible metals, such as platinum or gold, or of mercury, which too readily vaporize. Also the metallic sulphides, after the sulphur has been driven off. Also the salts of metals, after their acids are driven off by heat. Also the nitrates and carbonates, after their

5th PARAGRAPH SUMMARY:

6th PARAGRAPH SUMMARY:

7th PARAGRAPH SUMMARY:

8th PARAGRAPH SUMMARY:

acids are driven off during the fusion. Also the salts of the halogens, such as the chlorides, iodides, bromides, etc., of the metals. Also the silicates, but with great tardiness. Also the phosphates and borates that fuse in the bead without suffering decomposition. The metallic sulphides are insoluble in borax, and many of the metals in the pure state.

There are many substances which give clear beads with borax both while hot and cold, but which, upon being heated with the intermittent oxidation flame, become enamelled and opaque. The intermittent flame may be readily attained, not by varying the force of the air from the mouth, but by raising and depressing the bead before the point of the steady oxidating flame. The addition of a little nitrate of potash will often greatly facilitate the production of a color, as it oxidizes the metal. The hot bead should be pressed upon a small crystal of the nitrate, when the bead swells, intumesces, and the color is manifested in the surface of the bead.

Microcosmic salt is a better flux for many metallic oxides than borax, as the colors are exhibited in it with more strength and character. Microcosmic salt is the phosphate of soda and ammonia. When it is ignited it passes into the biphosphate of soda, the ammonia being driven off. This biphosphate of soda possesses an excess of phosphoric acid, and thus has the property of dissolving a great number of substances, in fact almost any one, with the exception of silica. If the substances treated with this salt consist of sulphides or arsenides, the bead must be heated on charcoal. But if the substance experimented upon consists of earthly ingredients or metallic oxides, the platinum wire is the best. If the latter is used a few additional turns should be given to the wire in consequence of the greater fluidity of the bead over that of borax.

The microcosmic salt bead possesses the advantage over that of borax, that the colors of many substances are better discerned in it, and that it separates the acids, the more volatile ones being dissipated, while the fixed ones combine with a portion of the base equally with the phosphoric acid, or else do not combine at all, but float about in the bead, as is the case particularly with silicic acid. Many of the silicates give with borax a

9th PARAGRAPH SUMMARY:

10th PARAGRAPH SUMMARY:

11th PARAGRAPH SUMMARY:

UNIT 8 - ADVANCED

clear bead, while they form with microcosmic salt an opalescent one.

It frequently happens, that if a metallic oxide will not give its peculiar color in one of the flames, that it will in the other, as the difference in degree with which the metal is oxidized often determines the color. If the bead is heated in the reducing flame, it is well that it should be cooled rapidly to prevent a reoxidation. Reduction is much facilitated by the employment of metallic tin, whereby the protoxide or the reduced metal may be obtained in a comparatively brief time. The carbonate of soda is pulverized and then kneaded to a paste with water; the substance to be examined, in fine powder, is also mixed with it.

A small portion of this paste is placed on the charcoal, and gradually heated until the moisture is expelled, when the heat is brought to the fusion of the bead, or as high as it can be raised. Several phenomena will take place, which must be closely observed. Notice whether the substance fuses with the bead, and if so, whether there is intumescence or not. Or, whether the substance undergoes reduction; or, whether neither of these reactions takes place, and, on the contrary, the soda sinks into the charcoal, leaving the substance intact upon its surface. If intumescence takes place, the presence of either tartaric acid, molybdic acid, silicic, or tungstic acid, is indicated. The silicic acid will fuse into a bead, which becomes clear when it is cold. Titanic acid will fuse into the bead, but may be easily distinguished from the silicic acid by the bead remaining opaque when cold.

Strontia and baryta will flow into the charcoal, but lime will not. The molybdic and tungstic acids combine with the soda, forming the respective salts. These salts are absorbed by the charcoal. If too great a quantity of soda is used, the bead will be quite likely to become opaque upon cooling, while, if too small a quantity of soda is used, a portion of the substance will remain undissolved. These can be equally avoided by either the addition of soda, or the substance experimented upon, as may be required. (System)

12th PARAGRAPH SUMMARY:

13th PARAGRAPH SUMMARY:

14th PARAGRAPH SUMMARY:

VISUAL MEMORY EXERCISE - ADVANCED LEVEL A

DIRECTIONS: This exercise is designed to improve your visual memory. Four grids of nine objects are presented. Look at each grid for one minute. Memorize as best you can the design and placement of each symbol. When you have all objects memorized for one grid, turn to the next page and draw the nine objects in the corresponding grid FROM MEMORY. If you need to look back at the grid, then document how many times you looked at the objects.

GRID 1

Э	π	Ψ
iЮ	Ø	3Ш
7.2	red	Nb

GRID 2

η	2λ	9Ω
g.5	ω	six
31	⅓	ר

GRID 3

Ξ	E	F
bee	т	Σ7
⅛	53	8%

GRID 4

Þ	¿	H√
≈	8.R	∂
ө	¥	≠

UNIT 8

VISUAL MEMORY *CONTINUED*

GRID 1   looked back _____ time(s)

GRID 2   looked back _____ time(s)

GRID 3   looked back _____ time(s)

GRID 4   looked back _____ time(s)

SENTENCE RECALL EXERCISE - ADVANCED LEVEL A

DIRECTIONS: This exercise is designed to improve your memory. Read each sentence carefully, remembering as much as possible. In the space immediately below, write the sentence FROM MEMORY, word-for-word. Resist the temptation to look back at the sentence after you have read it. Try to read each sentence only once.

___

Sentence #1:

Participation means love, hate, devotion and sacrifice, and only when all these powers of the soul are brought into play, together with the judgment, is the character strengthened and life more abundantly obtained. (Barnes)

Recall #1:

___

Sentence #2:

But gaze down for a moment from the cathedral platform upon the valley of the Arno, spread like a glowing picture at your feet, and see how immediately it resolves the doubt. (Allen)

Recall #2:

___

Sentence #3:

Upon meeting Ratu Pope every native dropped his burdens, stepped to the side of the wood-path and crouched down, softly chanting the words of the tame, muduo! (Mayer)

Recall #3:

___

Sentence #4:

Just as art is looking for help from the primitives, so these men are turning to half-forgotten times in order to get help from their half-forgotten methods. (Kandinsky)

Recall #4:

UNIT 8 - ADVANCED

Sentence #5:
From a practical and economic point of view, the work of the dairy consists in converting the milk of their buffaloes into the butter and buttermilk which constitute their staple diet. (Marett)

Recall #5:

Sentence #6:
Another name for those Amonian temples was Campi, of the same analogy, and nearly of the same purport, as Arpi above-mentioned. (Bryant)

Recall #6:

Sentence #7:
So shrewd an observer as Samuel Johnson once remarked that it was surprising to find how much more kindness than justice society contained. (Addams)

Recall #7:

Sentence #8:
The substances of this group cannot be reduced to the metallic state, neither by heating them per se, nor by fusing them with reagents. (System)

Recall #8:

Sentence #9:
Souls travel this closed cycle under the most diverse forms, from hell to the gods, advancing or retreating, in accordance with the good deeds or errors committed in previous existences. (Petrucci)

Recall #9:

SENTENCE RECALL *CONTINUED*

Sentence #10:
It is, of course, open to question whether either primitive or advanced morality is sufficiently of one piece to allow, as it were, a composite photograph to be framed of either. (Marett)

Recall #10:

_____

Sentence #11:
The saloons offer a common meeting ground, with stimulus enough to free the wits and tongues of the men who meet there. (Addams)

Recall #11:

_____

Sentence #12:
Sacred relics such as famous clubs, stones possessing miraculous powers, etc., were sometimes kept in Fijian temples, but there were no idols such as were prayed to by the Polynesians. (Mayer)

Recall #12:

_____

Sentence #13:
If literary art travelled by any such road as criticism would have it go, it would travel in a vicious circle, and would arrive only at the point of departure. (Howells)

Recall #13:

_____

Sentence #14:
When a child is named, a certain old man is required to sing songs outside of the camp, dropping some tobacco from his pipe down on the toes of his left foot as he sings each song. (Dorsey)

Recall #14:

_____

UNIT 9
ADVANCED LEVEL B

READING SPEED EXERCISE - ADVANCED LEVEL B

DIRECTIONS: This exercise is designed to measure your relative reading speed. Read the passage at an accelerated rate while monitoring your time. Be sure to comprehend as much material as possible. At the end of the passage, record the number of minutes and seconds you spent reading. Refer to the Appendix for your calculated reading rate.

More than that of any other modern people French art is a national expression. It epitomizes very definitely the national esthetic judgment and feeling, and if its manifestations are even more varied than are elsewhere to be met with, they share a certain character that is very salient. Of almost any French picture or statue of any modern epoch one's first thought is that it is French. The national quite overshadows the personal quality. In the field of the fine arts, as in nearly every other in which the French genius shows itself, the results are evident of an intellectual co-operation which insures the development of a common standard and tends to subordinate idiosyncrasy. The fine arts, as well as every other department of mental activity, reveal the effect of that social instinct which is so much more powerful in France than it is anywhere else, or has ever been elsewhere, except possibly in the case of the Athenian republic. Add to this influence that of the intellectual as distinguished from the sensuous instinct, and one has, I think, the key to this salient characteristic of French art which strikes one so sharply and always as so plainly French.

As one walks through the French rooms at the Louvre, through the galleries of the Luxembourg, through the unending rooms of the Salon he is impressed by the splendid competence everywhere displayed, the high standard of culture universally attested, by the overwhelming evidence that France stands at the head of the modern world esthetically— but not less, I think, does one feel the absence of imagination, opportunity, of spirituality, of poetry in a word. The French themselves feel something of this. At the great Exposition of 1889 no pictures were so much admired by them as the English, in which appeared, even to an excessive degree, just the qualities in which French art is lacking, and which less than those of any other school showed traces of the now all

but universal influence of French art. The most distinct and durable impression left by any exhibition of French pictures is that the French esthetic genius is at once admirably artistic and extremely little poetic.

It is a corollary of the predominance of the intellectual over the sensuous instinct that the true should be preferred to the beautiful, and some French critics are so far from denying this preference of French art that they express pride in it, and, indeed, defend it in a way that makes one feel slightly amateurish and fanciful in thinking of beauty apart from truth. A walk through the Louvre, however, suffices to restore one's confidence in his own convictions. The French rooms, at least until modern periods are reached, are a demonstration that in the sphere of esthetics science does not produce the greatest artists—that something other than intelligent interest and technical accomplishment are requisite to that end, and that system is fatal to spontaneity. M. Eugène Véron is the mouthpiece of his countrymen in asserting absolute beauty to be an abstraction, but the practice of the mass of French painters is, by comparison with that of the great Italians and Dutchmen, eloquent of the lack of poetry that results from a skepticism of abstractions.

The French classic painters—and the classic-spirit, in spite of every force that the modern world brings to its destruction, persists wonderfully in France—show little absorption, little delight in their subject. Contrasted with the great names in painting they are eclectic and traditional, too purely expert. They are too cultivated to invent. Selection has taken the place of discovery in their inspiration. They are addicted to the rational and the regulated. Their substance is never sentimental and incommunicable. Their works have a distinctly professional air. They distrust what cannot be expressed; what can only be suggested does not seem to them worth the trouble of trying to conceive. Beside the world of mystery and the wealth of emotion forming an imaginative penumbra around such a design as Raphael's Vision of Ezekiel, for instance, Poussin's treatment of essentially the same subject is a diagram.

On the other hand, qualities intimately associated with these defects are quite as noticeable in the old French rooms of the Louvre. Clearness, compactness, measure, and balance are evident in nearly every canvas. Everywhere is the air of reserve, of intellectual good-breeding, of avoidance of extravagance. That French painting is at the head of contemporary painting, as far and away incontestably it is, is due to the fact that it alone has kept alive the traditions of art which, elsewhere than in France, have given place to other and more material ideals. From the first its practitioners have been artists rather than poets, have possessed, that is to say, the constructive rather than the creative, the organizing rather than the imaginative temperament, but they have rarely been perfunctory and never common.

French painting in its preference of truth to beauty, of intelligence to the beatific vision, of form to color, in a word, has nevertheless, and perhaps à fortiori, always been the expression of ideas. These ideas almost invariably have been expressed in rigorous form—form which at times fringes the lifelessness of symbolism. But even less frequently, I think, than other peoples have the French exhibited in their painting that contentment with painting in itself that is the dry rot of art. With all their addiction to truth and form they have followed this ideal so systematically that they have never suffered it to become mechanical, merely formal—as is so often the case elsewhere (in England and among ourselves, everyone will have remarked) in instances where form has been mainly considered and where sentiment happens to be lacking.

Even when care for form is so excessive as to imply an absence of character, the form itself is apt to be so distinguished as itself to supply the element of character, and character consequently particularly refined and immaterial. And one quality is always present: elegance is always evidently aimed at and measurably achieved. Native or foreign, real or

factitious as the inspiration of French classicism may be, the sense of style and of that perfection of style which we know as elegance is invariably noticeable in its productions. So that, we may say, from Poussin to Puvis de Chavannes, from Clouet to Meissonier, taste—a refined and cultivated sense of what is sound, estimable, competent, reserved, satisfactory, up to the mark, and above all, elegant and distinguished—has been at once the arbiter and the stimulus of excellence in French painting. It is this which has made the France of the past three centuries, and especially the France of to-day—as we get farther and farther away from the great art epochs—both in amount and general excellence of artistic activity, comparable only with the Italy of the Renaissance and the Greece of antiquity.

Moreover, it is an error to assume, because form in French painting appeals to us more strikingly than substance, that French painting is lacking in substance. In its perfection form appeals to every appreciation; it is in art, one may say, the one universal language. But just in proportion as form in a work of art approaches perfection, or universality, just in that proportion does the substance which it clothes, which it expresses, seem unimportant to those to whom this substance is foreign. Some critics have even fancied, for example, that Greek architecture and sculpture—the only Greek art we know anything about—were chiefly concerned with form, and that the ideas behind their perfection of form were very simple and elementary ideas, not at all comparable in complexity and elaborateness with those that confuse and distinguish the modern world. When one comes to French art it is still more difficult for us to realize that the ideas underlying its expression are ideas of import, validity, and attachment.

The truth is largely that French ideas are not our ideas; not that the French who—except possibly the ancient Greeks and the modern Germans—of all peoples in the world are, as one may say, addicted to ideas, are lacking in them. Technical excellence is simply the inseparable accompaniment, the outward expression of the kind of esthetic ideas the French are enamored of. Their substance is not our substance, but while it is perfectly legitimate for us to criticize their substance it is idle to maintain that they are lacking in

READING SPEED *CONTINUED*

substance. If we call a painting by Poussin pure style, a composition of David merely the perfection of convention, one of M. Rochegrosse's dramatic canvasses the rhetoric of technique and that only, we miss something. We miss the idea, the substance, behind these varying expressions. These are not the less real for being foreign to us. They are less spiritual and more material, less poetic and spontaneous, more schooled and traditional than we like to see associated with such adequacy of expression, but they are not for that reason more mechanical. They are ideas and substance that lend themselves to technical expression a thousand times more readily than do ours. They are, in fact, exquisitely adapted to technical expression.

The substance and ideas which we desire fully expressed in color, form, or words are, indeed, very exactly in proportion to our esteem of them, inexpressible. We like hints of the unutterable, suggestions of significance that is mysterious and import that is incalculable. The light that "never was on sea or land" is the illumination we seek. The "Heaven," not the atmosphere that "lies about us" in our mature age as "in our infancy," is what appeals most strongly to our subordination of the intellect and the senses to the imagination and the soul. Nothing with us very deeply impresses the mind if it does not arouse the emotions. Naturally, thus, we are predisposed insensibly to infer from French articulateness the absence of substance, to assume from the triumphant facility and felicity of French expression a certain insignificance of what is expressed. Inferences and assumptions based on temperament, however, almost invariably have the vice of superficiality, and it takes no very prolonged study of French art for candor and intelligence to perceive that if its substance is weak on the sentimental, the emotional, the poetic, the spiritual side, it is exceptionally strong in rhetorical, artistic, cultivated, æsthetically elevated ideas, as well as in that technical excellence which alone, owing to our own inexpertness, first strikes and longest impresses us.

When we have no ideas to express, in a word, we rarely save our emptiness by any appearance of clever expression. When a Frenchman expresses ideas for which we do not care, with which we are

temperamentally out of sympathy, we assume that his expression is equally empty. Matthew Arnold cites a passage from Mr. Palgrave, and comments significantly on it, in this sense. "The style," exclaims Mr. Palgrave, "which has filled London with the dead monotony of Gower or Harley Streets, or the pale commonplace of Belgravia, Tyburnia, and Kensington; which has pierced Paris and Madrid with the feeble frivolities of the Rue Rivoli and the Strada de Toledo." Upon which Arnold observes that "the architecture of the Rue Rivoli expresses show, splendor, pleasure, unworthy things, perhaps, to express alone and for their own sakes, but it expresses them; whereas, the architecture of Gower Street and Belgravia merely expresses the impotence of the architect to express anything."

And in characterizing the turn for poetry in French painting as comparatively inferior, it will be understood at once, I hope, that I am comparing it with the imaginativeness of the great Italians and Dutchmen, and with Rubens and Holbein and Turner, and not asserting the supremacy in elevated sentiment over Claude and Corot, Chardin, and Cazin, of the Royal Academy, or the New York Society of American Artists. And so far as an absolute rather than a comparative standard may be applied in matters so much too vast for any hope of adequate treatment according to either method, we ought never to forget that in criticizing French painting, as well as other things French, we are measuring it by an ideal that now and then we may appreciate better than Frenchmen, but rarely illustrate as well.

Furthermore, the qualities and defects of French painting—the predominance in it of national over individual force and distinction, its turn for style, the kind of ideas that inspire its substance, its classic spirit in fine—are explained hardly less by its historic origin than by the character of the French genius itself. French painting really began in connoisseurship, one may say. It arose in appreciation, that faculty in which the French have always been, and still are, unrivalled. Its syntheses were based on elements already in combination. It originated nothing. It was eclectic at the outset. Compared with the slow and suave

UNIT 9 - ADVANCED

evolution of Italian art, in whose earliest dawn its borrowed Byzantine painting served as a stimulus and suggestion to original views of natural material rather than as a model for imitation and modification, the painting that sprang into existence, Minerva-like, in full armor, at Fontainebleau under Francis I, was of the essence of artificiality.

The court of France was far more splendid than, and equally enlightened with, that of Florence. The monarch felt his title to Mæcenasship as justified as that of the Medici. He created, accordingly, French painting out of hand—I mean, at all events, the French painting that stands at the beginning of the line of the present tradition. He summoned Leonardo, Andrea del Sarto, Rossi, Primaticcio, and founded the famous Fontainebleau school. Of necessity it was Italianate. It had no Giotto, Masaccio, Raphael behind it. Italian was the best art going; French appreciation was educated and keen; its choice between evolution and adoption was inevitable. It was very much in the position in which American appreciation finds itself to-day. Like our own painters, the French artists of the Renaissance found themselves familiar with masterpieces wholly beyond their power to create, and produced by a foreign people who had enjoyed the incomparable advantage of arriving at their artistic apogee through natural stages of growth, beginning with impulse and culminating in expertness.

The situation had its advantages as well as its drawbacks, certainly. It saved French painting an immense amount of fumbling, of laborious experimentation, of crudity, of failure. But it stamped it with an essential artificiality from which it did not fully recover for over two hundred years, until, insensibly, it had built up its own traditions and gradually brought about its own inherent development. In a word, French painting had an intellectual rather than an emotional origin. Its first practitioners were men of culture rather than of feeling; they were inspired by the artistic, the constructive, the fashioning, rather than the poetic, spirit. And so evident is this inclination in even contemporary French painting—and indeed in all French esthetic expression—that it cannot be ascribed wholly to the circumstances mentioned. The circumstances themselves need an explanation, and

find it in the constitution itself of the French mind, which (owing, doubtless, to other circumstances, but that is extraneous) is fundamentally less imaginative and creative than coordinating and constructive.

Naturally thus, when the Italian influence wore itself out, and the Fontainebleau school gave way to a more purely national art; when France had definitely entered into her Italian heritage and had learned the lessons that Holland and Flanders had to teach her as well; when, in fine, the art of the modern world began, it was an art of grammar, of rhetoric. Certainly up to the time of Géricault painting in general held itself rather pedantically aloof from poetry. Claude, Chardin, what may be called the illustrated vers de société of the Louis Quinze painters—of Watteau and Fragonard—even Prudhon, did little to change the prevailing color and tone. Claude's art is, in manner, thoroughly classic. His personal influence was perhaps first felt by Corot. He stands by himself, at any rate, quite apart. He was the first thoroughly original French painter, if indeed one may not say he was the first thoroughly original modern painter. He has been assigned to both the French and Italian schools—to the latter by Gallophobist critics, however, through a partisanship which in esthetic matters is ridiculous; there was in his day no Italian school for him to belong to.

The truth is that he passed a large part of his life in Italy and that his landscape is Italianate. But more conspicuously still, it is ideal—ideal in the sense intended by Goethe in saying, "There are no landscapes in nature like those of Claude." There are not, indeed. Nature has been transmuted by Claude's alchemy with lovelier results than any other painter— save always Corot, shall I say?—has ever achieved. Witness the pastorals at Madrid, in the Doria Gallery at Rome, the "Dido and Aeneas" at Dresden, the sweet and serene superiority of the National Gallery canvases over the struggling competition manifest in the Turners juxtaposed to them through the unlucky ambition of the great English painter. Mr. Ruskin says that Claude could paint a small wave very well, and acknowledges that he affected a revolution in art, which revolution "consisted mainly in setting the sun in heavens." "Mainly" is delightful, but Claude's

READING SPEED *CONTINUED*

excellence consists in his ability to paint visions of loveliness, pictures of pure beauty, not in his skill in observing the drawing of wavelets or his happy thought of painting sunlight. Mr. George Moore observes ironically of Mr. Ruskin that his grotesque depreciation of Mr. Whistler—"the lot of critics" being "to be remembered by what they have failed to understand"—"will survive his finest prose passage." I am not sure about Mr. Whistler.

Contemporaries are too near for a perfect critical perspective. But assuredly Mr. Ruskin's failure to perceive Claude's point of view—to perceive that Claude's aim and Stanfield's, say, were quite different; that Claude, in fact, was at the opposite pole from the botanist and the geologist whom Mr. Ruskin's "reverence for nature" would make of every landscape painter—is a failure in appreciation than to have shown which it would be better for him as a critic never to have been born. It seems hardly fanciful to say that the depreciation of Claude by Mr. Ruskin, who is a landscape painter himself, using the medium of words instead of pigments, is, so to speak, professionally unjust.

"Go out, in the springtime, among the meadows that slope from the shores of the Swiss lakes to the roots of their lower mountains. There, mingled with the taller gentians and the white narcissus, the grass grows deep and free; and as you follow the winding mountain paths, beneath arching boughs all veiled and dim with blossom—paths that forever droop and rise over the green banks and mounds sweeping down in scented undulation, steep to the blue water, studded here and there with new-mown heaps, filling the air with fainter sweetness—look up toward the higher hills, where the waves of everlasting green roll silently into their long inlets among the shadows of the pines."

Claude's landscape is not Swiss, but if it were it would awaken in the beholder a very similar sensation to that aroused in the reader of this famous passage. Claude indeed painted landscape in precisely this way. He was perhaps the first—though priority in such matters is trivial beside pre-eminence—who painted effects instead of things. Light and air were his

material, not ponds and rocks and clouds and trees and stretches of plain and mountain outlines. He first generalized the phenomena of inanimate nature, and in this he remains still unsurpassed. But, superficially, his scheme wore the classic aspect, and neither his contemporaries nor his successors, for over two hundred years, discovered the immense value of his point of view, and the puissant charm of his way of rendering nature.

Poussin, however, was the incarnation of the classic spirit, and perhaps the reason why a disinterested foreigner finds it difficult to appreciate the French estimate of him is that no foreigner, however disinterested, can quite appreciate the French appreciation of the classic spirit in and for itself. But when one listens to expressions of admiration for the one French "old master," as one may call Poussin without invidiousness, it is impossible not to scent chauvinism, as one scents it in the German panegyrics of Goethe, for example. He was a very great painter, beyond doubt. And as there were great men before Agamemnon there have been great painters since Raphael and Titian, even since Rembrandt and Velasquez. He had a strenuous personality, moreover. You know a Poussin at once when you see it. But to find the suggestion of the infinite, the Shakespearian touch in his work seems to demand the imaginativeness of M. Victor Cherbuliez.

When Mr. Matthew Arnold ventured to remark to Sainte-Beuve that he could not consider Lamartine as a very important poet, Sainte-Beuve replied: "He was important to us." Many critics, among them one severer than Sainte-Beuve, the late Edmond Scherer, have given excellent reasons for Lamartine's absolute as well as relative importance, and perhaps it is a failure in appreciation on our part that is really responsible for our feeling that Poussin is not quite the great master the French deem him. Assuredly he might justifiably apply to himself the "Et-Ego-in-Arcadia" inscription in one of his most famous paintings. And the specific service he performed for French painting and the relative rank he occupies in it ought not to obscure his purely personal qualities, which, if not transcendent, are incontestably elevated and fine.

UNIT 9 - ADVANCED

His qualities, however, are very thoroughly French qualities—poise, rationality, science, the artistic dominating the poetic faculty, and style quite outshining significance and suggestion. He learned all he knew of art, he said, from the Bacchus Torso at Naples. But he was eclectic rather than imitative, and certainly used the material he found in the works of his artistic ancestors as freely and personally as Raphael the frescos of the Baths of Titus, or Donatello the fragments of antique sculpture. From his time on, indeed, French painting dropped its Italian leading-strings. He might often suggest Raphael—and any painter who suggests Raphael inevitably suffers for it—but always with an individual, a native, a French difference, and he is as far removed in spirit and essence from the Fontainebleau school as the French genius itself is from the Italian which presided there. In Poussin, indeed, the French genius first asserts itself in painting. And it asserts itself splendidly in him.

We who ask to be moved as well as impressed, who demand satisfaction of the susceptibility as well as—shall we say rather than?—interest of the intelligence, may feel that for the qualities in which Poussin is lacking those in which he is rich afford no compensation whatever. But I confess that in the presence of even that portion of Poussin's magnificent accomplishment which is spread before one in the Louvre, to wish one's self in the Stanze of the Vatican or in the Sistine Chapel, seems to me an unintelligent sacrifice of one's opportunities.

It is a sure mark of narrowness and defective powers of perception to fail to discover the point of view even of what one disesteems. We talk of Poussin, of Louis Quatorze art—as of its revival under David and its continuance in Ingres—of, in general, modern classic art as if it were an art of convention merely; whereas, conventional as it is, its conventionality is—or was, certainly, in the seventeenth century—very far from being pure formulary. It was genuinely expressive of a certain order of ideas intelligently held, a certain set of principles sincerely believed in, a view of art as positive and genuine as the revolt against the tyrannous system into which it developed. We are simply out of sympathy with its aim, its ideal; perhaps, too, for that most frivolous of all reasons because we have grown tired of it.

But the business of intelligent criticism is to be in touch with everything. Of course, by "criticism" one does not mean pedagogy, as so many people constantly imagine, nor does justifying everything include bad drawing. But as Lebrun, for example, is not nowadays held up as a model to young painters, and is not to be accused of bad drawing, why do we so entirely dispense ourselves from comprehending him at all? Lebrun is, perhaps, not a painter of enough personal importance to repay attentive consideration, and historic importance does not greatly concern criticism. But we pass him by on the ground of his conventionality, without remembering that what appears conventional to us was in his case not only sincerity but aggressive enthusiasm.

If there ever was a painter who exercised what creative and imaginative faculty he had with an absolute gusto, Lebrun did so. He interested his contemporaries immensely; no painter ever ruled more unrivalled. He fails to interest us because we have another point of view. We believe in our point of view and disbelieve in his as a matter of course; and it would be self-contradictory to say, in the interests of critical catholicity, that in our opinion his may be as sound as our own. But to say that he has no point of view whatever—to say, in general, that modern classic art is perfunctory and mere formulary—is to be guilty of what has always been the inherent vice of Protestantism in all fields of mental activity. (Brownell)

TOTAL TIME:

....

PARAGRAPH SUMMARY EXERCISE - ADVANCED LEVEL B

DIRECTIONS: This exercise is designed to improve your ability to summarize main concepts. Read the material at a comfortable rate. After you have read EACH paragraph, write a brief summary of its key points in the right column. Include main ideas, conclusions, and opinions. Do not include details.

We have already agreed that the dramatist works ever under the sway of three influences which are not felt by exclusively literary artists like the poet and the novelist. The physical conditions of the theatre in any age affect to a great extent the form and structure of the drama; the conscious or unconscious demands of the audience, as we have observed in the preceding chapter, determine for the dramatist the themes he shall portray; and the range or restrictions of his actors have an immediate effect upon the dramatist's great task of character-creation. In fact, so potent is the influence of the actor upon the dramatist that the latter, in creating character, goes to work very differently from his literary fellow-artists,—the novelist, the story-writer, or the poet. Great characters in non-dramatic fiction have often resulted from abstract imagining, without direct reference to any actual person: Don Quixote, Tito Melema, Leatherstocking, sprang full-grown from their creators' minds and struck the world as strange and new.

1st PARAGRAPH SUMMARY:

But the greatest characters in the drama have almost always taken on the physical, and to a great extent the mental, characteristics of certain great actors for whom they have been fashioned. Cyrano is not merely Cyrano, but also Coquelin; Mascarille is not merely Mascarille, but also Molière; Hamlet is not merely Hamlet, but also Richard Burbage. Closet-students of the plays of Sophocles may miss a point or two if they fail to consider that the dramatist prepared the part of Oedipus in three successive dramas for a certain star-performer on the stage of Dionysus. The greatest dramatists have built their plays not so much for reading in the closet as for immediate presentation on the stage; they have grown to greatness only after having achieved an initial success that has given them the freedom of the theatre; and their conceptions of character have therefore crystallized around the actors

2nd PARAGRAPH SUMMARY:

UNIT 9 - ADVANCED

that they have found waiting to present their parts. A novelist may conceive his heroine freely as being tall or short, frail or firmly built; but if a dramatist is making a play for an actress like Maude Adams, an airy, slight physique is imposed upon his heroine in advance.

Shakespeare was, among other things, the director of the Lord Chamberlain's men, who performed in the Globe, upon the Bankside; and his plays are replete with evidences of the influence upon him of the actors whom he had in charge. It is patent, for example, that the same comedian must have created Launce in Two Gentlemen of Verona and Launcelot Gobbo in the Merchant of Venice; the low comic hit of one production was bodily repeated in the next. It is almost as obvious that the parts of Mercutio and Gratiano must have been entrusted to the same performer; both characters seem made to fit the same histrionic temperament. If Hamlet were the hero of a novel, we should all, I think, conceive of him as slender, and the author would agree with us; yet, in the last scene of the play, the Queen expressly says, "He's fat, and scant of breath." This line has puzzled many commentators, as seeming out of character; but it merely indicates that Richard Burbage was fleshy during the season of 1602.

The Elizabethan expedient of disguising the heroine as a boy, which was invented by John Lyly, made popular by Robert Greene, and eagerly adopted by Shakespeare and Fletcher, seems unconvincing on the modern stage. It is hard for us to imagine how Orlando can fail to recognize his love when he meets her clad as Ganymede in the forest of Arden, or how Bassanio can be blinded to the figure of his wife when she enters the court-room in the almost feminine robes of a doctor of laws. Clothes cannot make a man out of an actress; we recognize Ada Rehan or Julia Marlowe beneath the trappings and the suits of their disguises; and it might seem that Shakespeare was depending over-much upon the proverbial credulity of theatre audiences. But a glance at histrionic conditions in Shakespeare's day will show us immediately why he used this expedient of disguise not only for Portia and Rosalind, but for Viola and Imogen as well. Shakespeare wrote these parts to be played not by women but by boys. Now, when a boy playing a woman disguised himself as a woman playing a boy,

3rd PARAGRAPH SUMMARY:

4th PARAGRAPH SUMMARY:

the disguise must have seemed baffling, not only to Orlando and Bassanio on the stage, but also to the audience. It was Shakespeare's boy actors, rather than his narrative imagination, that made him recur repeatedly in this case to a dramatic expedient which he would certainly discard if he were writing for actresses to-day.

If we turn from the work of Shakespeare to that of Molière, we shall find many more evidences of the influence of the actor on the dramatist. In fact, Molière's entire scheme of character-creation cannot be understood without direct reference to the histrionic capabilities of the various members of the Troupe de Monsieur. Molière's immediate and practical concern was not so much to create comic characters for all time as to make effective parts for La Grange and Du Croisy and Magdeleine Béjart, for his wife and for himself. La Grange seems to have been the Charles Wyndham of his day,—every inch a gentleman; his part in any of the plays may be distinguished by its elegant urbanity. In Les Précieuses Ridicules the gentlemanly characters are actually named La Grange and Du Croisy; the actors walked on and played themselves; it is as if Augustus Thomas had called the hero of his best play, not Jack Brookfield, but John Mason.

In the early period of Molière's art, before he broadened as an actor, the parts that he wrote for himself were often so much alike from play to play that he called them by the same conventional theatric name of Mascarille or Sganarelle, and played them, doubtless, with the same costume and make-up. Later on, when he became more versatile as an actor, he wrote for himself a wider range of parts and individualized them in name as well as in nature. His growth in depicting the characters of young women is curiously coincident with the growth of his wife as an actress for whom to devise such characters. Molière's best woman—Célimène, in Le Misanthrope—was created for Mlle. Molière at the height of her career, and is endowed with all her physical and mental traits.

The reason why so many of the Queen Anne dramatists in England wrote comedies setting forth a dandified and foppish gentleman is that Colley Cibber,

5th PARAGRAPH SUMMARY:

6th PARAGRAPH SUMMARY:

UNIT 9 - ADVANCED

the foremost actor of the time, could play the fop better than he could play anything else. The reason why there is no love scene between Charles Surface and Maria in The School for Scandal is that Sheridan knew that the actor and the actress who were cast for these respective roles were incapable of making love gracefully upon the stage. The reason why Victor Hugo's Cromwell overleaped itself in composition and became impossible for purposes of stage production is that Talma, for whom the character of Cromwell was designed, died before the piece was finished, and Hugo, despairing of having the part adequately acted, completed the play for the closet instead of for the stage. But it is unnecessary to cull from the past further instances of the direct dependence of the dramatist upon his actors. We have only to look about us at the present day to see the same influence at work.

But the contemporary English-speaking stage furnishes examples just as striking of the influence of the actor on the dramatist. Sir Arthur Wing Pinero's greatest heroine, Paula Tanqueray, wore from her inception the physical aspect of Mrs. Patrick Campbell. Many of the most effective dramas of Mr. Henry Arthur Jones have been built around the personality of Sir Charles Wyndham. The Wyndham part in Mr. Jones's plays is always a gentleman of the world, who understands life because he has lived it, and is "wise with the quiet memory of old pain." He is moral because he knows the futility of immorality. He is lonely, lovable, dignified, reliable, and sound. By serene and unobtrusive understanding he straightens out the difficulties in which the other people of the play have willfully become entangled. He shows them the error of their follies, preaches a worldly-wise little sermon to each one, and sends them back to their true places in life, sadder and wiser men and women. (Hamilton)

7th PARAGRAPH SUMMARY:

8th PARAGRAPH SUMMARY:

VISUAL MEMORY EXERCISE - ADVANCED LEVEL B

DIRECTIONS: This exercise is designed to improve your visual memory. Four grids of nine objects are presented. Look at each grid for one minute. Memorize as best you can the design and placement of each symbol. When you have all objects memorized for one grid, turn to the next page and draw the nine objects in the corresponding grid FROM MEMORY. If you need to look back at the grid, then document how many times you looked at the objects.

GRID 1

ς	C	][
Λ	bβ	Æ
^	sűń	I͡Ξ

GRID 2

Ā	%	⌂ⁿ
Ł7	7d	EШ
(o)	Ψ	ĕ

GRID 3

Ч	4λ	θ.σ
bЭ	k∂	Σ
ž>	Φ	9.3

GRID 4

U	5+4	⅞
∩	ε	T.8
Ŧ	⊥	П

UNIT 9

VISUAL MEMORY *CONTINUED*

GRID 1   looked back _____ time(s)

GRID 2   looked back _____ time(s)

GRID 3   looked back _____ time(s)

GRID 4   looked back _____ time(s)

SENTENCE RECALL EXERCISE - ADVANCED LEVEL B

DIRECTIONS: This exercise is designed to improve your memory. Read each sentence carefully, remembering as much as possible. In the space immediately below, write the sentence FROM MEMORY, word-for-word. Resist the temptation to look back at the sentence after you have read it. Try to read each sentence only once.

Sentence #1:
He ingenuously owns, that not only the Grecian writers, but even the priests of Egypt, and the bards of the same country varied in the accounts which they gave of this hero. (Bryant)

Recall #1:

Sentence #2:
Chinese books state that between the fourth and the eighth centuries "the art of painting man and things underwent a vital change." (Petrucci)

Recall #2:

Sentence #3:
The tendency to order, said Sénancour, should form "an essential part of our inclinations, of our instinct, like the tendencies to self-preservation and to reproduction." (Brownell)

Recall #3:

Sentence #4:
They delighted in painting fanciful landscapes and were inclined toward images that were more external and less inspired than in the past. (Petrucci)

Recall #4:

UNIT 9 - ADVANCED

Sentence #5:
It is a well-established and indisputable truth that from the Sun, the solar center of our system, is derived all force, every power and variety of phenomena that manifests itself upon Mother Earth. (Wagner)

Recall #5:

Sentence #6:
Of course, I kept up with 'Our Mutual Friend,' which Dickens was then writing, and with 'Philip,' which was to be the last of Thackeray. (Howells)

Recall #6:

Sentence #7:
The mask is certainly one of the stock properties of the subject, but notice how it is used to confer upon the whole work a character of mysterious witchery. (Brownell)

Recall #7:

Sentence #8:
The Euskarian neolithic population of Britain - a dark white race, like the modern Basques - had settlements in Sussex, at least in the coast district between the Downs and the sea. (Allen)

Recall #8:

Sentence #9:
The astronomer-priests of the hoary past, when language was figurative, and often pictorial, had recourse to a system of symbols to express abstract truths and ideas. (Wagner)

Recall #9:

SENTENCE RECALL *CONTINUED*

Sentence #10:

It gives us no account whatever of the origin of matter, but assumes that it was already in existence at the time from which the theory takes its point of departure. (Ackland)

Recall #10:

Sentence #11:

As the initial stiffness disappears, and the vocal action gradually becomes smooth and automatic, the voice begins to take on the characteristics of perfect tone-production. (Taylor)

Recall #11:

Sentence #12:

A painter, who finds no satisfaction in mere representation, however artistic, in his longing to express his inner life, cannot but envy the ease with which music, the most non-material of the arts today, achieves this end. (Kandinsky)

Recall #12:

Sentence #13:

Mercury and Mars, the smallest planets, should have, according to this principle, the largest eccentricities and orbital inclinations of any of the major planets. (Campbell)

Recall #13:

Sentence #14:

They were ignorant of the spherical form of the earth, and so could not have attached any idea whatever to a statement that it revolved about its axis. (Ackland)

Recall #14:

UNIT 10
ADVANCED LEVEL C

READING SPEED EXERCISE - ADVANCED LEVEL C

DIRECTIONS: This exercise is designed to measure your relative reading speed. Read the passage at an accelerated rate while monitoring your time. Be sure to comprehend as much material as possible. At the end of the passage, record the number of minutes and seconds you spent reading. Refer to the Appendix for your calculated reading rate.

To study Scott's relations with contemporary writers is a very pleasant task because nothing shows better the greatness of his heart. His admirable freedom from literary jealousy was an innate virtue which he deliberately increased by cultivation, taking care, also, never to subject himself to the conditions which he thought accounted for the faults of Pope, who had "neither the business nor the idleness of life to divide his mind from his Parnassian pursuits." "Those who have not his genius may be so far compensated by avoiding his foibles," Scott said; and some years later he wrote,—"When I first saw that a literary profession was to be my fate, I endeavored by all efforts of stoicism to divest myself of that irritable degree of sensibility—or, to speak plainly, of vanity—which makes the poetical race miserable and ridiculous." The record of his life clearly shows that his kindness towards other men of letters was not limited to words. One who received his good offices has written,—"The sternest words I ever heard him utter were concerning a certain poet: 'That man,' he said, 'has had much in his power, but he never befriended rising genius yet' "We may safely say that Scott enjoyed liking the work of other men. "I am most delighted with praise from those who convince me of their good taste by admiring the genius of my contemporaries," he once wrote to Southey.

It is commonly supposed that Scott's amiability led him into absurd excesses of praise for the works of his fellow-craftsmen, and indeed he did say some very surprising things. But when all his references to any one man are brought together, they will be found, with a few exceptions, pretty fairly to characterize the writer. His obiter dicta must be read in the light of one another, and in the light, also, of his known principles. Temperamentally modest about his own work, he was also habitually optimistic, and the combination gave him an utterly different quality from that of the typical Edinburgh or Quarterly critics.

His disapproval of their point of view he expressed more than once. It seemed to him futile and ungentlemanly for the anonymous reviewer to seek primarily for faults, or "to wound any person's feelings ... unless where conceit or false doctrine strongly calls for reprobation." "Where praise can be conscientiously mingled in a larger proportion than blame," he said, "there is always some amusement in throwing together our ideas upon the works of our fellow-labourers."

He thought, indeed, that vituperative and satiric criticism was defeating its own end, in the case of the Edinburgh Review since it was overworked to the point of monotony. Such criticism he considered futile as well on this account as because he thought it likely to have an injurious effect on the work of really gifted writers.

An admirer of both Jeffrey and Scott, who once heard a conversation between the two men, has recorded a distinction which is exactly what we should expect. He says: "Jeffrey, for the most part, entertained us, when books were under discussion, with the detection of faults, blunders, absurdities, or plagiarisms: Scott took up the matter where he left it, recalled some compensating beauty or excellence for which no credit had been allowed, and by the recitation, perhaps, of one fine stanza, set the poor victim on his legs again."

On Jeffrey Scott's verdict was, "There is something in his mode of reasoning that leads me greatly to doubt whether, notwithstanding the vivacity of his imagination, he really has any feeling of poetical genius, or whether he has worn it all off by perpetually

UNIT 10 - ADVANCED

sharpening his wit on the grindstone of criticism." His comment on Gifford's reviews was to the effect that people were more moved to dislike the critic for his savagery than the guilty victim whom he flagellated. In the early days of Blackwood's Magazine Scott often tried to repress Lockhart's "wicked wit," and when Lockhart became editor of the Quarterly his father-in-law did not always approve of his work. "Don't like his article on Sheridan's life," says the Journal. "There is no breadth in it, no general views, the whole flung away in smart but party criticism. Now, no man can take more general and liberal views of literature than J.G.L."

With these opinions, Scott was not likely often to undertake the reviewing of books that did not, in one way or another interest him or move his admiration; and he would lay as much stress as possible on their good points. Gifford told him that "fun and feeling" were his forte. In his early days he was probably somewhat influenced by Jeffrey's method, and his articles on Todd's Spenser and Godwin's Life of Chaucer indicate that he could occasionally adopt something of the tone of the Edinburgh Review. Years afterwards he refused to write an article that Lockhart wanted for the Quarterly, saying, "I cannot write anything about the author unless I know it can hurt no one alive" but for the first volume of the Quarterly he reviewed Sir John Carr's Caledonian Sketches in a way that Sharon Turner seriously objected to, because it made Sir John seem ridiculous.

Some of Scott's critics would perhaps apply one of the strictures to himself: "Although Sir John quotes Horace, he has yet to learn that a wise man should not admire too easily; for he frequently falls into a state of wonderment at what appears to us neither very new nor very extraordinary." But if admiration seems to characterize too great a proportion of Scott's critical work, it is because he usually preferred to ignore such books as demanded the sarcastic treatment which he reprehended, but which he felt perfectly capable of applying when he wished.

Speaking of a fulsome biography he once said, "I can no more sympathize with a mere eulogist than I can with a ranting hero upon the stage; and it unfortunately

happens that some of our disrespect is apt, rather unjustly, to be transferred to the subject of the panegyric in the one case, and to poor Cato in the other."

Besides Scott's formal reviews, we find cited as evidence of his extreme amiability his letters, his journal, and the remarks he made to friends in moments of enthusiasm. These do indeed contain some sweeping statements, but in almost every case one can see some reason, other than the desire to be obliging, why he made them. He was not double-faced. One of the nearest approaches to it seems to have been in the case of Miss Seward's poetry, for which he wrote such an introduction as hardly prepares the reader for the remark he made to Miss Baillie, that most of it was "absolutely execrable." His comment in the edition of the poems—the publication of which Miss Seward really forced upon him as a dying request—is sedulously kind, and in Waverley he quotes from her a couple of lines which he calls "beautiful." But the essay is most carefully guarded, and throughout it the editor implies that the woman was more admirable than the poetry. Personally, indeed, he seems to have liked and admired her.

The catalogue of Scott's contemporaries is so full of important names that his genius for the enjoyment of other men's work had a wide opportunity to display itself without becoming absurd. An argument early used to prove that Scott was the author of Waverley was the frequency of quotation in the novels from all living poets except Scott himself, and he felt constrained to throw in a reference or two to his own poetry in order to weaken the force of the evidence. The reader is irresistibly reminded of the following description, given by Lockhart in a letter to his wife, of a morning walk taken by Wordsworth and Scott in company: "The Unknown was continually quoting Wordsworth's Poetry and Wordsworth ditto, but the great Laker never uttered one syllable by which it might have been intimated to a stranger that your Papa had ever written a line either of verse or prose since he was born."

Scott's opinions in regard to his fellow craftsmen may best be given largely in his own words—words which cannot fail to be interesting, however little evidence they show of any attempt to make them quotable.

In considering Scott's estimation of his contemporaries it is chronologically proper to mention Burns first. As a boy of fifteen Scott met Burns, an event which filled him with the suitable amount of awe. He was most favorably impressed with the poet's appearance and with everything in his manner. The boy thought, however, that "Burns' acquaintance with English poetry was rather limited, and also, that having twenty times the abilities of Allan Ramsay and of Ferguson, he talked of them with too much humility as his models." Scott's admiration of Burns was always expressed in the highest and, if one may say so, the most affectionate terms. He refused to let himself be named "in the same day" with Burns. "Long life to thy fame and peace to thy soul, Rob Burns!" he exclaimed, in his Journal; "when I want to express a sentiment which I feel strongly, I find the phrase in Shakespeare—or thee." On another day he compared Burns with Shakespeare as excelling all other poets in "the power of exciting the most varied and discordant emotions with such rapid transitions." Again, "The Jolly Beggars, for humorous description and nice discrimination of character, is inferior to no poem of the same length in the whole range of English poetry." Scott wished that Burns might have carried out his plan of dramatic composition, and regretted, from that point of view, the excessive labor at songs which in the nature of things could not all be masterpieces.

Of writers who were more precisely contemporaries of Scott, the Lake Poets and Byron are the most important. The precedence ought to be given to Coleridge because of the suggestion Scott caught from a chance recitation of Christabel for the meter he made so popular in the Lay. Fragments from Christabel are quoted or alluded to so often in the novels and throughout Scott's work that we should conclude it had made a greater impression upon him than any other single poem written in his own time, if Lockhart had not spoken of Wordsworth's sonnet on Neidpath Castle as one which Scott was perhaps fondest of quoting. Christabel is not the only one of Coleridge's poems

which Scott used for allusion or reference, but it was the favorite. "He is naturally a grand poet," Scott once wrote to a friend. "His verses on Love, I think, are among the most beautiful in the English language. Let me know if you have seen them, as I have a copy of them as they stood in their original form, which was afterwards altered for the worse." The Ancient Mariner also made a decided impression on him, if we judge from the fact that he quoted from it several times. Scott evidently felt that Coleridge was a most tantalizing poet, and once intimated that future generations would in regard to him feel something like Milton's desire "to call up him who left half told the story of Cambuscan bold." "No man has all the resources of poetry in such profusion, but he cannot manage them so as to bring out anything of his own on a large scale at all worthy of his genius.... His fancy and diction would have long ago placed him above all his contemporaries, had they been under the direction of a sound judgment and a steady will."

Such, in effect, was the opinion that Scott always expressed concerning Coleridge, and it is practically that of posterity. In The Monastery Coleridge is called "the most imaginative of our modern bards." In another connection, after speaking of the "exquisite powers of poetry he has suffered to remain uncultivated," Scott adds, "Let us be thankful for what we have received, however. The unfashioned ore, drawn from so rich a mine, is worth all to which art can add its highest decorations, when drawn from less abundant sources." These remarks are worth quoting, not only because of their wisdom, but also because Scott had small personal acquaintance with Coleridge and was rather repelled than attracted by what he knew of the character of the author of Christabel. His praises cannot in this case be called the tribute of friendship, and his own remarkable power of self-control might have made him a stern judge of Coleridge's shortcomings.

One of his most interesting comments on Coleridge is contained in a discussion of Byron's Darkness, a poem which to his mind recalled "the wild, unbridled, and fiery imagination of Coleridge." Darkness is characterized as a mass of images and

UNIT 10 - ADVANCED

ideas, unarranged, and the critic goes on to warn the author against indulging in this sort of poetry. He says: "The feeling of reverence which we entertain for that which is difficult of comprehension, gives way to weariness whenever we begin to suspect that it cannot be distinctly comprehended by anyone.... The strength of poetical conception and beauty of diction bestowed upon such prolusions [sic], is as much thrown away as the colors of a painter, could he take a cloud of mist or a wreath of smoke for his canvas." It is disappointing that we have no comment from Scott upon Shelley's poetry, but we can imagine what is would have been. Scott's position as the great popularizer of the Romantic movement in poetry makes particularly interesting his very evident though not often expressed repugnance to the more extreme development of that movement.

Wordsworth's peculiar theory of poetry seemed to Scott superfluous and unnecessary, though he was never, so far as we can judge, especially irritated by it. Of Wordsworth and Southey he wrote to Miss Seward: "Were it not for the unfortunate idea of forming a new school of poetry, these men are calculated to give it a new impulse; but I think they sometimes lose their energy in trying to find not a better but a different path from what has been traveled by their predecessors." Scott paid tribute in the introduction to The Antiquary to as much of Wordsworth's poetical creed as he could acquiesce in when he said, "The lower orders are less restrained by the habit of suppressing their feelings, and ... I agree with my friend Wordsworth that they seldom fail to express them in the strongest and most powerful language." In a letter to Southey Scott calls Wordsworth "a great master of the passions," and in his Journal he said: His imagination "is naturally exquisite, and highly cultivated by constant exercise." At another time he compared Wordsworth and Southey as scholars and commented on the "freshness, vivacity, and spring" of Wordsworth's mind.

The personal relations between Scott and Wordsworth were, as Wordsworth's tribute in Yarrow Revisited would indicate, those of affectionate intimacy. And if Scott took exception to Wordsworth's choice of subjects and manner, Wordsworth used the same freedom in disagreeing with Scott's poetical ideals. "Thank you," he wrote in 1808, "for Marmion,

which I have read with lively pleasure. I think your end has been attained. That it is not in every respect the end which I should wish you to purpose to yourself, you will be well aware, from what you know of my notions of composition, both as to matter and manner." When, in 1821, Chantrey was about to exhibit together his busts of the two poets, Scott wrote: "I am happy my effigy is to go with that of Wordsworth, for (differing from him in very many points of taste) I do not know a man more to be venerated for uprightness of heart and loftiness of genius. Why he will sometimes choose to crawl upon all fours, when God has given him so noble a countenance to lift to heaven, I am as little able to account for as for his quarrelling (as you tell me) with the wrinkles which time and meditation have stamped his brow withal."

These remarks upon Wordsworth and Coleridge touch merely the fringe of the subject, and indeed we do not find that Scott exercised any such sublimated ingenuity in appreciating these men as has often been considered essential. We can see that he admired certain parts of their work intensely, but we look in vain for any real analysis of their quality. But as he never had occasion to write essays upon their poetry, it is perhaps hardly fair to expect anything more than the general remarks that we actually do find, and as far as they go they are satisfactory.

His full-blooded enjoyment of life and literature tempered without obscuring his critical instinct, and though he was "willing to be pleased by those who were desirous to give pleasure", he noted the weak points of men to whose power he gladly paid tribute. Wordsworth, Coleridge, Southey, and Byron, whom he classed as the great English poets of his time, may, with the exception of Southey, be given the places he assigned to them. In regard to Byron, Scott expressed a critical estimate that the public is only now getting ready to accept after a long period of depreciating Byron's genius. The men whose work Scott judged fairly and sympathetically represent widely different types. With some of them he was connected by the new impulse that they were imparting to English poetry, but he was so close to the transition period that he could look backward to his predecessors with no sense of strangeness. He was never inclined to quarrel with the "erroneous system" of a poem which he really liked. His comments on Byron's Darkness suggest that if he had read more than he did of Shelley and others among his younger contemporaries he might have found much to reprehend, but he held that "we must not limit poetical merit to the class of composition which exactly suits one's own particular taste." Among novelists even less than among poets can we trace a "school" to which he paid special allegiance. He read and enjoyed all sorts of good stories, growing in this respect more catholic in his tastes, though perhaps more severe in his standards, as he grew older.

In speaking of Scott's relations with his contemporaries, we must especially remember his ardent interest in those realities of life which he considered greater than the greatest books. In one of his reviews he laid stress on the merit of writing on contemporary events, and he seemed to think there was too little of such celebration. There are many evidences of his great admiration for those of his contemporaries who were men of action, but it is sufficient to remember that the only man in whose presence Scott felt abashed was the Duke of Wellington, for he counted that famous commander the greatest man of his time.

Important as Scott's poetry was in the English Romantic revival, as a critic he can hardly be counted among the Romanticists. His attitude, nevertheless, differed radically from that of the school represented by Jeffrey and Gifford. We have already seen that he disliked their manner of reviewing, and that he was conscious of complete disagreement with Jeffrey in regard to poetic ideals. Of Jeffrey Mr. Gates has said: "[He] rarely appreciates a piece of literature.... He is always for or against his author; he is always making points." That Scott was influenced in his early critical work by the tone of the Edinburgh Review is undeniable, but temperamentally he was inclined to give any writer a fair chance to stir his emotions; and he did not adopt the magisterial mood that dictated the famous remark, "This will never do." Scott's style lacked the adroitness and pungency which helped

Jeffrey successfully to take the attitude of the censor, and which made his satire triumphant among his contemporaries. Scott declined, moreover, to cultivate skill in a method which he considered unfair. Compared with Jeffrey's his criticism wanted incisiveness, but it wears better.

The period was transitional, and Jeffrey did not go so far as Scott in breaking away from the dictation of his predecessors. But his attitude was on the whole more modern than the reader would infer from the following sentence in one of his earliest reviews: "Poetry has this much at least in common with religion, that its standards were fixed long ago by certain inspired writers, whose authority it is no longer lawful to call in question.

"He considered himself rather an interpreter of public opinion than a judge defining ancient legislation, but he used the opinion of himself and like-minded men as an unimpeachable test of what the greater public ought to believe in regard to literature. We may remember that the enthusiasm over the Elizabethan dramatists which seems a special property of Lamb and Hazlitt, and which Scott shared, was characteristic also of Jeffrey himself. It was Jeffrey's dogmatism and his repugnance to certain fundamental ideas which were to become dominant in the poetry of the nineteenth century that lead us to consider him one of the last representatives of the eighteenth century critical tradition. Scott praised the Augustan writers as warmly as Jeffrey did, but he was more hospitable to the newer literary impulse. "Perhaps the most damaging accusation that can be made against Jeffrey as a critic," says Mr. Gates, "is inability to read and interpret the age in which he lived."

Scott's criticism was largely appreciative, but appreciative on a somewhat different plane from that of the contemporary critics whom we are accustomed to place in a more modern school: Hazlitt, Hunt, Lamb, and Coleridge. His judgments were less delicate and subtle than the judgments of these men were apt to be, and more "reasonable" in the eighteenth-century sense; they were marked, however, by a regard for the imagination that would have seemed most unreasonable to many men of the eighteenth century.

Scott had not a fixed theory of literature which could dominate his mind when he approached any work. He was open-minded, and in spite of his extreme fondness for the poetry of Dr. Johnson he was apt to be on the Romantic side in any specific critical utterance. We have seen also that he resembled the Romanticists in his power to disengage his verdicts on literature from ethical considerations. On the other hand he seems always to have deferred to the standard authorities of the classical criticism of his time when his own knowledge was not sufficient to guide him. In discussing Roscommon's Essay on Translated Verse he wrote: "It must be remembered that the rules of criticism, now so well known as to be even trite and hackneyed, were then almost new to the literary world."

Perhaps the main reason why one would not class Scott's critical work with that of the Romanticists is that he had no desire to proclaim a new era in creative literature or in criticism. Like the Romanticists he was ready to substitute "for the absolute method of judging by reference to an external standard of 'taste,' a method at once imaginative and historical"; yet he talked less about imagination than about good sense. The comparison with Boileau suggests itself, for Scott admired that critic in the conventional fashion, calling him "a supereminent authority," and Boileau also had said much about "reason and good sense." But Scott had an appreciation of the furor poeticus that made "good sense" quite a different thing to him from what it was to Boileau. He did not say, moreover, that the poet should be supremely characterized by good sense, but that the critic, recognizing the facts about human emotion, should make use of that quality.

The subjective process by which experience is transmuted into literature engaged Scott's attention very little: in this respect also he stands apart from the newer school of critics. The metaphysical description of imagination or fancy interested him less than the piece of literature in which these qualities were exhibited. His own mental activities were more easily set in motion than analyzed, and the introspective or philosophical attitude of mind was unnatural to him. Because of his

adoption of the historical method of studying literature, and the similarity of many of his judgments to those which were in general characteristic of the Romantic school, we may say that Scott's criticism looks forward; but it shows the influence of the earlier period in its acceptance of traditional judgments based on external standards which disregarded the nature of the creative process.

From Coleridge Scott is separated in the most definite way. Coleridge began at the foundation, building up a set of principles such as the new impulse in literature seemed to demand. Scott preferred the concrete, and was stimulated by the particular book to express opinions that would never have come to his mind as the result of pursuing a train of unembodied ideas. Coleridge's judgments, moreover, would be unaffected by public estimation, for he sought to found them on the spiritual and philosophic consciousness that exists apart from the crowd. Scott, on the other hand, was ready to use popular judgment as an important test of his opinions. Coleridge himself pointed out another interesting contrast. He wrote: "Dear Sir Walter Scott and myself were exact, but harmonious opposites in this;—that every old ruin, hill, river, or tree, called up in his mind a host of historical or biographical associations, ... whereas, for myself, notwithstanding Dr. Johnson, I believe I should walk over the plain of Marathon without taking more interest in it than in any other plain of similar features." We might perhaps say that Coleridge's affection was given to ideas, Scott's, to objects; hence Coleridge was a critic of literary principles and theories, Scott a critic of individual books and writers. It follows that Scott was on the whole an impressionistic critic.

A study of his personality is essential to a consideration of his critical work, for he was not so much a systematic student of literature, guided by fixed principles, as a man of a certain temperament who read particular things and made particular remarks about them as he felt inclined. The inconsistencies and contradictions which would naturally result from such a procedure are occasionally noticeable, but they are fewer than would occur in the work of a less well-balanced man than himself.

His ideas about criticism were influenced by his feeling that the judgment of the public would after all take its own course, and that it was in the long run the best criterion. He used his opinion that an author, even in his own lifetime, commonly receives fair treatment from the public, as an argument against establishing in England any literary body having the power of pensioning literary men. On this subject he said, "There is ... really no occasion for encouraging by a society the competition of authors. The land is before them, and if they really have merit they seldom fail to conquer their share of public applause and private profit.... I cannot, in my knowledge of letters, recollect more than two men whose merit is undeniable while, I am afraid, their circumstances are narrow. I mean Coleridge and Maturin."

Scott's whole attitude toward criticism shows that he felt its supreme function to be elucidation. It should also, he believed, warn the world against books that were foolish, or pernicious, intellectually or morally; but unless there were good reason for issuing such warnings the bad books should be ignored and the good treated sympathetically, not without such discrimination as should distinguish between the better and the worse in them, but with emphasis on the better. His literary creed, though not formulated into a system, was conscious and fairly definite; but it consisted of general principles which never resolved themselves into intricate subtleties requiring great space for their development. Scott could not think in that way, and he felt convinced that such thinking was useless and worse than useless. A magazine-writer of his own period who said of him,—"The author of Waverley, we apprehend, has neither the patience nor the disposition requisite for writing philosophically upon any subject," was mistaken, for much of Scott's criticism, without making any pretensions, is really philosophical. But any fine-drawn analysis seemed to him to serve the vanity of the critic rather than the need of the public; and he despised that arrogance in the critic which leads him to assume to direct literary taste.

Historical illustration was that kind of editorial work which he found most congenial, and which harmonized best with his critical principles; for when

he could bring definite facts to the service of elucidation he felt that he was doing something worth while. Among all the introductions and annotations that we have from his hand, including those of the Dryden and the Swift, this kind of explanation greatly predominates over the more strictly literary comment; in his reviews, also, it is evident that he seized every opportunity for turning from literary to historical discussion. He was in the habit of "embroidering the subject, whatever it might be, with lively anecdotic illustration," as one of his biographers says. We are not to conclude that in writing on specifically literary subjects he felt ill at ease. He felt, on the contrary, that the objection lay in the too great ease with which the critic might become dictatorial. He was fond enough of details when they were concrete and vital.

The facts of literary history were in this category to him, as distinguished from the notions of literary theory; and we find that his critical principles are apt to appear incidentally among remarks on what seemed to him the more tangible and important facts of literary and social history. The books he chose to review were chiefly those which gave him a chance to use his historical information and imagination. His ideas were concrete, as those of a great novelist must inevitably be. Indeed the dividing line between creative work and criticism seems often to be obliterated in Scott's literary discussions, since he was inclined to amplify and illustrate instead of dissecting the book under consideration. As a critic he was distinguished by the qualities which appear in his novels, and which may be described in Hazlitt's words, as "the most amazing retentiveness of memory, and vividness of conception of what would happen, be seen, and felt by everybody in given circumstances."

Scott felt that there was especial danger of futile theorizing in the criticism of poetry. In writing about Alexander's Feast he discussed for a moment the possibility of detecting points at which the author had paused in his work, but almost immediately he stopped himself with the characteristic remark—"There may be something fanciful ... in this reasoning, which I therefore abandon to the reader's mercy; only begging him to observe, that we have no mode of

UNIT 10 - ADVANCED

estimating the exertions of a quality so capricious as a poetic imagination." Early in his career he gave this rather over-amiable explanation of the fact that he had never undertaken to review poetry: "I am sensible there is a greater difference of tastes in that department than in any other, and that there is much excellent poetry which I am not nowadays able to read without falling asleep, and which would nevertheless have given me great pleasure at an earlier period of my life. Now I think there is something hard in blaming the poor cook for the fault of our own palate or deficiency of appetite." We have seen that he did review poetry afterwards, but that he was inclined to do it with the least possible emphasis on the specifically aesthetic elements. On the subject of novel-writing he developed a somewhat fuller critical theory, but here also his discussions concerned themselves rather with the kind of ideas set forth than with the manner of presentation.

It does indeed seem as if Scott's feelings were more easily aroused to the point of formulating "laws" in the field of political criticism than in that which appears to us his more legitimate sphere. He has his fling, to be sure, at Madame de Staël, because she "lived and died in the belief that revolutions were to be effected, and countries governed, by a proper succession of clever pamphlets." But in proposing the establishment of the Quarterly Review he made no secret of the fact that his motives were political. The literary aspect of the periodical was thought of as a subordinate, though a necessary and not unimportant phase of the undertaking. The Letters of Malachi Malagrowther contain some very definite maxims on the subject of political economy, and just as decided are the remarks made in the last of Paul's Letters, as well as in the Life of Napoleon and elsewhere, as to how Louis XVIII ought to set about the task of calming his distracted kingdom of France. But however emphatic Scott may be in the comments on government which appear throughout his writings, he was as strongly averse in this matter as in literary affairs to any separation of philosophy from fact: his maxims are always derived from experience. The following statement of opinion is typical: "In legislating for an ancient people, the question is not, what is the best possible system of law, but what is the best they can bear. Their habitudes and prejudices must always be respected; and, whenever it

is practicable, those prejudices, instead of being destroyed, ought to be taken as the basis of the new regulations."

It was Scott's political creed that roused the ire of such men as Hazlitt and Hunt, though they may also have been exasperated at the unprecedented success of poetry which seemed so facile and so superficial to them as Scott's. Leigh Hunt calls him "a poet of a purely conventional order," "a bitter and not very large-minded politician," "a critic more agreeable than subtle." But Scott's politics may be looked at in another way. "In his patriotism," says Mr. Courthope, "his passionate love of the past, and his reverence for established authority, literary or political, Scott is the best representative among English men of letters of Conservatism in its most generous form."

Though it seems to have been a common opinion among the literary men of his own time that Scott's criticism was superficial, his knowledge of mediaeval literature was, as we have seen, recognized and respected. Favorable comments by his contemporaries on other parts of his critical work are not difficult to find. For example, Gifford wrote to Murray in regard to the article on Lady Suffolk's Correspondence: "Scott's paper is a clever, sensible thing—the work of a man who knows what he is about." Isaac D'Israeli made the following observation on another of Scott's papers: "The article on Pepys, after so many have been written, is the only one which, in the most charming manner possible, shows the real value of these works, which I can assure you many good scholars have no idea of." A more recent verdict may be set beside those just quoted, and it is in perfect agreement with them. "His critical faculty," says Professor Saintsbury, "if not extraordinarily subtle, was always as sound and shrewd as it was good-natured." (Ball)

TOTAL TIME:

....

PARAGRAPH SUMMARY EXERCISE - ADVANCED LEVEL C

DIRECTIONS: This exercise is designed to improve your ability to summarize main concepts. Read the material at a comfortable rate. After you have read EACH paragraph, write a brief summary of its key points in the right column. Include main ideas, conclusions, and opinions. Do not include details.

Although proverbial philosophy warns us never to prophesy unless we know, experience has shown that political prophets have often made singularly correct forecasts of the future. Lord Chesterfield, and at a much earlier period Marshal Vauban, foretold the French Revolution, whilst the impending ruin of the Ottoman Empire has formed the theme of numerous prophecies made by close observers of contemporaneous events from the days of Horace Walpole downwards. "It is of no use," Napoleon wrote to the Directory, "to try to maintain the Turkish Empire; we shall witness its fall in our time." During the War of Greek Independence the Duke of Wellington believed that the end of Turkey was at hand. Where the prophets have for the most part failed is not so much in making a mistaken estimate of the effects likely to be produced by the causes which they saw were acting on the body politic, as in not allowing sufficient time for the operation of those causes. Political evolution in its early stages is generally very slow. It is only after long internal travail that it moves with vertiginous rapidity.

1st PARAGRAPH SUMMARY:

De Tocqueville cast a remarkably accurate horoscope of the course which would be run by the Second Empire, but it took some seventeen years to bring about results which he thought would be accomplished in a much shorter period. It has been reserved for the present generation to witness the fulfillment of prophecy in the case of European Turkey. The blindness displayed by Turkish statesmen to the lessons taught by history, their complete sterility in the domain of political thought, and their inability to adapt themselves and the institutions of their country to the growing requirements of the age, might almost lead an historical student to suppose that they were bent on committing political suicide. The combined diplomatists of Europe, Lord Salisbury sorrowfully remarked in 1877, "all tried to save Turkey," but she

2nd PARAGRAPH SUMMARY:

UNIT 10 - ADVANCED

scorned salvation and persisted in a course of action which could lead to but one result. That result has now been attained. The dismemberment of European Turkey, begun so long ago as the Peace of Karlovitz in 1699, is now almost complete. "Modern history," Lord Acton said, "begins under the stress of the Ottoman conquest." Whatever troubles the future may have in store, Europe has at last thrown off the Ottoman incubus. A new chapter in modern history has thus been opened. Henceforth, if Ottoman power is to survive at all, it must be in Asia, albeit the conflicting jealousies of the European Powers allow for the time being the maintenance of an Asiatic outpost on European soil.

3rd PARAGRAPH SUMMARY:

It is as yet too early to expect any complete or philosophic account of this stupendous occurrence, which the future historian will rank with the unification first of Italy and later of Germany, as one of the most epoch-making events of the later nineteenth and early twentieth centuries. Notably, there are two subjects which require much further elucidation before the final verdict of contemporaries or posterity can be passed upon them. In the first place, the causes which have led to the military humiliation of a race which, whatever may be its defects, has been noted in history for its martial virility, require to be differentiated. Was the collapse of the Turkish army due merely to incapacity and mismanagement on the part of the commanders, aided by the corruption which has eaten like a canker into the whole Ottoman system of government and administration? Or must the causes be sought deeper, and, if so, was it the palsy of an unbridled and malevolent despotism which in itself produced the result, or did the sudden downfall of the despot, by the removal of a time-honored, if unworthy, symbol of government, abstract the corner-stone from the tottering political edifice, and thus, by disarranging the whole administrative gear of the Empire at a critical moment, render the catastrophe inevitable? Further information is required before a matured opinion on this point, which possesses more than a mere academic importance, can be formed.

4th PARAGRAPH SUMMARY:

There is yet another subject which, if only from a biographical point of view, is of great interest. Two untoward circumstances have caused Turkish domination in Europe to survive, and to resist the pressure of the civilization by which it was surrounded, but which seemed at one time doomed to thunder ineffectually at its gates. One was excessive jealousy— in Solomon's words, "as cruel as the grave"—amongst European States, which would not permit of any political advantage being gained by a rival nation. The other, and, as subsequent events proved, more potent consideration, was the fratricidal jealousy which the populations of the Balkan Peninsula mutually entertained towards each other. The maintenance and encouragement of mutual suspicions was, in either case, sedulously fostered by Turkish Sultans, the last of whom, more especially, acted throughout his inglorious career in the firm belief that mere mediaeval diplomatic trickery could be made to take the place of statesmanship. He must have chuckled when he joyously put his hand to the firman creating a Bulgarian Exarch, who was forthwith excommunicated by the Greek Patriarch, with the result, as Mr. Miller tells us, that "peasants killed each other in the name of contending ecclesiastical establishments."

5th PARAGRAPH SUMMARY:

In the early days of the last century the poet Rhigas, who was to Greece what Arndt was to Germany and Rouget de Lisle to Revolutionary France, appealed to all Balkan Christians to rise on behalf of the liberties of Greece. But the hour had not yet come for any such unity to be cemented. At that time, and for many years afterwards, Europe was scarcely conscious of the fact that there existed "a long-forgotten, silent nationality" which, after a lapse of nearly five centuries, would again spring into existence and bear a leading part in the liberation of the Balkan populations. But the rise of Bulgaria, far from bringing unity in its wake, appeared at first only to exacerbate not merely the mercurial Greek, proud of the intellectual and political primacy which he had heretofore enjoyed, but also the brother Slav, with whom differences arose which necessitated an appeal to the arbitrage of arms.

6th PARAGRAPH SUMMARY:

Although the thunder of the guns of Kirk Kilisse and Lüle Burgas proclaimed to Europe, in the words of the English Prime Minister, that "the map of Eastern Europe had to be recast," it is none the less true that the cause of the Turk was doomed from the moment when Balkan discord ceased, and when the Greek, the

UNIT 10 - ADVANCED

Bulgarian, the Serb, and the Montenegrin agreed to sink their differences and to act together against the common enemy. Who was it who accomplished this miracle? Mr. Miller says, "the authorship of this marvellous work, hitherto the despair of statesmen, is uncertain, but it has been ascribed chiefly to M. Venezélos." All, therefore, that can now be said is that it was the brain, or possibly brains, of some master-workers which gave liberty to the Balkan populations as surely as it was the brain of Cavour which united Italy.

Although these and possibly other points will, without doubt, eventually receive more ample treatment at the hands of some future historian, Mr. Miller has performed a most useful service in affording a guide by the aid of which the historical student can find his way through the labyrinthine maze of Balkan politics. He begins his story about the time when Napoleon had appeared like a comet in the political firmament, and by his erratic movements had caused all the statesmen of Europe to diverge temporarily from their normal and conventional orbits, one result being that the British Admiral Duckworth wandered in a somewhat aimless fashion through the Dardanelles to Constantinople, and had very little idea of what to do when he got there.

Mr. Miller reminds us of events of great importance in their day, but now almost wholly forgotten: of how the ancient Republic of Ragusa, which had existed for eleven centuries and which had earned the title of the "South Slavonic Athens," was crushed out of existence under the iron heel of Marmont, who forthwith proceeded to make some good roads and to vaccinate the Dalmatians; of how Napoleon tried to partition the Balkans, but found, with all his political and administrative genius, that he was face to face with an "insoluble problem"; of how that rough man of genius, Mahmoud II., hanged the Greek Patriarch from the gate of his palace, but between the interludes of massacres and executions, brought his "energy and indomitable force of will" to bear on the introduction of reforms; of how the Venetian Count Capo d'Istria, who was eventually assassinated, produced a local revolt by a well-intentioned attempt to amend the primitive ethics of the Mainote Greeks—a tale which is not without its

7th PARAGRAPH SUMMARY:

8th PARAGRAPH SUMMARY:

warning if ever the time comes for dealing with a cognate question amongst the wild tribes of Albania; and of how, amidst the ever-shifting vicissitudes of Eastern politics, the Tsar of Russia, who had heretofore posed as the "protector" of Roumans and Serbs against their sovereign, sent his fleet to the Bosphorus in 1833 in order to "protect" the sovereign against his rebellious vassal, Mehemet Ali, and exacted a reward for his services in the shape of the leonine arrangement signed at Hunkiar-Iskelesi.

And so Mr. Miller carries us on from massacre to massacre, from murder to murder, and from one bewildering treaty to another, all of which, however, present this feature of uniformity, that the Turk, signing of his own free will, but with an unwilling mind made on each occasion either some new concession to the ever-rising tide of Christian demand, or ratified the loss of a province which had been forcibly torn from his flank. Finally, we get to the period when the tragedy connected with the name of Queen Draga acted like an electric shock on Europe, and when the accession of King Peter, "who had translated Mill On Liberty," to the blood-stained Servian throne, revealed to an astonished world that the processes of Byzantinism survived to the present day. Five years later followed the assumption by Prince Ferdinand of the title of "Tsar of the Bulgarians," and it then only required the occurrence of some opportunity and the appearance on the scene of some Balkan Cavour to bring the struggle of centuries to the final issue of a death-grapple between the followers of aggressive Christianity and those of stagnant Islamism.

The whole tale is at once dramatic and dreary, dramatic because it is occasionally illumined by acts of real heroism, such as the gallant defense of Plevna by Ghazi Osman, a graphic account of which was written by an adventurous young Englishman (Mr. W.V. Herbert) who served in the Turkish army, or again as the conduct of the Cretan Abbot Máneses who, in 1866, rather than surrender to the Turks, "put a match to the powder-magazine, thus uniting defenders and assailants in one common hecatomb." It is dreary because the mind turns with horror and disgust from the endless record of government by massacre, in which, it is to be

9th PARAGRAPH SUMMARY:

10th PARAGRAPH SUMMARY:

UNIT 10 - ADVANCED

observed, the crime of blood guiltiness can by no means be laid exclusively at the door of the dominant race, whilst Mr. Miller's somber but perfectly true remark that "assassination or abdication, execution or exile, has been the normal fate of Balkan rulers," throws a lurid light on the whole state of Balkan society.

But how does the work of diplomacy, and especially of British diplomacy, stand revealed by the light of the history of the past century? The point is one of importance, all the more so because there is a tendency on the part of some British politicians to mistrust diplomatists, to think that, either from incapacity or design, they serve as agents to stimulate war rather than as peace-makers, and to hold that a more minute interference by the House of Commons in the details of diplomatic negotiations would be useful and beneficial.

It would be impossible within the limits of an ordinary newspaper article to deal adequately with this question. This much, however, may be said—that, even taking the most unfavorable view of the results achieved by diplomacy, there is nothing whatever in Mr. Miller's history to engender the belief that better results would have been obtained by shifting the responsibility to a greater degree from the shoulders of the executive to those of Parliament. The evidence indeed rather points to an opposite conclusion. For instance, Mr. Miller informs us that inopportune action taken in England was one of the causes which contributed to the outbreak of hostilities between Greece and Turkey in 1897. "An address from a hundred British members of Parliament encouraged the masses, ignorant of the true condition of British politics, to count upon the help of Great Britain." (Baring)

11th PARAGRAPH SUMMARY:

12th PARAGRAPH SUMMARY:

VISUAL MEMORY EXERCISE - ADVANCED LEVEL C

DIRECTIONS: This exercise is designed to improve your visual memory. Four grids of nine objects are presented. Look at each grid for one minute. Memorize as best you can the design and placement of each symbol. When you have all objects memorized for one grid, turn to the next page and draw the nine objects in the corresponding grid FROM MEMORY. If you need to look back at the grid, then document how many times you looked at the objects.

GRID 1

φ	Θ8	‡
[»]	Ћ	Kẅ
?¿	Ξ	Σ

GRID 2

ğ2	♥	6.Υ
N	Ꝇ	∩U
И	śaw	↓ą

GRID 3

Ψ	Ц	ɔ
kęn	Я	^>v
Λ	Δ	b.9

GRID 4

4β	‰	DĐ
ň3	△	ШI
≈	ΞE	Ħ

UNIT 10

VISUAL MEMORY *CONTINUED*

GRID 1   looked back _____ time(s)

GRID 2   looked back _____ time(s)

GRID 3   looked back _____ time(s)

GRID 4   looked back _____ time(s)

SENTENCE RECALL EXERCISE - ADVANCED LEVEL C

DIRECTIONS: This exercise is designed to improve your memory. Read each sentence carefully, remembering as much as possible. In the space immediately below, write the sentence FROM MEMORY, word-for-word. Resist the temptation to look back at the sentence after you have read it. Try to read each sentence only once.

Sentence #1:

The power to distinguish between the genuine effort and the adventitious mistakes is perhaps the most difficult test which comes to our fallible intelligence. (Addams)

Recall #1:

Sentence #2:

He agreed with Percy that ballads were composed and sung by minstrels, and based his discussion on the materials brought forward by Percy and Ritson for use in their great controversy. (Ball)

Recall #2:

Sentence #3:

To make full use of the conception of the organism as an historical being it is necessary then to understand the causal nexus between ontogeny and phylogeny. (Russell)

Recall #3:

Sentence #4:

It is doubtless true at this day that "no race inhabits Greece," and the main difference between Greeks and other Balkan peoples is that, inhabiting the mountains and valleys of Hellas, they speak in dialects of the ancient tongue. (Jordan)

Recall #4:

UNIT 10 - ADVANCED

Sentence #5:
That the content rather than the literary turn of dialogue is the thing that counts most in the theatre will be felt emphatically if we compare the mere writing of Molière with that of his successor and imitator, Regnard. (Hamilton)

Recall #5:

Sentence #6:
The inevitable desire for outward expression of the objective element is the impulse here defined as the "inner need." (Kandinsky)

Recall #6:

Sentence #7:
He does not content himself with telling us, for example, that one of his characters is a good man or a bad man, an able, a selfish, a tall, a blonde, or a stupid man, as the case may be. (Brownell)

Recall #7:

Sentence #8:
There are many persons who suppose that the highest proof an artist can give of his fantasy is the invention of a complicated plot, spiced with perils, surprises, and suspenses. (Howells)

Recall #8:

Sentence #9:
All the probabilities against the separate variations must be combined, not by addition, but by multiplication, so that the probabilities against the production of all these separate forms become enormous. (Ackland)

Recall #9:

SENTENCE RECALL *CONTINUED*

Sentence #10:
The fatigue was wholesome, and I was so bad a shot that no other creature suffered loss from my gain except one hapless wild pigeon. (Howells)

Recall #10:

Sentence #11:
Pictures painted in shades of green are passive and tend to be wearisome; this contrasts with the active warmth of yellow or the active coolness of blue. (Kandinsky)

Recall #11:

Sentence #12:
They fail to be content with the fulfillment of their family and personal obligations, and find themselves striving to respond to a new demand involving a social obligation. (Addams)

Recall #12:

Sentence #13:
A music-lover whose experience of hearing singing and instrumental music has been wide enough to develop the mental voice in a fair degree, possesses in this faculty a valuable means for judging singers. (Taylor)

Recall #13:

Sentence #14:
Below that, again, was a mass, six to eight feet deep, of the characteristic yellow clay with far-carried fragments of rock in it that is associated with the great floods of the ice-age. (Marett)

Recall #14:

References

Ackland, T. S. <u>The Story of Creation as told by Theology and by Science</u>. October, 2003 [Etext #4598] <www.gutenberg.net>

Addams, Jane. <u>Democracy and Social Ethics</u>. March 28, 2005 [EBook #15487] <www.gutenberg.net>

Allen, Grant. <u>Science in Arcady</u>. July 18, 2005 [EBook #16325] <www.gutenberg.net>

Anonymous. <u>A System of Instruction in the Practical Use of the Blowpipe</u>. April 7, 2005 [EBook #15576] <www.gutenberg.net>

Ball, Margaret. <u>Sir Walter Scott as a Critic of Literature</u>. September 18, 2005 [EBook #16715] <www.gutenberg.net>

Baring, Evelyn. <u>Political and Literary essays</u>. December 16, 2005 [EBook #17320] <www.gutenberg.net>

Barnes, Earl. <u>Woman in Modern Society</u>. April 23, 2005 [EBook #15691] <www.gutenberg.net>

Berens, E.M. <u>A Hand-Book of Mythology: Myths and Legends of Ancient Greece and Rome</u>. New York: Maynard, Merrill, & Co, 1894.

Brownell, W. C. <u>French Art: Classic and Contemporary Painting and Sculpture</u>. December 6, 2005 [EBook #17244] <www.gutenberg.net>

Bryant, Jacob. <u>A New System; or, an Analysis of Ancient Mythology</u>. Vol II. October 18, 2006 [EBook #19584] <www.gutenberg.net>

Campbell, W. W. "The Evolution of the Stars and the Formation of the Earth." <u>Popular Science Monthly</u>. Vol 86. July, 1997 [Etext #987] <www.gutenberg.net>

Cushman, A.S. Chemistry and Civilization. Boston: Gorham, 1920.

Dorsey, James Owen. Siouan Sociology. October 10, 2006 [Ebook #19518]
    <www.gutenberg.net>

Gillette, John. "The Conservation of Talent Through Utilization." Popular Science Monthly.
    Vol 86. July, 1997 [Etext #987] <www.gutenberg.net>

Griggs, Edward Howard. The Philosophy of Art: the Meaning and Relations of Sculpture,
    Painting, Poetry, and Music. New York: Huebsch, 1913

Hamilton, Clayton. The Theory of the Theatre. October 3, 2004 [EBook #13589]
    <www.gutenberg.net>

Howells, William Dean. Literature and Life. October 28, 2006 [EBook #3389]
    <www.gutenberg.net>

Jordan, David Starr. "War Selection in the Ancient World." Popular Science Monthly. Vol 86.
    July, 1997 [Etext #987] <www.gutenberg.net>

Kandinsky, Wassily. Concerning the Spiritual in Art. March, 2004 [EBook #5321]
    <www.gutenberg.net>

Ladd, Adoniram Judson. On the Firing Line in Education. June 7, 2007 [EBook #21762]
    <www.gutenberg.net>

Marett, Robert. Anthropology. December 11, 2005 [EBook #17280] <www.gutenberg.net>

Mayer, A.G. "A History of Fiji." Popular Science Monthly. Vol 86. July, 1997 [Etext #987]
    <www.gutenberg.net>

Petrucci, Raphael. Chinese Painters, A Critical Study. August 9, 2007 [EBook #22288]
    <www.gutenberg.net>

Robertson, T. B. "The Cash Value of Scientific Research." Popular Science Monthly. Vol 86.
    July, 1997 [Etext #987] <www.gutenberg.net>

Rogers, James Frederick. "The Physical Michelangelo." <u>Popular Science Monthly</u>. Vol 86. July, 1997 [Etext #987] <www.gutenberg.net>

Russell, Edward Stuart. <u>Form and Function: A Contribution to the History of Animal Morphology</u>. January 23, 2007 [EBook #20426] <www.gutenberg.net>

Snider, Denton J. <u>Modern European Philosophy: the History of Modern Philosophy Psychologically Treated</u>. St. Louis: Sigma, 1904.

Taylor, David C. <u>The Psychology of Singing</u>. June 28, 2007 [eBook #21957] <www.gutenberg.net>

Wagner, Henry O. et al. <u>The Light of Egypt</u>. Vol II. February, 1999 [Etext #1650] <www.gutenberg.net>

Zimmermann, E. W. <u>Zimmermann On Ocean Shipping</u>. New York: Prentice-Hall, 1923.

Appendix

Answers to Quiz Questions in Chapter 5

1. Direct Comprehension question

2. New Information question, Strengthen and Weaken question

3. Direct Reference question, Strengthen and Weaken question

4. Structure and Function question

5. Direct Reference question, New Information question

6. Inference question, Direct Reference question

7. Direct Comprehension question

8. Inference question

9. Direct Reference question, About the Author question

10. Main Idea question

11. Inference question

12. About the Author question

13. Direct Comprehension question, Direct Reference question

14. Inference question, New Information question

15. Direct Comprehension question

16. About the Author question

17. Structure and Function question

18. Structure and Function question

19. About the Author question

20. Direct Comprehension question

21. Strengthen and Weaken question, Inference question

22. Direct Comprehension question, Direct Reference question

23. Inference question, Direct Reference question

Words Per Minute Grid for Reading Speed Exercises

Reading Speed Passage versus Total Reading Duration

For example: finishing the reading speed exercise in Unit 1 in 8:00 minutes translates to 144 wpm.

	UNIT 1	UNIT 2	UNIT 3	UNIT 4	UNIT 5	UNIT 6	UNIT 7	UNIT 8	UNIT 9	UNIT 10
3:00	377	459	933	914	956	907	1000	1465	1424	1969
3:30	323	394	800	783	819	778	857	1256	1221	1688
4:00	283	345	700	686	717	681	750	1099	1068	1477
4:30	252	306	622	609	637	605	667	977	950	1313
5:00	226	276	560	548	574	544	600	879	855	1181
5:30	206	251	509	499	521	495	545	799	777	1074
6:00	189	230	467	457	478	454	500	733	712	985
6:30	174	212	431	422	441	419	462	676	657	909
7:00	162	197	400	392	410	389	429	628	610	844
7:30	151	184	373	366	382	363	400	586	570	788
8:00	142	172	350	343	359	340	375	550	534	738
8:30	133	162	329	323	337	320	353	517	503	695
9:00	126	153	311	305	319	302	333	488	475	656
9:30	119	145	295	289	302	287	316	463	450	622
10:00	113	138	280	274	287	272	300	440	427	591
10:30	108	131	267	261	273	259	286	419	407	563
11:00	103	125	255	249	261	247	273	400	388	537
11:30	98	120	243	238	249	237	261	382	372	514
12:00	94	115	233	229	239	227	250	366	356	492
12:30	91	110	224	219	229	218	240	352	342	473
13:00	87	106	215	211	221	209	231	338	329	454
13:30	84	102	207	203	212	202	222	326	317	438
14:00	81	98	200	196	205	194	214	314	305	422
14:30	78	95	193	189	198	188	207	303	295	407
15:00	75	92	187	183	191	181	200	293	285	394
15:30	73	89	181	177	185	176	194	284	276	381
16:00	71	86	175	171	179	170	188	275	267	369
16:30	68	83	169	165	173	164	181	265	257	356
17:00	67	81	165	161	169	160	176	259	251	347
17:30	65	79	160	157	164	156	171	251	244	338
18:00	63	77	156	152	159	151	167	244	237	328
18:30	61	74	151	148	155	147	162	238	231	319
19:00	60	73	147	144	151	143	158	231	225	311
19:30	58	71	144	141	147	140	154	225	219	303
20:00	57	69	140	137	143	136	150	220	214	295

Words Per Minute Grid for Reading Speed Exercises

continued...

	UNIT 1	UNIT 2	UNIT 3	UNIT 4	UNIT 5	UNIT 6	UNIT 7	UNIT 8	UNIT 9	UNIT 10
20:30	55	67	137	134	140	133	146	214	208	288
21:00	54	66	133	131	137	130	143	209	203	281
21:30	53	64	130	128	133	127	140	204	199	275
22:00	51	63	127	125	130	124	136	200	194	269
22:30	50	61	124	122	127	121	133	195	190	263
23:00	49	60	122	119	125	118	130	191	186	257
23:30	48	59	119	117	122	116	128	187	182	251
24:00	47	57	117	114	120	113	125	183	178	246
24:30	46	56	114	112	117	111	122	179	174	241
25:00	45	55	112	110	115	109	120	176	171	236
25:30	44	54	110	108	112	107	118	172	168	232
26:00	44	53	108	105	110	105	115	169	164	227
26:30	43	52	105	103	108	102	113	165	161	222
27:00	42	51	104	102	106	101	111	163	158	219
27:30	41	50	102	100	104	99	109	160	155	215
28:00	40	49	100	98	102	97	107	157	153	211
28:30	40	48	98	96	101	96	105	154	150	207
29:00	39	48	97	95	99	94	103	152	147	204
29:30	38	47	95	93	97	92	102	149	145	200
30:00	38	46	93	91	96	91	100	147	142	197

Reading Program Training Schedule: 6-Month

Sample schedule for examinees taking a summer MCAT, starting in January of the year of the test.

January

Improve Mechanics:

- ☐ 30 minutes of force reading daily, at comfortable pace.
- ☐ 1 hour of normal reading in the morning, at comfortable pace.
- ☐ 1 hour of normal reading in the evening, at comfortable pace.

= 2.5 hours daily reading

February

Improve Memory and Comprehension:

- ☐ 30 minutes of sentence recall and paragraph summary daily.
- ☐ 30 minutes of force reading daily, at comfortable pace.
- ☐ 1 hour of reading in the morning, using TSM analysis.
- ☐ 1 hour of reading in the evening, using TSM analysis.

= 3 hours daily reading

March - April

Improve Memory and Comprehension:

- ☐ 1.5 hours of force reading with NVP in the morning.
- ☐ 1.5 hours of force reading with NVP in the evening.

= 3 hours daily reading

May - June

Improve Speed and MCAT Familiarity:

- ☐ 30 minutes reading at 400 words per minute in the morning.
- ☐ 1 hour reading at 200 words per minute in the morning using NVP.
- ☐ 30 minutes reading at 400 words per minute in the evening.
- ☐ 1 hour reading at 200 words per minute in the evening using NVP.
- ☐ Two sample Verbal Reasoning passages daily.

= 3 hours daily reading + passages

Reading Program Training Schedule: 8-Month

Sample schedule for examinees taking a summer MCAT, starting in
October of the year prior to the test:

October (of year prior to test)

Improve Mechanics:

☐ 30 minutes of force reading daily, at comfortable pace.

☐ 1 hour of normal reading in the morning, at comfortable pace.

☐ 1 hour of normal reading in the evening, at comfortable pace.

= 2.5 hours daily reading

November (of year prior to test)

Improve Memory and Comprehension:

☐ 30 minutes of sentence recall and paragraph summary daily.

☐ 30 minutes of force reading daily, at comfortable pace.

☐ 1 hour of reading in the morning, using TSM analysis.

☐ 1 hour of reading in the evening, using TSM analysis.

= 3 hours daily reading

December - March

Improve Memory and Comprehension:

☐ 1.5 hours of force reading with NVP in the morning.

☐ 1.5 hours of force reading with NVP in the evening.

= 3 hours daily reading

April - May

Improve Speed and MCAT Familiarity:

☐ 30 minutes reading at 400 words per minute in the morning.

☐ 1 hour reading at 200 words per minute in the morning using NVP.

☐ 30 minutes reading at 400 words per minute in the evening.

☐ 1 hour reading at 200 words per minute in the evening using NVP.

☐ Two sample Verbal Reasoning passages daily.

= 3 hours daily reading + passages

Summary of Reading Comprehension Techniques, Skills, and Methods

FOR PRACTICE:

☐ read challenging academic material - see book list (Chapter 11)

☐ read two to three hours daily for six to eight months

AS YOU READ, BE SURE TO USE:

✓ **Clutch Reading** - improve focus (use always)

✓ **Sentence Recall** - improve memory (15 min/day)

✓ **Paragraph Summary** - boost comprehension (30 min/day)

✓ **Anticipation** - improve comprehension (always)

✓ **Three Point Analysis** - improve comprehension (always)

✓ **TSM Analysis** - improve comprehension (always)

✓ **Neuro-Visual Programming** - retain all details (always)

KEEP AT THE FOREFRONT OF YOUR MIND:

• key questions about the material - see list (page 96)

• topic, setting, and main idea (TSM analysis)

• the Interpretive and Applied Levels of reading

• your mental dialogue with the author

• interest in the material

• awareness of your thoughts and focus level

Index